interactive SCIENCE

Scenario Based Investigations

Boston, Massachusetts Chandler, Arizona Glenview, Illinois Upper Saddle River, New Jersey

Note to Teachers

This book is designed to provide you with engaging activities that allow students to apply their knowledge to investigate the chapter concepts in the *Interactive Science* program. You can use this book as a means of reinforcing inquiry, critical thinking, real-world application, and cooperative learning skills in your classroom.

Extensive Teacher Support

The first page of each project is a guide for you. The overview contains helpful notes to guide students and smoothly conduct each investigation. It also may include suggestions for preparation, materials, and interesting background information. A rubric is included to help you evaluate the final assignment for each investigation. Additionally, there are extensions with every investigation. Students can complete an assignment outside the classroom that applies what they've learned. You can alter or extend an investigation to incorporate collaboration and differentiated instruction. Finally, there are suggestions for field trips and guest speakers to delve further into the real-world topics.

Real-World Connections

Each investigation contains a two-page worksheet for your students. The highlight of the activity is the Scenario, an exciting, real-world story relevant to the science content of each chapter. Generally, students must assume a role to fix a problem or explain an event. The Procedure then directs students through the investigation and asks them to collect scientific evidence. The Conclusion wraps up the activity with questions that create a basis for an in-class discussion and a final, communication-based assignment.

Flexible Activities

The activities in this book vary in structure and can be done independently, in small groups, or as homework. The investigation itself can be completed within a class period, but you can incorporate class discussion, homework assignments, and cooperative activities to solidify students' understanding, problem-solving skills, and interest in science. Typically, an investigation requires some knowledge of the chapter content, so activities generally should be done after you have covered the corresponding information in your textbook.

Copyright © Pearson Education, Inc., or its affiliates. All Rights Reserved. Printed in the United States of America. This publication is protected by copyright, and permission should be obtained from the publisher prior to any prohibited reproduction, storage in a retrieval system, or transmission in any form or by any means, electronic, mechanical, photocopying, recording, or likewise. The publisher hereby grants permission to reproduce these pages, in part or in whole, for classroom use only, the number not to exceed the number of students in each class. Notice of copyright must appear on all copies. For information regarding permissions, write to Pearson Curriculum Group Rights & Permissions, One Lake Street, Upper Saddle River, New Jersey 07458.

Pearson, Prentice Hall, Pearson Prentice Hall, and Lab Zone are trademarks, in the U.S. and/or other countries, of Pearson Education, Inc., or its affiliates.

ISBN-13: 978-0-13-369878-7
ISBN-10: 0-13-369878-5

12 V001 15

Science Inquiry and Processes

Ecology and the Environment

Cells and Heredity

The Diversity of Life

Human Body Systems

Earth's Structure

Copyright © Pearson Education, Inc., or its affiliates. All Rights Reserved.

Contents

Copyright © Pearson Education, Inc., or its affiliates. All Rights Reserved.

Casting a Vote That Makes Sense

Investigation Overview

- This investigation features an issue that was the subject of a real question on the ballot in Northampton, Massachusetts. When the votes were counted, 63.8 percent were against expanding the landfill.
- The passage quoted in "Are Landfills Safe?" is from an EPA report, which you can find at http://www.epa.gov/climatechange/emissions/downloads09/documents/SubpartHH-Landfills.pdf
- Prior to the investigation, create a ballot box in which students can drop their votes at the end of the Conclusion. Make sure you have enough index cards for each student to cast a ballot.
- You may need to review the concept of aquifers with your students. An aquifer is an underground layer of cracked rock or other porous material (gravel, sand, silt, or clay) that is saturated with water. The water in an aquifer is called groundwater. Wells are used to extract drinking water from an aquifer. Aquifers are recharged by rain and snowmelt.
- To begin the investigation, have students form groups of two or three to read and discuss the Scenario and Steps 1–4. Answer all questions, and tell students that although they are working together on the Procedure, they will each privately cast a vote on an index card as part of the Conclusion.
- After all votes have been cast, count the votes, announce the results, and reveal Northampton's actual vote.

SCORING RUBRIC	
SCORE 4	The student writes a vote of *yes* or *no* on one side of an index card, and on the other side gives a valid scientific reason that supports the vote. The reason is written in a complete sentence.
SCORE 3	The student's ballot meets the content criteria for a score of 4, but the reason is not a complete sentence or contains errors.
SCORE 2	The student's reason supports the vote but is not scientific.
SCORE 1	The student gives a vote without a valid reason, or the reason contradicts the vote.

Extension Activities

Assignment Have students list other ways in which having a good understanding of scientific concepts and/or thinking scientifically can help solve problems and answer real-life questions.

Cooperative Learning Have students work in teams to create posters featuring a profession that requires the use of scientific knowledge on a regular basis. Each poster should include a description of the profession and how it requires the use of scientific knowledge, the educational requirements of the job, its salary range, and a relevant illustration.

Field Trip Arrange a field trip to a company where students can observe workers applying scientific knowledge to complete various tasks. Have the people there explain their jobs with a focus on how they use scientific knowledge in their work.

Copyright © Pearson Education, Inc., or its affiliates. All Rights Reserved.

Name _______________________ Date ___________ Class ___________

Casting a Vote That Makes Sense

Purpose To investigate the role of science in society

Materials • index card

Scenario

On Tuesday, residents of Northampton, Massachusetts, will be voting on this question:

Should the city of Northampton expand the Northampton landfill over the Barnes Aquifer?

The state of Massachusetts wants to expand the landfill. It now occupies 52 acres, but after the expansion, the landfill will cover 81.5 acres. Guess what? Many people are against the idea.

Are Landfills Safe?

Landfills produce large amounts of methane gas, along with a poisonous liquid that seeps from the compressed trash. Landfills often have liners and pipes that collect the toxic liquid to keep it from contaminating groundwater. But according to the Environmental Protection Agency (EPA), even the best collection systems and landfill liners deteriorate and leak:

> "No liner ... can keep all liquids out of the ground for all time. Eventually liners will either degrade, tear, or crack and will allow liquids to migrate out of the unit. Some have argued that liners are devices that provide a perpetual seal against any migration from a waste management unit. EPA has concluded that the more reasonable assumption, based on what is known about the pressures placed on liners over time, is that any liner will begin to leak eventually."

When a landfill liner does leak, poisons escape directly into the environment, where they can contaminate air, water, and soil.

The landfill has served Northampton, Easthampton, and several other communities in Western Massachusetts for 40 years. If nothing is done, the landfill will be full in two years. If it is expanded, it can last another 20 years. But the proposed expansion lies on top of the recharge area of the aquifer that supplies drinking water to four cities and towns.

Supporters of the expansion say not to worry because studies have shown no evidence of increased cancer rates due to contamination in the area. But the Barnes Aquifer Protection Committee warns that the long-term costs of expanding the landfill far outweigh any short-term benefits.

Copyright © Pearson Education, Inc., or its affiliates. All Rights Reserved.

Name ______________________ Date____________ Class____________

Scenario *(continued)*

The Northampton City Council had a chance to put the question on the ballot last summer, but the council members voted it down. Then a group of citizens got enough signatures on a petition to put the question on the ballot anyway. The group wanted the citizens of Northampton to be heard on this important environmental issue.

You live in Northampton and you really want to vote the right way on this important issue. But what is the right way? What are the risks? What are the benefits? You must understand the issue better before you cast a vote.

Procedure

1. **Are Landfills Always Safe?** Read the information in "Are Landfills Safe?" Do you think landfills are always safe? Explain.

   ____

2. **What Is an Aquifer?** Before you can cast a well-informed vote, you have to make sure you understand the vocabulary used. What is an aquifer?

   ____

3. **The Recharge Area** Why is it important to protect an aquifer's recharge area?

   ____

   ____

4. **Before You Cast Your Vote** This question is a very important one. There are costs and there are benefits to expanding the landfill. In your notebook, make a table that lists the costs in one column and the benefits in another column.

Conclusion

Let's see what you learned about the importance of thinking scientifically when voting on an important issue.

1. Why is it important to understand the scientific terms before you vote?

   ____

   ____

2. How did your scientific knowledge help you decide on your vote? What scientific evidence or data influenced your vote the most?

   ____

   ____

Now, write your vote on an index card. On the back, write your name and a complete sentence explaining the main *scientific* reason for your vote. Drop your completed ballot in the ballot box.

Copyright © Pearson Education, Inc., or its affiliates. All Rights Reserved.

Bias, Anyone?

Investigation Overview

- Students should have learned about personal, cultural, and experimental bias before doing this investigation.
- Several weeks before conducting this investigation, begin collecting news articles about scientific findings and claims. Each student will need a copy of one article to analyze.
- Have students read the Scenario and Steps 1–5, and then answer all questions.
- Now tell your students to begin individually rereading the news story about Dr. Profit's findings, highlighting the signs of bias they find there.
- Once everyone has finished, ask for volunteers to each give one sign of bias they found in the article. If the class is divided on whether or not bias is indicated, have both sides voice their opinions, and then take a vote. Encourage students to highlight or underline any sign of bias they missed.
- Now distribute a science news article to each student. Tell them to analyze the article, and then highlight or underline all signs of bias they find.

SCORING RUBRIC	
SCORE 4	Student writes a summary of a science article and describes the signs of bias found or describes the features of the research that indicate a lack of bias.
SCORE 3	The summary meets the content standards for a score of 4 but contains some errors.
SCORE 2	The summary demonstrates some understanding of the meaning of bias.
SCORE 1	The summary demonstrates minimal understanding of the meaning of bias.

Extension Activities

Assignment Successful scientists share important attitudes (curiosity, honesty, creativity, open-mindedness, skepticism, and good ethics). Have each student select one of these attitudes and write about a situation in which the attitude influenced his or her actions in some way.

Cooperative Learning Have students work together in three-person teams to create a tri-fold brochure about the attitudes and qualities that make a good scientist (mentioned above). One member of each team should be responsible for the layout of the brochure and for drawing or finding pictures to illustrate the different attitudes. The other members should be responsible for researching and writing about three of the attitudes. Together the team should decide on a clever title for the brochure.

Guest Speaker Invite spokespeople from two or three organizations with divergent views (different biases) regarding an issue that affects your community. Have each spokesperson explain his or her organization's position. Conclude by having students cast votes on the issue and explain their reasoning.

Copyright © Pearson Education, Inc., or its affiliates. All Rights Reserved.

Name ______________________________ Date ______________ Class ______________

Bias, Anyone?

Purpose
To investigate how bias influences scientific claims

Materials
- science news article
- highlighter

Scenario

Boulder, CO At a press conference today, Dr. Seymour Profit, senior scientist at Larry Heartmore Laboratories, announced a breakthrough. Dr. Profit was so excited by his findings that he couldn't wait for a science journal to report the results. In his study of an experimental blood-pressure medicine, Dr. Profit found that the medicine lowered blood pressure an average of ten percent in the 17 women he studied. "Not only that, these drops happened in just one week," Dr. Profit said. (The women were also placed on a reduced-salt diet, but according to Dr. Profit, the diet alone only lowered blood pressure by five percent in a control group of six men and four women.)

Dr. Profit went on to say, "The effectiveness of the new drug has now been scientifically proven, and once it becomes available to the public, it will surely save the lives of millions of men and women." Although the same company that invented the drug paid for Dr. Profit's study, he assured the reporters that the money in no way influenced the results.

This is exciting news! Or is it? Sometimes the science news we see on television or read about in the newspaper is exaggerated. Sometimes it's biased.

Personal bias, cultural bias, and experimental bias are three different kinds of bias that can influence the results of a science experiment. But when you read a news story, how can you tell that bias is present?

You should suspect that a science claim is inaccurate or exaggerated if it is announced to the media rather than reported in a science journal. Are there other signs to look for? The answer is yes! Any of the three kinds of bias can lead to similar problems that you can spot.

Procedure

1. **What Are the Signs?** In this investigation you will search for signs of bias in a real science article. First, you need to practice finding bias by carefully rereading the article above. Signs of bias come in three forms: the *language* used, the *data* reported, and the *source* of the study. In the next four steps you will read about what makes good science, and then you will identify evidence of bias in the article above.

2. **The Language of Science** Good scientists choose their words carefully. They do not exaggerate their claims or make strong emotional statements, and their conclusions are always supported by data. The words "scientifically proven" are a potential sign that something is wrong. A real scientist tries to find evidence that supports the hypothesis being tested, but support *never* proves the hypothesis.

3. **Looking At the Sample** Is the sample appropriate? A *sample* is a small group selected from a larger group called the *population*. Sampling bias occurs when a sample does not reflect the entire population being studied.

Copyright © Pearson Education, Inc., or its affiliates. All Rights Reserved.

Procedure *(continued)*

4. **Looking At the Measurements** Are the measurements appropriate for the conclusion presented? Does the experiment take into account the effect of other factors? Did the experiment run long enough? Were the measurements accurate? You may not find this information in a news story. But if the story says that the findings were reported in the *New England Journal of Medicine*—or another science journal—that's a good sign. The scientific community uses peer-reviewed journals, checked and approved by experts, to ensure the quality of the science.
5. **Looking At the Source** Where was the study done, and who paid for it? Scientists do their research at universities, corporations, and at government agencies. Money for the research comes from special-interest groups, corporations, and the government. Any organization can run a good experiment and produce unbiased data, but the need to promote a special interest or make a profit may lead to bias. The source doesn't prove bias, but it should make the reader skeptical.
6. **Discussing What Was Found** Your teacher will now ask for volunteers to identify signs of bias they found in the article. If not everyone agrees about whether or not something is a sign of bias, listen to both sides and vote on the issue.
7. **Analyzing a Real Science Article** Now read a real science article and highlight any sign of bias you find.

Conclusion

Let's see what you learned about bias.

1. Why is an exaggerated claim a sign of bias?

____

2. What is one sign that might indicate experimental bias?

____

3. Is it possible for a scientist to be unbiased when working on research funded by a special-interest group? Explain.

____

____

4. If a newspaper article reports a science finding that was first published in a peer-reviewed journal, is it most likely biased or unbiased? Explain.

____

____

____

Write a brief summary of the article you read. In a concluding paragraph, describe the signs of bias you found or the features of the research that indicate a lack of bias.

Copyright © Pearson Education, Inc., or its affiliates. All Rights Reserved.

This Isn't Science!

Investigation Overview

- To prepare for this investigation, make identical kits for each team by placing all required materials except the egg in a box or bag. Purchase one egg for each group, plus extras in case some break during the design process.
- Prior to the investigation, prepare the drop area. Mark one-foot intervals along the height of a wall, and place a bucket on the floor to catch groups' eggs.
- Make a three-column table where students can record their test results. Label the columns "Team #," "Scientific Reasons," and "Height." Post the chart and a pen or marker near the drop area.
- Divide the class into teams and have students read the Scenario and Procedure. As students read, distribute materials.
- Answer all questions and stress the need to base all design decisions on the listed scientific discoveries.
- Give each group one egg and have them complete Steps 1–4. Remind students not to drop the egg until the contest begins.
- Once all teams have built their carriers, take the class to the drop area to test the designs. Have each team record their information on the chart and test their design by dropping the carrier from a height of three feet. If the egg does not break, repeat the test, increasing the drop height by one foot until the egg breaks.
- The winner is the team whose egg survives the drop from the greatest height. Ask the winning team to explain which scientific reason was most important to their success.

SCORING RUBRIC	
SCORE 4	Final report includes a correctly labeled diagram, a chart listing the scientific discovery related to each design feature, and a paragraph explaining which science discovery was most important to the design's success.
SCORE 3	Final report meets all content standards required for a score of 4 but may contain errors.
SCORE 2	The chart does not include scientific discoveries for every design feature, or the paragraph does not explain how each discovery helped in the design of the carrier.
SCORE 1	The chart and/or paragraph are largely incomplete or contain significant errors.

Extension Activities

Assignment Have each student select one technology from around the school or his or her home and identify a scientific discovery that makes the technology possible.

Field Trip Arrange a field trip to a business, factory, or construction site where many different technologies are used on a daily basis. Have spokespeople explain the science behind each of the technologies used there. (For example, the crane at a construction site uses simple machines to gain mechanical advantage and lift heavy weights.)

Copyright © Pearson Education, Inc., or its affiliates. All Rights Reserved.

Name ______________________ Date ____________ Class ____________

This Isn't Science!

Purpose To investigate how science relates to technology

Materials

- egg
- plastic foam cup
- five cotton balls
- four toothpicks
- blank paper
- scissors
- one foot of masking tape
- two rubber bands

Scenario

So far, your science class has been fun and interesting. Today's lesson involves building a container to protect a falling egg. This isn't science! Or is it?

When you asked why you are doing an egg-drop experiment in a science class, your teacher said that once scientific discoveries are confirmed, they can be useful. Your teacher knows the egg-drop experiment is an example of using scientific discoveries to design a successful technology to solve a problem. The more you apply scientific knowledge to your design, the better your results should be.

To show the class how they can use their knowledge of scientific discoveries to design useful technologies, your teacher is holding a contest. Groups will use their scientific knowledge to design egg carriers. The winner is the group whose egg carrier protects their egg from the highest drop.

Procedure

1. **Reading the Science** The box below contains a list of four scientific discoveries that may help you design a more successful egg-protection device. Each member of your team should read one of the discoveries and think about how it may influence the design of your egg carrier.

Scientific Discoveries

Force – Force is a push or pull. It can change the movement of an object by causing it to speed up, slow down, or change direction. Sir Isaac Newton discovered that force equals mass multiplied by acceleration.

Gravity – Newton also discovered that all objects are attracted to other objects by a force he called gravity. The more massive the objects, the greater the attraction. Every second an egg falls, gravity increases the egg's velocity.

Inertia – Newton also discovered that an object in motion stays in motion unless it encounters an opposing force. The greater the opposing force, the faster the moving object comes to a stop. If an egg stops too quickly, the force will break the egg.

Stress – Stress is force divided by area. This means that when a force is spread out over a larger area there is less stress. Stress on the egg will cause it to break.

Copyright © Pearson Education, Inc., or its affiliates. All Rights Reserved.

Procedure *(continued)*

2. **Explain the Science to Your Team** Take turns explaining to each other the scientific discovery you read. After each explanation, discuss how you can use the information to design a better egg carrier. Record this information in your notebook.
3. **Building an Egg Carrier** Once you receive your egg, you will have 15 minutes to design a carrier that will protect it from the fall. Base each design choice on one or more of the scientific discoveries listed.
4. **Recording Design Choices** As you build your carrier, record each design feature and any scientific reasons for including the feature. Count the total number of scientific reasons used in your design and record it in your notebook.
5. **Testing Your Carrier** When everyone is ready, teams will take turns dropping their egg carriers from a height of one meter. After each drop, your teacher will check the egg for damage. If the egg is still intact, the team will drop its egg from one-quarter meter higher until it breaks. Record the highest successful drop for your team.
6. **Declaring a Winner** If your egg survives the greatest height, you win! Be prepared to explain which scientific discovery was most helpful in designing your carrier.

Conclusion

Let's see what you learned about the difference between science and technology.

1. Which field involves trying to understand how the natural world works? ______
2. Which field involves designing a solution to a problem? ______
3. How are science and technology related?

______

______

4. What field involves using science and technological knowledge together to solve a problem?

______

Now, you will prepare a final report that includes

- a diagram of your finished carrier with each design feature labeled
- a neat version of your chart stating the scientific discovery behind each feature
- a paragraph that explains which science discovery was most helpful in designing your egg carrier

Copyright © Pearson Education, Inc., or its affiliates. All Rights Reserved.

Name ______________________________ Date__________ Class__________

Procedure *(continued)*

Williamsport, PA	
Year	**Five-Year Average Annual Temperature (°C)**
1914	10.3
1919	9.9
1924	10.3
1929	9.9
1934	10.7
1939	10.0
1944	9.7
1949	10.3
1954	10.4
1959	10.2
1964	9.7
1969	9.6
1974	9.9
1979	9.8
1984	9.7
1989	10.0
1994	10.2
1999	10.3
2004	10.4
2009	10.7

4. **Dividing the Data in Thirds** On your graph, divide the data points into three approximately equal groups by drawing a vertical line between 1944 and 1949 and another vertical line between 1974 and 1979. (This places seven points in the early years, seven points in the recent years, and six points in between.)

5. **Finding the Median Points** A *median* is the midpoint in a set of ordered data. To find the median for the early years, use a pencil to draw a horizontal line on your graph with half the points above the line and half below it. Next, draw a vertical line with half of the points on either side. The lines intersect at the *median point*. Mark it in black pen. Repeat this process to find the median points for the recent and in-between years.

6. **Plotting a Median-Median Line** Place your ruler so that it connects the early and recent median points, but don't draw a line yet! If the in-between median point is below the line, move the straightedge downward slightly. If the in-between point is above the line, adjust upward. *Do not tilt the straightedge. Slide the whole thing up or down.* Draw your median-median line in red. Exactly half of the data points should be above the line, and half below it.

Conclusion

Let's see what you learned about finding a trend in nonlinear data.

1. The first step in finding a trend is making a special kind of graph called a ____________.

2. One way to describe data is to find the median. What is a median?

   ____

3. How is the placement of the trend line affected by extreme data points?

   ____

4. Is your trend line the same as the trend lines drawn by other students? Whose trend line is most accurate? Explain.

   ____

   ____

Your article is complete, and now you just have to get your graph ready for publication. Create a caption for your graph that describes what the graph shows.

Copyright © Pearson Education, Inc., or its affiliates. All Rights Reserved.

Fantasy Food Chain

Investigation Overview

- Students should complete this investigation in groups of four. You will use colored index cards to assign each student his or her role, so you will need index cards in four different colors, and enough of each color to give one card to every fourth student. Additionally, each student will need one white index card.
- Have students read the Scenario and the Procedure. Answer any questions, and randomly distribute the colored cards.
- Tell students to form groups of four with each person having a different colored card. Then announce which color represents each organism's role in the ecosystem (producer, herbivore, carnivore, or scavenger).
- As groups conclude the activity, they will add to their poster one index card for each fictional organism. Although these cards will contain fictional information, the relative population sizes must be accurate with respect to the role each organism plays in the ecosystem. You should discuss this requirement with your students before they begin working on their cards.

SCORING RUBRIC	
SCORE 4	The student's drawing of a fictional organism is neat, detailed, and creative. The index card contains all of the required information, and the relative population size supports the organism's role in the food chain. The student actively participates in creating the team poster.
SCORE 3	The student completes the drawing and index card, but the organism is not very creative and/or detailed. The student participates in creating the poster.
SCORE 2	The student completes the drawing, and the index card contains most of the required information. The student did not fully participate in creating the poster.
SCORE 1	The index card is mostly incomplete or incorrect, or the student did not contribute to the poster.

Extension Activities

Assignment Have students identify a real plant or animal that lives near your school, research its role in the ecosystem, and write a one-paragraph report.

Cooperative Learning This investigation provides an excellent opportunity to use the *Jigsaw* strategy. After Step 4, and once students know the role their organism will be playing, regroup the class into four expert groups based on those role designations. Each expert group should discuss and review the important features of that particular role in an ecosystem. This strategy will help make students more prepared and productive when they return to their four-person teams.

Field Trip Arrange a field trip to a local zoo or animal preserve and have students find a representative of each of the three animal roles (herbivore, carnivore, and scavenger). For the herbivore, identify the producer that serves as its main source of food.

Copyright © Pearson Education, Inc., or its affiliates. All Rights Reserved.

Name ______________________ Date __________ Class __________

Fantasy Food Chain

Purpose To investigate the roles of different organisms in a food chain

Materials
- colored index cards (4 different colors)
- white index cards
- white copier paper
- colored pencils or markers
- poster board or newsprint

Scenario

You are an ecologist. Your specialty is ecosystems. Normally that means investigating relationships among the plants and animals that live together in an area. Your work involves food chains and food webs.

Today, you and three of your colleagues were given a different kind of job to do. You have been asked to create three imaginary animals and one imaginary plant for a new children's book.

Stories by Curtis Larking in *The Adventures of Henry Porter* are all set in a fantasy world that the author creates in his mind. After writing fourteen novels, he is looking for some original ideas. That's where you come in. Larking plans to use the three animals and one plant that you invent as he writes about a fictional food chain in his new book.

Larking needs a fictional plant to be the producer and three levels of animal consumers—one species of herbivore, one species of carnivore, and one species of scavenger. Although these organisms are fictional, Larking wants the food chain to be scientifically accurate.

That means the largest amount of available energy should be at the producer level. It also means that as you move up the food chain, the available energy must decrease, so consumer populations will get smaller.

Procedure

1. **Forming Your Fantasy Team** Your teacher has given each student in your class a card. The cards come in four colors. When your teacher tells you, form a team in which each person on your team has a different color card.
2. **Who's Inventing What?** Your teacher will tell you which color card represents which organism (plant, herbivore, carnivore, and scavenger).
3. **Creating an Organism** The organisms your team is creating need to be imaginative—even the plant. (After all, the organisms are going to inhabit an ecosystem in a fantasy world.) You can create an organism that no one has ever seen before, or you can create an organism by combining parts of real animals or real plants. Work together with your partners to make sure your organisms can live together in the same kind of environment. Also, remember that the herbivores will eat the plants, the carnivores will eat both the herbivores and the scavengers, and the scavengers will eat any dead animals (carnivores, herbivores, and even other scavengers).
4. **Drawing Your Organism** Draw a picture of your organism. Make each picture large enough to fill a sheet of copier paper.

Copyright © Pearson Education, Inc., or its affiliates. All Rights Reserved.

Name ______________________ Date ______________ Class ______________

Conclusion

Let's see what you learned about food chains.

1. What role do producers play in an ecosystem?

____

2. Which level in a food chain has the most available energy?

____

3. Which level in a food chain has the least available energy?

____

4. If Curtis Larking asks you to suggest decomposers, what will their role be?

____

Now mount your group's four organisms on a poster to show the food chain. Arrange them so that producers are on the bottom, carnivores and scavengers are at the top, and herbivores are in the middle. Leave room for labels and arrows to show the relationships that exist in the food chain.

Next to each organism, Larking wants an index card with the following information:

- role in the food chain
- population size (make sure it is appropriate for the role in the food chain)
- litter size (for plants, give the number of germinated seeds it produces)
- life expectancy
- any strange behaviors it exhibits

Once you have added all of the index cards to your poster, add arrows to show the flow of energy through your food chain.

Copyright © Pearson Education, Inc., or its affiliates. All Rights Reserved.

Light Bulbs Can't Use Much Energy

Investigation Overview

- To prepare for this investigation, you will need examples of both incandescent and fluorescent light bulbs. (If possible, have a sample of a tubular fluorescent and a compact fluorescent.)
- Since this investigation requires students to complete a survey of the incandescent light bulbs in their homes, you should begin approximately ten minutes before the end of the period and complete the activity when class next meets. Begin by having students read the Scenario and Steps 1–3.
- Before Day 2, find out the kilowatt-hour (kWh) cost of electricity in your community. Check your most recent electric bill or call the electric company. Students will need this information to complete the Conclusion.
- On Day 2, post the kWh cost in your community on the board or on chart paper, and have your students complete Step 4 and the Conclusion.
- Some households may not have any incandescent light bulbs. You may want to have students count the CFL bulbs too, and then they can do a cost comparison. Let students alter the chart as necessary to represent the light bulbs in their homes.

SCORING RUBRIC	
SCORE 4	Student prepares an index card with answers to all five questions. Each answer provides additional detail. The answers are stated in complete sentences.
SCORE 3	Student answers at least four questions, and most answers provide additional detail. The answers are stated in complete sentences but may contain minor errors.
SCORE 2	Student answers at least three questions and uses complete sentences, but there is no additional detail.
SCORE 1	Student answers some questions but provides no extra detail and/or does not use complete sentences.

Extension Activities

Cooperative Learning Have your class survey the school for cases of inefficient or unnecessary use of lights (lights left on when there is plenty of sunlight, using brighter lights than necessary, etc.) Have the class summarize their findings and prepare a report for the principal, including suggestions for how to reduce energy use in the school.

Field Trip Find a green building (designed with conservation in mind) in your community and arrange a field trip. Have someone who helped design the building meet your class there to explain the features that make it green.

Copyright © Pearson Education, Inc., or its affiliates. All Rights Reserved.

Name ______________________ Date ____________ Class ____________

Light Bulbs Can't Use Much Energy

Purpose To calculate the energy consumption of household light bulbs

Materials
- calculator
- index card (one for each student)

Scenario

Your mother is always getting on your case about something. If your shower lasts more than two minutes, she tells you to stop wasting water. If you leave the lights on in a room, she accuses you of wasting electricity. You defend yourself as best you can, but you wonder how much it really costs to leave the lights on. It can't cost very much, can it?

Believe it or not, incandescent light bulbs use a lot of energy. A single 100-watt bulb left on 24 hours a day for a whole year would cost about $100.00 to operate. That seems like too much, doesn't it? The average cost of electricity in the United States is $0.113 per kilowatt hour (kWh). See for yourself:

$$100 \text{ watts} \times \frac{24 \text{ hours}}{\cancel{\text{day}}} \times \frac{365 \cancel{\text{ days}}}{\text{year}} = \frac{876{,}000 \text{ watt-hours}}{\text{year}}$$

$$\frac{876{,}000 \cancel{\text{ watt-hours}}}{\text{year}} \times \frac{1 \text{ kWh}}{1000 \cancel{\text{ watt hours}}} = \frac{876 \text{ kWh}}{\text{year}}$$

$$\frac{\$0.113}{\cancel{\text{kWh}}} \times \frac{876 \cancel{\text{ kWh}}}{\text{year}} = \$98.99/\text{year}$$

Today your science teacher issued a challenge: Count the number of incandescent light bulbs in your home and determine the total cost of leaving all the light bulbs on for one year.

Procedure

1. **Counting Your Bulbs** Use the chart below to record the number of incandescent light bulbs used in your home. Keep track of how many bulbs are of each wattage (the number should be on the light bulb).

Watts	Total Bulbs	Total Watts
25		
40		
60		
75		
100		
150		
Total		

Why Compact Fluorescent Bulbs?

Incandescent bulbs produce light by passing electricity through a thin filament. The filament is heated until it glows. Fluorescent bulbs (CFLs) use electricity to excite the atoms of mercury vapor that fill the tube. The excited mercury atoms cause the phosphorus coating on the inside of the CFL to give off visible light.

Fluorescent bulbs convert more of the electricity into visible light and less into heat. A fluorescent bulb can produce the same amount of light as an incandescent bulb for about half the cost.

Copyright © Pearson Education, Inc., or its affiliates. All Rights Reserved.

Name ______________________ Date ______________ Class ______________

Procedure *(continued)*

2. **The Totals** Multiply the number of bulbs by the number of watts for each size bulb. Next, add the total number of watts of all bulbs in your home. Record your results in the table.

3. **Kilowatt Hours** Now calculate the number of kilowatt-hours your light bulbs could possibly use in a year.

   First multiply the total number of watts from your chart by 24 hours: ______________

   Multiply this number by 365 days: ______________

   Divide this number by 1,000: ______________ kWh in a year

4. **Lighting 24/7** To determine what it would cost to have all of your lights burning 24 hours a day, seven days a week, for an entire year, you need to make one more calculation. Multiply the final number from Step 3 by the cost of a kilowatt hour in your community. (Your teacher will tell you that number.) ______________

Conclusion

Let's see what you learned about the cost of operating incandescent light bulbs.

1. How much would it cost to leave your incandescent lights on 24/7? ______________

2. How do incandescent and fluorescent light bulbs transform electrical energy into light energy?

   ____

   ____

3. Why are fluorescent bulbs cheaper to operate?

   ____

   ____

The news anchor at your local TV station wants you to explain your findings on the evening news. Prepare an index card with your answers to the following questions:

- How many incandescent light bulbs do you use in your home?
- What is the wattage of the highest-wattage bulb?
- Do you have any compact fluorescent bulbs? If so, how many?
- How many kilowatts would your light bulbs draw per hour if they were all turned on?
- What would it cost to leave all of your incandescent lights on 24/7 for a whole year?

Since the news anchor wants more than one-word answers, try to think of ways to expand your answers. (For example, for the first question, you could also tell how many bulbs you have of each size.) Write your answers in complete sentences.

Copyright © Pearson Education, Inc., or its affiliates. All Rights Reserved.

The Problem with Runoff

Investigation Overview

- Before the investigation, use a mapping web site to print a satellite image of your school and the surrounding property. Make eight copies for the class.
- Arrange with your school's support staff to provide access to the locker or closet where lawn-and-garden products are stored.
- On the day of the investigation, have the class brainstorm what characteristics of the school and its surroundings might contribute to the contamination of a nearby stream after a heavy rain. Record students' ideas on the board or chart paper. (This question provides students with an opportunity to recall that stormwater runoff can carry many things into nearby streams. Sediments, toxic chemicals, and even nutrients can be harmful. Also, the faster the water moves, the more it will carry.)
- After you are satisfied with the list, have the class read the Scenario, the Procedure, and "Schoolyard Stormwater Survey."
- Ask if there are any characteristics not already on the class list. Add to the class list, if necessary.
- Designate eight meeting areas in your classroom and label them "A" through "H." Assign each student a letter and have students move to the area labeled with their letter. Each group will survey the schoolyard for the problem that corresponds to their group's letter.
- Give each team one copy of the school map and tell them they will be going outside to complete Step 2. Lead the class outside and allow them to use the remainder of the class period to conduct their surveys.
- The next time your class meets, give each group five minutes to present their findings. They should describe the focus of their search, what they found, and their recommendations for solving any problems.

SCORING RUBRIC	
SCORE 4	Student's letter is well written and identifies the most serious runoff problem, explains why it is harmful, and outlines what steps should be taken to solve the problem. The letter also lists which people should help and, if necessary, suggests fundraising ideas.
SCORE 3	Student's letter indentifies the most serious problem, explains why it is harmful, and proposes a solution. It does not include details such as who should help or how to raise funds. There may be minor errors.
SCORE 2	Student's letter identifies the most serious problem and either explains why it is harmful or proposes a solution. No other details are included.
SCORE 1	Student's letter identifies the most serious problem, but contains little or no additional information.

Extension Activities

Assignment Have students identify similar problems near their homes and develop a plan for addressing one of those problems.

Field Trip Contact your local water department and arrange a trip to their water treatment facility. While there, ask the staff to describe the impact of stormwater runoff on water quality and the steps they take to make the water suitable for human consumption.

Copyright © Pearson Education, Inc., or its affiliates. All Rights Reserved.

Name ______________________ Date ____________ Class ____________

The Problem with Runoff

Purpose To investigate how runoff can affect the water quality of nearby lakes and streams

Materials

- school map (one per team)
- chalkboard, whiteboard, or chart paper
- measuring tape
- camera (optional)

Scenario

As hydrologists (water scientists), you and your partners are experts in stormwater runoff. You know that runoff can carry bad things into nearby streams. Sediments, toxic chemicals, and even nutrients can cause problems for animals and people who live in and near the streams.

Students at your local middle school are worried that their schoolyard may be causing a problem. They have asked your company to check for runoff problems on the school property.

Procedure

1. **Runoff Problems** Work together with your class to make a list of characteristics of your school's property that might lead to contamination of the water in a nearby stream or pond.
2. **Surveying the Schoolyard** Your teacher will divide the class into groups and assign each group one runoff problem from "Schoolyard Stormwater Survey." Once you receive your assignment, review its description with your group. Use a map of your school's property to survey for the location of your assigned problem.

Schoolyard Stormwater Survey

A. **Car and Truck Waste**
Stormwater can carry spilled motor oil, antifreeze, brake fluid, and other automotive fluids to nearby streams. Examine paved surfaces for spills.

B. **Yard and Garden Waste**
Grass clippings and other yard wastes can wash away and pollute streams and lakes. Search for yard waste.

C. **Roof Surfaces**
If downspouts empty onto hard surfaces, the water quickly runs off without soaking into the ground. Check the downspouts.

D. **Animal Waste**
Animal waste contains nutrients that promote the growth of algae in streams and also contains bacteria that can cause disease. Look for signs of animal waste that could contaminate streams.

E. **Lawn Chemicals**
Herbicides, insecticides, fungicides, and fertilizers must be stored in waterproof containers and out of the path of runoff. Check how the products your school has on site are stored.

F. **Bare Soil**
Water from rain and snow can erode bare soil and wash it into streams. Search for bare soil around the school.

G. **Paved Surfaces**
Paved surfaces prevent rainwater from soaking into the ground. Where does water from the parking lot or driveway go?

H. **Landscaping**
Lawns that slope the wrong way direct water onto neighboring property or streets. Terracing hills can slow the flow of runoff. A *rain garden* (a strip of thick vegetation) can slow or filter runoff.

Copyright © Pearson Education, Inc., or its affiliates. All Rights Reserved.

Name ______________________ Date __________ Class __________

Procedure *(continued)*

3. **Recording the Evidence** Record all evidence of your assigned runoff problem by marking the sites on your team's map and labeling the problem.
4. **The Report** Each group will have five minutes to explain to the whole class the focus of their search, what they found, and their recommendations for solving any problems they found. Plan your presentation together and make sure that everyone has a role to play.
5. **Ranking and Remediation** As you listen to the reports of other groups, pay close attention. Which problems seem the most severe, and which are the least severe?

Conclusion

Let's see what you learned about the runoff problems around your school.

1. What problem were you looking for, and what evidence did you find? ______________________

____

____

____

2. Of the problems that your class investigated, which do you consider most severe and why?

____

____

3. List one action that your school community (students, teachers, parents) can take to fix the problem.

____

____

Write a brief letter to your school's principal. Explain the most serious problem your class found, and why animals, plants, or people in your community are at risk. Tell your principal what can be done to solve the problem and which members of the school community should be asked to help. If there will be any cost involved or any materials or equipment needed (seeds, plants, shovels, etc.), be sure to suggest fundraising ideas.

Copyright © Pearson Education, Inc., or its affiliates. All Rights Reserved.

That Can't Possibly Work!

Investigation Overview

- Before you begin this investigation, you will need to make up one population bag for each student pair or group of 3-4. Dried beans or uncooked macaroni work well, but small plastic insects from a toy store are ideal. If you use plastic bugs, make sure the markers that students use have washable ink so the marks can be washed off and the bugs reused by the next class.
- Before students begin, point out that accurately counting all individuals in a population may not be possible or practical. Ask students for possible reasons why this is the case. For example, researchers cannot find all the individuals because they live underground, or it may not be possible to count all individuals because they move too quickly or are too numerous.
- Next, have your students read "Scientists Are Skeptical" and discuss times when they have been skeptical. Tell them they are being good scientists when they are skeptical.
- Have students read and discuss the Procedure. Answer all questions before distributing the bags and markers. Stress the importance of thoroughly mixing the population before each trial.
- Before collecting the bags at the end of the activity, have students discard all marked individuals (or wash the marks off plastic bugs). This is easiest to do when students are counting the actual population size in Step 9. You may or may not wish to replenish the lost beans or macaroni before each new class arrives.

SCORING RUBRIC	
SCORE 4	Student states that the friend is wrong and that the correct estimate is 600. The e-mail identifies the mistake: transposing the numbers of marked individuals.
SCORE 3	Student states that the friend is wrong and that the correct estimate is 600. The e-mail does not identify the source of the mistake.
SCORE 2	Student states that the friend is wrong but does not give the correct estimate. The e-mail does not identify the source of the mistake.
SCORE 1	Student states that the friend is wrong but does not give the correct estimate and/or writes an inadequate e-mail.

Extension Activities

Cooperative Learning Wild animal populations are increasing in urban and suburban environments. Chipmunks, coyotes, deer, and bears are now common in areas where they were rare only 10 years ago. Have the class investigate the wild animals in your community to determine whether their population sizes are changing. Students should work together in teams to investigate the reason(s) for any changes that are occurring.

Field Trip Arrange a trip to a field or wooded area near your school where your students can practice sampling techniques for estimating the size of a plant population. An example is the quadrat (a measured rectangle or square that is used to sample the abundance of a particular plant species within a larger area). By sampling many quadrats, ecologists can generate data sets for analysis. A common plant such as the dandelion is a good species to practice on. Students can also investigate other population-estimating techniques, such as the line transect or point sampling methods.

Copyright © Pearson Education, Inc., or its affiliates. All Rights Reserved.

Name ______________________ Date ____________ Class ____________

That Can't Possibly Work!

Purpose To investigate the accuracy of the Mark and Recapture population estimating method

Materials
- 15 plastic zipper storage bags
- felt-tip marker
- small items to fill the bags (dried beans, uncooked macaroni, etc.)

Scenario

You have just learned about a method for estimating the size of a population called "Mark and Recapture." Ecologists use Mark and Recapture when it isn't practical for them to count all the individuals in a population. Mark and Recapture involves estimating the size of a population by capturing, marking, and then recapturing some members of the population. This technique can yield a very accurate estimate. Perhaps you are skeptical? You need to see for yourself that this can work.

Mark and Recapture

1. To estimate the size of a population, a researcher visits the study area and uses traps to capture a group of individuals. Each individual is marked with a numbered tag or band and then released unharmed back into the environment.
2. The researcher goes away to allow time for the marked individuals to mix back into the population.
3. When the researcher returns, he or she captures another sample of individuals. Some of the individuals in this second sample will already be marked. The rest will not be marked.
4. The researcher records the number of marked and unmarked individuals in each sample. The researcher then uses a mathematical formula to calculate the size of the population. The researcher can estimate population size from as few as two visits to the study area, but more visits provide a more accurate estimate.

Scientists Are Skeptical

Scientists like to see evidence. When they read or hear about a new claim, their first reaction is to examine the evidence to see if the facts support the claim. When scientists read about a new way of doing something, they are skeptical about that, too. They ask, "Does the new way work as well as the older way of doing the same thing? Is the new way better?"

Procedure

1. **The Population** Your teacher will give you a bag filled with small objects. The objects represent a population of lively animals.
2. **The Capture and Mark** Capture 10 animals by reaching into the bag and removing them one at a time. (It's okay to look during this step.)
3. **The Mark** Mark the captured animals with the marker and return them to the bag.
4. **The Mix** Allow the population to mix. Stir them or shake them to get them to move.
5. **The Recapture** With your eyes closed, reach into the bag and remove 15 animals.

Copyright © Pearson Education, Inc., or its affiliates. All Rights Reserved.

Name ______________________ Date ______________ Class ______________

Procedure *(continued)*

6. Recording the Data Record on the data table the number of the recaptured animals that already have a mark.

7. Return and Repeat Return the animals to the bag and repeat Steps 4 and 5. Complete a total of 10 recaptures.

8. Total the Results After you have entered the counts from the 10 recaptures, add them and record the total number of recaptured animals that had a mark on them.

9. Calculate and Count Use the formula below to calculate your estimate of the population size, and then check your estimate by counting the actual number of animals in the bag:

Trial Number	Total Recaptured	Number Recaptured with a mark
1	15	
2	15	
3	15	
4	15	
5	15	
6	15	
7	15	
8	15	
9	15	
10	15	
Total:	150	

$$\text{Estimate of Total Population} = \frac{\text{(total number recaptured)} \times \text{(number originally marked)}}{\text{(total number recaptured with a mark)}}$$

Estimated size: ____________ Actual size: ____________

Conclusion

Let's see what you learned about estimating the size of a population using the Mark and Recapture method. Compare the actual size to the estimated size and answer the following questions.

1. How close was your estimate? ______________________
2. Was your estimate too high or too low? ______________________
3. Explain how you could make the estimate more accurate. ______________________
4. Are you still skeptical? Explain. ______________________

A friend of yours is using the Mark and Recapture technique to study the butterfly population in the area around his school. He first marked and released 50 butterflies. For four weeks, he checked his traps daily, counted the butterflies in the traps, and then released them. He caught a total of 300 butterflies, and 25 of them were marked. He determined that the total population of butterflies is 150. Is he correct? If not, what is the size of the butterfly population he is studying, and what mistake did he make? Prepare a brief answer to send to your friend by e-mail. Show all calculations.

Copyright © Pearson Education, Inc., or its affiliates. All Rights Reserved.

Some Resources Are Worth Saving

Investigation Overview

- Prepare blank public service announcement (PSA) placards by cutting large construction paper sheets into 36" × 11" strips. You will need one strip for each student.
- Have your students read the Scenario and Procedure. Review the meanings of the following terms: natural resource, renewable, nonrenewable, sustainable.
- If your students have trouble selecting three natural resources commonly used in your community, you may brainstorm with the whole class before they begin Step 2. Ask for suggestions and list them on the board or chart paper. Before moving on, ask if there are any items on the list for which there are no sustainable alternatives. Eliminate those and tell your students to begin working on their placards.

SCORING RUBRIC	
SCORE 4	Student produces a placard that clearly identifies a commonly used natural resource and encourages its conservation and sustainable use. The placard is colorful and neat, and uses a clever picture and/or humorous words to convey its message. The picture and lettering are easily visible from 10 feet, and there is no writing or image too close to the edge.
SCORE 3	Student's placard meets the standards for a score of 4, but the student did not deliver the message in a clever or humorous way, or there are minor errors.
SCORE 2	Student's placard meets the standards for a score of 3, but there are errors that demonstrate only partial understanding of conservation and sustainable use.
SCORE 1	Student's placard identifies a natural resource but does not address conservation or sustainable use. The design may be sloppy and/or contain significant errors.

Extension Activities

Assignment Have students investigate your community's waste transfer center, recycling center, water and/or sewage treatment plant(s), or any factory or business that extensively uses recycled material. They should search for statistics about one of these facilities and prepare a one-page report on their findings.

Cooperative Learning Have your students work together in teams of three to plan and conduct field trips to one of the facilities mentioned above. Team members should have specific roles. The team leader should make contact with an official at the site and schedule the trip. While at the site, one student should interview the official while the third student takes notes. Following the trip, the team should prepare a brief presentation for the rest of the class.

Field Trip Arrange a trip to one of the facilities mentioned at the left. (For example, most commercial car washes use less water, recycle what they do use, and send dirty water into the sewer system for treatment.) If your town has many of these facilities, and some students' parents are willing to drive, this is a perfect opportunity for multiple field trips. Divide the class into teams and have each team arrange for a parent to drive them. A student leader from each team can make the contact with an official at the site and schedule the trip. While at the site, students should take notes and prepare a brief group presentation for the class.

Copyright © Pearson Education, Inc., or its affiliates. All Rights Reserved.

Name ______________________________ Date______________ Class______________

Some Resources Are Worth Saving

Purpose To investigate ways to use sustainable resources

Materials
- markers and/or crayons
- construction paper strip (36" × 11")

Scenario

The news is full of stories about natural resources. As demand for them grows, some of our natural resources are becoming scarce! Since you are an environmental scientist, you know this problem well.

Although some natural resources are renewed by nature, many are not. When we use nonrenewable resources, they are gone forever. But there is good news: Some nonrenewable resources have substitutes that are renewable.

In your job, you study the sustainable use of our resources. Now you've been asked to encourage regular citizens to help. How can you make people want to conserve, recycle, and behave in ways that support sustainability? Perhaps advertising on city buses is an answer.

Public Service Announcement

Thousands of people use buses to get around town. Many cities keep bus fares low by selling advertising space. These ads, called *placard ads,* go in slots above the buses' windows. If you have been on a bus before, you have probably seen them.

If the ads are not sold, the city still uses the space. They can promote the bus service itself or worthwhile causes. These unpaid ads are called *public service announcements*, or PSAs.

The city has asked your company to create three PSAs to encourage people to use sustainable resources whenever possible. You and two partners have this important task, and you don't have much time! Your placards must meet certain size requirements, and they must be ready by tomorrow.

Size: 36 inches long by 11 inches high.

(Because the grooves that hold the placard in place will cover a half inch of every edge, the visible area is actually 35" × 10".)

Procedure

1. **Sustainable Resources** You and your two partners must work quickly. You will each select a different natural resource used by your community.
2. **Clever and Humorous** You will each design a placard to encourage conserving, recycling, or in some way promoting sustainable use of the resource you selected. Your placard should use a combination of clever and/or humorous pictures and words. Most importantly, your placard should catch the attention of as many bus riders as possible.

Copyright © Pearson Education, Inc., or its affiliates. All Rights Reserved.

Name ______________________ Date ____________ Class ____________

Procedure *(continued)*

3. **Helping Is Not Cheating** Although you will each design your own placard, please help your partner(s). Helping can include sharing ideas, proofreading, and even contributing skills like drawing or lettering.

4. **Making It Fit** Be sure the placard you design fits in the space allowed.

Conclusion

Let's see what you learned about conserving natural resources in your community.

1. What does sustainable mean?

____

____

2. Name a renewable natural resource and explain how it can be used in a sustainable way.

____

____

3. Name one nonrenewable natural resource and a renewable alternative for it.

____

____

4. Explain how population growth threatens natural resources.

____

____

____

Your finished placard must clearly identify a natural resource commonly used in your community and encourage its conservation and sustainable use. The placard must be colorful and neat, and include a clever picture and/or humorous words. The picture and lettering must be big enough to be visible from 10 feet away, but there should be no writing or image that will be covered up by the grooves.

Copyright © Pearson Education, Inc., or its affiliates. All Rights Reserved.

Just Count the Bubbles

Investigation Overview

- Prior to the investigation, obtain all materials including the *Elodea* and the baking soda you will add to the water. *Elodea* (American waterweed) is a freshwater plant that is available in most pet or aquarium supply stores. Each student pair will need one healthy *Elodea* sprig about 10 cm long. Keep the *Elodea* underwater in a lighted room or on a windowsill until you need it.
- Add approximately 1.5 teaspoons of sodium bicarbonate (baking soda) to a gallon of tap water. In water, baking soda breaks down and releases sodium ions, hydroxide ions, and carbon dioxide molecules. This ensures that there will be enough carbon dioxide available for the *Elodea* to carry out photosynthesis at a rapid pace.
- On the day of the investigation, have students begin by reading the Scenario and Steps 1–5. Answer any questions.
- Keep the classroom lights low and the plants out of direct sunlight so that most of the light the plant receives is coming from the 100-watt bulb in the lamp.
- Your students may question the statement in Step 4 that they only have to count one stream of bubbles. Tell them that what they are measuring is the rate of photosynthesis at different distances, and not the volume of the bubbles created.
- Remind students to turn off the bulb after every measurement. Students should wait until the bubbles have stopped before beginning the next measurement.

SCORING RUBRIC	
SCORE 4	The report follows the correct format and contains all required elements. All findings are supported by evidence, a properly labeled graph is included, and the recommendation is logical based on the evidence.
SCORE 3	The report meets all content standards required for a score of 4 but contains minor errors.
SCORE 2	The report either states findings or makes a recommendation. The findings or recommendation are supported by evidence. There may be several errors.
SCORE 1	The report is poorly written and has many errors. The report states findings or makes a recommendation, but there is insufficient supporting evidence.

Extension Activities

Cooperative Learning Have your students work in groups of three to design a spaceship that could produce enough oxygen to carry them on a deep-space mission. Have them consider the following questions:

- What materials and equipment will they need to bring on the mission?
- What skills will the people require to maintain the oxygen supplies?
- Where should the oxygen production system be stored on the ship?

Field Trip Arrange a field trip to a local arboretum, botanical garden, or farm. Have a spokesperson explain to your students which plants store their surplus food in a form that is used by people.

Copyright © Pearson Education, Inc., or its affiliates. All Rights Reserved.

Name ______________________ Date ______________ Class ______________

Just Count the Bubbles

Purpose To measure the effect of light intensity on the rate of photosynthesis

Materials

- lamp with a bare 100-watt lightbulb
- meter stick
- test tube rack
- test tube
- stopwatch
- 10-cm piece of *Elodea*
- 100 mL of baking soda and water solution

Scenario

As a botanist, you are an expert on plants. You know everything about their roots, stems, and leaves. You know that fossil evidence suggests that flowering plants were the most recent plants to appear on Earth. You also know that plants make their own food from light, water, and carbon dioxide—a process called *photosynthesis*—and give off oxygen during this process.

Since you know all of this, why were you stumped today when a NASA engineer emailed you with a simple question:

> How much light does it take before photosynthesis starts to work?

Of course you know the basic answer: It depends on the kind of plant. Some plants grow better in partial shade, and other plants grow better in direct sunlight.

NASA doesn't like that answer. They are planning a manned probe into deep space and will be using plants to supply the oxygen that the astronauts will need on the long journey. The NASA engineers have already picked the plant. They need to know how much light it needs before it will start to produce oxygen.

You and your partner have been given the very important job of finding an answer to this question.

Procedure

1. **Checking the List** Make sure you have the first five materials you will need to conduct this investigation. Plug in the lamp to check that it works, and then turn it off until you need it.
2. ***Elodea* Anyone?** Once you are ready, your teacher will give you a sprig of a freshwater plant called *Elodea* and a container of water. Place the *Elodea* upside down in a test tube and cover it with the baking soda and water solution. (When mixed with water, baking soda releases carbon dioxide.)
3. **Setting up the Lamp** The easiest way to vary the strength of the light is to change its distance from the plant. As you move the lamp farther away from the plant, the intensity of the light reaching the plant decreases. You will start by placing the lamp so that the tip of the bulb is 20 cm from the nearest point on the test tube. Measure carefully.
4. **Adjusting to the Light** Now turn on the lamp and wait five minutes. This will allow the plant time to adjust to the new amount of light it's exposed to. While the plant adjusts, observe it carefully. You should be able to see bubbles rising from it. NOTE: You will only count the bubbles coming from one spot on the plant.

Copyright © Pearson Education, Inc., or its affiliates. All Rights Reserved.

Name ______________________ Date ____________ Class ____________

Procedure *(continued)*

5. **Counting the Bubbles** After waiting five minutes, count the bubbles for exactly one minute. Record the number of bubbles per minute and record it in the 20-cm column in the chart below. Turn the lamp off after counting the bubbles.

6. **Dimmer and Dimmer** Now repeat Steps 3–5 at distances of 30, 40, and 50 cm. You are trying to find the greatest distance that the light can be from the plant and still produce a stream of bubbles. If your plant stops producing bubbles at 40 cm, there is no need to continue. On the other hand, if you still see bubbles at 50 cm, you will need to continue until they stop, or until there is no longer a decrease in the number of bubbles.

	Plant Distance from Lamp					
	20 cm	30 cm	40 cm	50 cm	60 cm	70 cm
Bubbles Per Minute						

Conclusion

Let's see what you learned about photosynthesis.

1. Why did your teacher add baking soda to the water?

____

2. What gas is inside of the bubbles formed by the plant?

____

3. What is the name of the process that is producing the bubbles?

____

4. Write the general formula for that process.

____

Write a report of your findings to the NASA engineers. Begin with this opening statement:

> My colleague and I tested the rate of oxygen production by *Elodea* at several light intensities. We found that, at a distance of ____ cm, the plant stopped producing oxygen bubbles.

Next, draw a graph to show your data. On the *x*-axis, show the distance from the light source. Begin with 20 cm and end with the largest distance you used. On the *y*-axis, show bubbles per minute. Start with zero at the bottom and number the axis up to the highest bubble rate that you measured. Be sure to provide a label on each axis of the graph and give your graph a title.

In the final paragraph, state your recommendation for the lowest practical minimum light level that should be used on the deep-space mission. You must each write your own report to the NASA engineers.

Copyright © Pearson Education, Inc., or its affiliates. All Rights Reserved.

The Cell Game

Investigation Overview

- Gather enough materials so that students can complete this investigation in groups of three. Each group will need a supply of markers or colored pencils, poster board, index cards, and materials for constructing a spinner.
- Have students read the Scenario and Procedure. Answer any questions.
- This activity will require little guidance from you as long as your students are familiar with board games. It is a good idea to have a simple game available for students to examine.
- Be prepared to direct students to the appropriate pages of their textbook to find information they can use to write questions.

SCORING RUBRIC	
SCORE 4	The board game meets the stated requirements: one easy and one hard question with correct answers for each cell part; game board with at least five cell part drawings; and designated places for question cards and spinner.
SCORE 3	The board game meets the stated requirements for a score of 4, but the student did not contribute equally.
SCORE 2	The board game meets the stated requirements for a score of 4, but the student's questions are of poor quality, incomplete, or incorrect.
SCORE 1	The board game is of poor quality and fails to meet multiple requirements, or the student contributed little to the game or questions.

Extension Activities

Assignment Have students design flash cards with pictures of each cell part on the front, and a description of the part's function on the back.

Cooperative Learning Before your students begin to design the board game, assign each a specific role to play. One student can have the title of game designer and be in charge of laying out the board. Another student can be in charge of creating a spinner and decorating the board with cell part drawings, and the third student can be responsible for designing and writing the game rules.

Field Trip Take your students on a field trip to a local pond or stream where they can collect water samples. Have each student collect a sample from a different location and record a detailed description of the location. When you return to the classroom, have your students examine drops of water under the microscope and contrast the different kinds of cells they find in different locations.

Copyright © Pearson Education, Inc., or its affiliates. All Rights Reserved.

Name ______________________ Date ____________ Class ____________

The Cell Game

Purpose To examine the parts and functions of animal cells and plant cells

Materials
- twelve index cards
- poster board
- pencils, pens, and markers
- thumbtack and other materials to construct spinner

Scenario

Suppose you're a biologist during the day, but at night you have hobby: You love to play board games. A famous board game company has asked you to help with a new project. They are designing a science board game just for middle school students. The game will require answering questions about the parts of a cell to move a game piece forward.

A series of squares will extend from the start square to the winner's circle. A spinner will determine the number of squares a player can move. After a player spins, an opponent will draw a card with two questions on it from the question bank. The opponent will say, "The questions are about [the cell part on the card]." If the player chooses the easy question and answers it correctly, the player will move forward exactly the number of squares on the spinner. If the player instead chooses the hard question and answers it correctly, the player moves forward the number on the spinner plus two bonus squares.

You may also add a penalty for wrong answers and an option to pass for a player who doesn't want to attempt to answer either question.

What the company wants from you is twelve question cards, one card for each cell part. Each card needs the name of the cell part, one hard question, one easy question, and the correct answers to both questions. They also want you to design the actual playing board for the game.

Procedure

1. **One Part Per Card** You will complete this investigation with your partners. Divide up the cell parts equally among the members of the group. Each group member will write question cards for his or her cell parts. Each question card should contain a hard question, an easy question, and answers for each. Write your questions on a piece of paper first. If you need help thinking of questions, use your textbook.

Parts of a Eukaryotic Cell

cell wall	endoplasmic reticulum (ER)	nucleolus
chloroplast	Golgi apparatus	nucleus
chromosome	lysosome	ribosome
cytoplasm	mitochondrion	vacuole

Copyright © Pearson Education, Inc., or its affiliates. All Rights Reserved.

Name ______________________ Date __________ Class __________

Procedure *(continued)*

2. **Testing Your Questions** Review your questions by reading them one at a time to your partners. If the wording confuses one or both of your partners, let them help you reword that question. If they think your questions are too hard or too easy, have them help you make them better.

3. **Neatness Counts** Once you and your partners are satisfied with the questions, write them on your cards as neatly as possible.

Conclusion

Let's see what you learned about the parts of cells.

1. Which cell parts from the list are only found in plant cells?

____

____

2. Which cell parts from the list are only found in animal cells?

____

____

3. Which cell parts from the eukaryote list would be missing from a list of prokaryote cell parts?

____

____

4. Some cells have special structures that help them move. Name one such structure and an example of a cell that has that structure.

____

____

Now create a board game like the one described by the game company. Be sure to decorate the game with drawings of at least five of the cell parts listed. Make a space on the board for the stack of question cards and label it "Question Bank." Also make a space for used question cards labeled "Question Dump" and a spinner with the numbers 1–4.

Copyright © Pearson Education, Inc., or its affiliates. All Rights Reserved.

Worms Under Attack!

Investigation Overview

- At least one day before the investigation, buy 1,000 wooden toothpicks. Stain 500 of them green by soaking them in food coloring and allowing them to dry overnight on newspaper. On the morning of the investigation, randomly spread the toothpicks throughout a grassy area of your schoolyard with well-defined boundaries.
- Ask your students to read the Scenario and think about the question asked at the end. Their answers to this question will become their hypotheses for the investigation. This will also be the first step in a think-pair-share strategy. (Note: Although Foa is one of the 171 islands in the South Pacific that form the Tonga archipelago, the story is fictional.)
- Have each student discuss his or her hypothesis with another student for one minute and be prepared to share their ideas with the class. Record students' ideas on chart paper.
- Give each student a clear plastic collection bag and have them read Step 1. Explain that you will be taking them to the area where you have spread the toothpicks. Once there, they will have 60 seconds to find as many toothpicks as they can.
- Escort your class to the hunting field. Signal them to start the hunt and begin timing. When time is up, signal the students to stop gathering toothpicks and return to class.
- Once back in the class, have your students complete Step 2. When all data have been recorded, compile class totals for use in Step 3.

SCORING RUBRIC	
SCORE 4	Student pair has produced an effective outline or script including a well-supported, logical prediction of how the pickworm population may change in the future. The terms *adaptation, survival of the fittest,* and *natural selection* are used correctly. Any visuals included are relevant to the presentation.
SCORE 3	All requirements for a score of 4 are met, but the written product may contain minor errors.
SCORE 2	The written product meets all requirements, but only correctly uses two of the three terms.
SCORE 1	The written product is inadequate and correctly uses at most one of the required terms.

Extension Activities

Assignment Have each student select one endangered animal in your state (a list is available at www.fws.gov) and write a brief report describing the changes in the environment that are making survival more difficult for the animal.

Cooperative Learning Have students work together in teams of three to create a *Survival of the Fittest* board game. Each student should have a specific role to play, so form teams that have students with the skills needed to complete the task.

Copyright © Pearson Education, Inc., or its affiliates. All Rights Reserved.

Name ______________________ Date ____________ Class ____________

Worms Under Attack!

Purpose
To investigate species diversity and adaptation

Materials
- 1,000 wooden toothpicks (500 dyed green and 500 left their natural color)
- one clear plastic collection bag for each member of the class

Scenario

The Foa Island Pickworm

Pickworms (*Toothpickidus wormosum*) are the biggest tourist attraction on Foa Island in the Kingdom of Tonga. They are skinny, straight worms that live on Foa's grassy lawns. Pickworms feed on the surface in the daytime. They retreat below ground at night. The worms' main predators are wild pigs, which are nocturnal (they only come out at night).

Pickworms are all nearly identical, except for their color. About half of all pickworms are green, and the other half are tan. Until now, the pickworms have had no daytime enemy. That just changed!

An oil tanker passing near Foa during last night's storm was the home of two rare East Texas worm hawks. The birds had been hanging around the tanker for years because of the captain's hobby. Breeding mealworms on the ship's deck provided many hours of enjoyment for the captain and plenty of food for the hawks.

But during the storm, a violent gust of wind lifted the worm hawks high into the air and carried them far from the tanker. When the storm ended, the hungry and dazed hawks found themselves on the front lawn of the governor's mansion on Foa Island. They were surrounded by pickworms!

As the official Foa Island naturalist, you have a job to do: The Governor wants you to find out what will become of Foa's famous pickworms. Are they safe, or should the East Texas worm hawks be captured before it's too late?

Procedure

1. **A worm disaster?** In the first part of this investigation, you and the other naturalists will pretend to be worm hawks. You will swoop down on an area where your teacher has placed 1,000 toothpicks that match the natural colors of the Foa Island pickworms. Your job is to catch as many model pickworms as you can.

2. **Your Data**
   - Number of tan pickworms caught ________
   - Number of green pickworms caught ________
   - Total pickworms you caught ________

3. **Class Data**
   - Total tan pickworms caught ________
   - Total green pickworms caught ________
   - Total pickworms caught by the class ________

Copyright © Pearson Education, Inc., or its affiliates. All Rights Reserved.

Name ______________________ Date ______________ Class ______________

Conclusion

Let's see what you learned about the diversity and adaptation of the pickworms. As you answer these questions, assume that pickworms reproduce very rapidly and easily feed the worm hawks.

1. Why were different numbers of tan and green pickworms collected?

____

____

2. If the hawks are captured, and the surviving pickworms are allowed to grow and reproduce, what will the population probably look like after several years? Explain.

____

____

____

3. A change in the environment can stimulate the process of natural selection. How did the environment on Foa Island change today?

____

____

4. How might the result of this experiment be different if the grass was dead and brown? Explain your reasoning.

____

____

____

5. How would an evolutionary biologist explain the worms' adaptations over several years?

____

____

The National Academy of Sciences has asked you and a partner to make a presentation at the next meeting. They are interested in the effects of predation on the pickworm population. Use your data to show any effects you found. Predict how future generations may differ from the present. Think about and use these terms and phrases as you prepare your talk: *adaptation, survival of the fittest,* and *natural selection*. Prepare a written outline or a script for your presentation. (Optional: You may want to present graphics or charts to illustrate your findings.)

Only one or two teams will be asked to present their findings at the meeting. However, all teams must be prepared, and all written work will be collected.

Copyright © Pearson Education, Inc., or its affiliates. All Rights Reserved.

The WWGP Is Coming

Investigation Overview

- The World-Wide Genome Project is not a real organization. However, the description of its work provided in the Scenario represents real scientific work that is going on in similar organizations around the world.
- Several days prior to the investigation, assemble the materials. You will need to dye half of the foam packing peanuts to distinguish deoxyribose from phosphate molecules.
- Make a supply bag for each student pair. Each bag should include 16 foam packing peanuts (8 dyed, 8 undyed), dried beans (two pieces each of four different beans), four toothpicks, and two 20-cm pieces of thread.
- Provide extra materials for students to make the key for their model.
- Students will complete this investigation in pairs. On the day of the investigation, have students read the Scenario and Procedure. Answer all questions, and then tell students to begin.
- As your students work, circulate among them and make sure they are following the directions.
- When students near the end of the model-building phase of the investigation, caution them not to twist their model too much, or it could fall apart.

SCORING RUBRIC	
SCORE 4	The DNA model is accurate (base pairs are connected from sugar to sugar to form a ladder), and bases are correctly paired (adenine with thymine, cytosine with guanine). The title and labels are printed neatly and spelled correctly, and a sample is mounted next to each label.
SCORE 3	The model meets all criteria for a score of 4, but has minor errors.
SCORE 2	The model contains a significant error or omission.
SCORE 1	The model is poorly made, with significant errors or omissions.

Extension Activities

Assignment Scientists do genome sequencing to study genetic diseases in humans and animals, and to learn about the genes that code for useful traits in plants and animals. Have students select an animal or plant whose genome they think should be sequenced next and explain why they selected it. They should name a disease or an important trait that should be studied in the organism.

Cooperative Learning You may expand the cooperative nature of this investigation by having four pairs join forces to link their models. If you plan to extend the investigation this way, make sure all color-coding is agreed upon before pairs build their individual models. Instruct pairs to check the accuracy of each other's models before joining them together.

Field Trip Arrange a field trip to a university or commercial laboratory where genetic research is taking place. Students will be able to see scientists using gene sequencers, electrophoresis, and other procedures. If there is no such research laboratory in your community, many science museums have a section dealing with DNA or genetics.

Copyright © Pearson Education, Inc., or its affiliates. All Rights Reserved.

Name ________________________ Date ____________ Class ____________

The WWGP Is Coming

Purpose To build a model of a DNA molecule

Materials

- 16 foam packing peanuts (8 plain, 8 dyed)
- 8 dried beans (4 types, 2 of each type)
- 4 toothpicks
- two 20-cm pieces of thread
- needle
- scissors

Scenario

The unique genetic code that determines the appearance and characteristics of every living organism is called its *genome*. You have a genome, and so does your dog. The African violet growing in your window has a totally different genome. The genome of every living thing is found in the DNA molecules that make up every chromosome in every cell.

Scientists around the world are busy sequencing the genomes of different organisms. In 1995, the first genome was published. It was the genome of a simple bacterium. Now, genome sequences have been completed for animals, plants, and fungi. For example, we now know the complete genetic codes for the rice plant, honeybee, mouse, cow, dog, cat, guinea pig, and human.

The World-Wide Genome Project (WWGP) is coordinating the mapping of all of these genomes, and it has decided to build its headquarters in your town. The building will be the storage place for all successfully mapped genomes. It will be like a library. Instead of words, sentences, and paragraphs, this library will hold codes made of long chains of these four letters: A, T, C, and G.

Here's where you come in. The architect designing the WWGP headquarters has hired your company to produce a model of a DNA molecule to hang in the lobby of the new building. You and your partner are master model builders, and you want the contract for this important job. The WWGP president will choose the best design from all of the models submitted, and he wants them by tomorrow.

If you are going to win the $500,000 contract, you need to work quickly.

Procedure

1. **Gathering the Materials** To build a model of a DNA molecule, you will need to represent each of the components that make up the real thing. DNA is composed of nucleotide bases (adenine, cytosine, guanine and thymine), a sugar called deoxyribose, and phosphate molecules. For your model, you will use foam packing peanuts to represent molecules of deoxyribose, and dyed foam packing peanuts to represent phosphate molecules. You will use four different types of dried beans to represent the bases. String and toothpicks will hold everything together.

2. **Building the Backbones** A DNA molecule is supported by two strands of alternating sugar and phosphate molecules. To build the supporting backbones for your model, alternate dyed and undyed foam packing peanuts in two rows of eight peanuts. For each strand, use the needle and thread to connect four dyed pieces and four undyed pieces lengthwise.

Copyright © Pearson Education, Inc., or its affiliates. All Rights Reserved.

Name ______________________ Date__________ Class__________

Procedure *(continued)*

3. **Connecting the Base Pairs** The dried beans represent the bases (adenine, cytosine, guanine, and thymine). Decide which bean you want to represent each base, and then connect each pair of bases using a toothpick. Be sure to pair your bases accurately. Remember, adenine only pairs with thymine, and cytosine only pairs with guanine.

4. **Putting It All Together** Next, you will connect the two strands of peanuts together. In a molecule of DNA, base pairs are attached to the deoxyribose sugar molecules in each strand. It resembles a ladder, with the paired bases acting as the rungs of the ladder. In your model, use the dried-bean base pairs to connect the two strands of peanuts. The two strands of peanuts represent the sugar molecules.

5. **Giving It a Twist** Hold the ends of your model and give it a slight twist so that it has the double-helix shape of a DNA molecule.

Conclusion

Let's see what you learned about DNA.

1. What makes up the supporting strands of a DNA molecule?

____

2. Name the nucleotide bases that join the two DNA strands.

____

3. What nucleotide can form a pair with adenine?

____

4. What nucleotide can form a pair with cytosine?

____

5. What is a genome?

____

____

The president of WWGP not only wants to make sure your model is accurate but also wants you to have a title for your model and a key to the meaning of each color.

Give your model a descriptive title and create a key that explains the parts of your model. (You have heard that the president prefers that you use an actual sample of the substance used in the model for your key). Make sure all words are printed neatly and spelled correctly.

Copyright © Pearson Education, Inc., or its affiliates. All Rights Reserved.

We All Have It, So It Must Be Dominant!

Investigation Overview

- Engage your students by explaining that, even though most people think that dominant traits are always the most common traits (for example, brown eyes), this is not always the case. Sometimes a recessive trait is more common than the dominant form. Examples include the genes for Type "O" blood, polydactyly (extra fingers and/or toes), and achondroplasia (a common cause of dwarfism).
- Have your students read the Scenario and Procedure. Answer any questions, assign student pairs, and instruct the class to proceed with Steps 1 and 2.
- As students complete Step 2, post a table where the entire class can record their results. As students finish, have them record their results on the chart. Calculate and post the total for each trait.
- Explain to students that the reason a recessive trait can be more common than the dominant form relates to the gene pool (all of the possible alleles for a particular gene in a given population). Any particular allele can be more or less common in the gene pool. If the recessive allele represents 90 percent of the alleles in the gene pool, it will be the most commonly expressed. Unless the dominant gene provides a selection advantage, the relative percentages will remain constant over very long periods of time.

SCORING RUBRIC	
SCORE 4	Student writes a brief e-mail using complete sentences that explains why there is no relationship between dominance and the frequency of a trait, mentions the "gene pool," and gives two or more examples of recessive human traits that are more common than corresponding dominant traits.
SCORE 3	Student's e-mail meets the content standards for a score of 4 but contains minor errors.
SCORE 2	Student's e-mail gives only one example of a recessive trait that is more common than the dominant one.
SCORE 1	Student's e-mail is missing more than one required element or contains incorrect information.

Extension Activities

Assignment Have students estimate the frequency of each recessive trait in the human gene pool. To do this, first calculate the fraction of students in the class with the trait. This is the probability of two recessive genes occurring together in the same individual. The square root of this number is the fraction of the allele in the gene pool. For example, if 13 students in a class of 28 have Type O blood, then the fraction of the class with Type O blood is 13/28, or 0.46. The percent of genes in the gene pool that are Type O, however, is the square root of 0.46, which is 0.68, or 68 percent.

Field Trip Arrange a trip to a zoo that is breeding endangered animals so they can be released back into the wild. Such breeding programs strive to select animals with genetic traits that will ensure a high likelihood of survival for the offspring. Have a representative of the zoo speak to your class about its breeding program.

Copyright © Pearson Education, Inc., or its affiliates. All Rights Reserved.

Name ______________________ Date ____________ Class ____________

We All Have It, So It Must Be Dominant!

Purpose To investigate the relationship between the frequency and dominance of genetic traits

Materials
- paper
- pen or pencil

Scenario

In your science class, you are learning about inheritance. Today your teacher told the class that just because a trait is the most common, that doesn't mean it's a dominant allele. Sometimes the most common trait is recessive.

How can that be true? It makes much more sense that the most common trait should be the one that is dominant. Like a good scientist, you have decided to investigate on your own before you accept what your teacher told you.

Procedure

1. **Check Yourself** Work with a partner to determine whether or not you have the dominant or the recessive trait for each of these six common human characteristics. Record your results in your notebook.

Some Human Characteristics

Dimples: Dimples (dominant) vs. No dimples (recessive)

A dimple is a dent that appears on your right and/or left cheek when you smile.

Earlobes: Free earlobes (dominant) vs. Attached earlobes (recessive)

Free earlobes hang below the point where they join the head. Attached earlobes do not.

Mid-digit hair: Mid-digit hair (dominant) vs. No mid-digit hair (recessive)

Look at the finger next to your pinky. If hair is growing on the back of your finger between the second and third knuckles, it's called mid-digit hair.

Forelock: White forelock (dominant) vs. No white forelock (recessive)

A white forelock is a patch of white hair located just above the forehead.

Pinky: Straight pinky (recessive) vs. Bent pinky (dominant)

Hold your hands tightly together (pinky against pinky) with your palms facing up and your fingers extended. If the tips of your pinkies begin to point away from one another at the last knuckle, they are bent.

Thumbs: Straight thumb (dominant) vs. Curved thumb (recessive)

Hold one hand out in front of you with your palm facing away. Keep your fingers together but stick your thumb out as far as possible. Look at the line from the bottom of your hand up to the tip of your thumb. Does it make a straight line, or is there a major curve?

Copyright © Pearson Education, Inc., or its affiliates. All Rights Reserved.

Name ______________________ Date ______________ Class ______________

Tay-Sachs

Purpose

To examine the probability of carrying the gene for Tay-Sachs disease

Materials

- paper
- pen
- computer and printer (optional)

Scenario

You are a genetic counselor. Your job is to evaluate clients' family histories and medical records, order genetic tests, evaluate the results, and advise parents if they have or are carriers for a genetic disease.

John and Mary Klein are new clients who were referred to you for help. They are a newly-married couple who are considering having children. They are concerned because genetic tests have shown that they are both carriers for Tay-Sachs disease.

John and Mary want to know more about Tay-Sachs. They are especially interested in the probability that their children will have Tay-Sachs or be carriers.

Tay-Sachs Disease

Tay-Sachs disease is a devastating genetic disorder caused by an autosomal-recessive mutation. Babies born with Tay-Sachs develop normally for the first few months of life, but then development slows and eventually reverses.

In Tay-Sachs patients, fat begins to build up in the nerve cells in the brain. This buildup leads to problems such as blindness, paralysis, and eventually, death.

There is no cure for Tay-Sachs, but it is possible to identify carriers for the disease. This means parents can know if they are at risk for having a child with Tay-Sachs.

Procedure

1. Just the Facts In order to answer John and Mary's questions, you have researched the following facts about Tay-Sachs:

The Facts About Tay-Sachs

- Tay-Sachs disease is a hereditary disease that is most common in people with Eastern European ancestry.
- Tay-Sachs disease is caused by a recessive allele on chromosome 15.
- In order for a child to inherit Tay-Sachs disease, both parents must be carriers of the gene. Being a carrier means that a person's phenotype is normal, but his or her genotype is heterozygous.
- Carriers of Tay-Sachs have no symptoms of the disease.

Copyright © Pearson Education, Inc., or its affiliates. All Rights Reserved.

Name ______________________ Date ______________ Class ______________

Procedure *(continued)*

2. **The Tay-Sachs Square** Draw a Punnett square to show a cross between parents who are both carrying the Tay-Sachs allele (they are heterozygous). Let "H" stand for the normal, healthy allele, and "h" stand for Tay-Sachs.

   What is the probability that a child in this family will have Tay-Sachs? ______________

   What is the probability that a child in this family child will be heterozygous? ______________

   What is the probability that a child in this family will not carry the allele? ______________

Conclusion

Let's see what you learned about heredity.

1. Write a question that you will ask John and Mary about their family history.

   ____

   ____

2. Is Tay-Sachs caused by a recessive allele or a dominant allele? Explain.

   ____

3. Is Tay-Sachs a sex-linked disease? Explain.

   ____

   ____

4. Babies who suffer from Tay-Sachs disease always die before they reach reproductive age. That means that no person with Tay-Sachs disease is ever a parent. Why doesn't Tay-Sachs disappear from the human genome?

   ____

   ____

   ____

   ____

When John and Mary come for their appointment, you need to give them a handout. Make a handout that explains Tay-Sachs is a recessive hereditary disease. Your pamphlet should also include a Punnett square to demonstrate the possible genotypes of the children carrier parents may have. Finally, state the probability that their child will have Tay-Sachs disease and the probability that their child will be a carrier.

Copyright © Pearson Education, Inc., or its affiliates. All Rights Reserved.

The Stomach Stone Controversy

Investigation Overview

- At least one day before investigation, obtain one index card for each student.
- Begin the investigation by having students read the Scenario and Procedure. You may want to demonstrate how a stomach stone works using a rough stone and a plant, such as celery.
- Explain to your students that many animals that swallow their food whole have a special kind of muscular stomach called a gizzard. The gizzard grinds whole food, often with the help of small rocks or grit that the animal swallows. Birds, crocodiles, most invertebrates, and some fish have gizzards.
- You can let students work together in pairs to complete the Procedure, but each student should work individually to complete the Conclusion.

SCORING RUBRIC	
SCORE 4	Student accurately and effectively states on an index card two reasons why sauropods needed stomach stones.
SCORE 3	Student states two reasons why sauropods needed stomach stones, but the reasons are vague or contain minor errors.
SCORE 2	Student gives one correct reason why sauropods needed stomach stones.
SCORE 1	Student's reason(s) demonstrate minimal understanding of the lesson's concepts.

Extension Activities

Assignment Have students work in teams of two to design and build a working model of a gizzard with stomach stones. They should test their model's ability to grind different types of food and report their findings.

Cooperative Learning Have students work in teams of four to create a poster explaining the digestive system of a sponge, hydra, earthworm, fish, chicken, or cow. They should include a labeled drawing of the animal and its digestive system, a description of the digestion process, and a list of the food the animal eats.

Field Trip Arrange a trip to a farm where the farmer can explain the special digestive system in a cow or steer and the role of grit in the diet of the chickens.

Copyright © Pearson Education, Inc., or its affiliates. All Rights Reserved.

Name ______________________ Date ____________ Class ____________

The Stomach Stone Controversy

Purpose To investigate the effectiveness of gastroliths as a means of digestion

Materials
- Student Edition
- index cards
- pencil or pen

Scenario

John is a fast eater. His parents complain that he gulps down his food faster than they can put it on the table. His mother is constantly saying, "John! Chew your food!" He ignores his mother and goes on eating as quickly as ever.

John thinks that the only point of chewing is to make food easier to swallow. As long as he swallows without choking, what's the big deal?

Chewing is more than preparation for swallowing. Chewing breaks down large pieces of food into smaller particles. This gives the food more surface area. The more surface area, the better the food particles mix with digestive chemicals in the mouth, stomach, and intestines. Better mixing means more contact with the chemicals, and that means better digestion.

But some animals don't have teeth. How do they grind their food into smaller particles? Birds, for example, have muscular organs called gizzards that do the work. Birds that eat seeds must also eat grit. Grit is small bits of rocks that birds swallow for use in their gizzards. Grit helps break up the hard seeds that birds eat. After a time, these stomach stones (also known as gastroliths) become smooth and polished.

Highly polished stones that are unlike others in the area are sometimes found near fossilized skeletons of sauropods and other plant-eating dinosaurs. Some scientists think the reason the stones are round and polished is that they came from the dinosaurs' gizzards. There's a problem! Birds have gizzards because they don't have teeth, but dinosaurs had teeth. Why would sauropods need gizzards and stomach stones to grind their food? Wouldn't their teeth do the job?

Procedure

1. **Human Teeth** Humans have four different kinds of teeth, and each has a different purpose. Adult humans have 32 teeth—eight incisors, four canines, eight premolars, and 12 molars. Incisors are located in the front of the mouth and have a sharp chisel-like edge used to cut food. On either side of the incisors are the canines, which tear food. Premolars mash and grind food, and molars are used for big grinding jobs.

2. **Different Teeth for Different Foods** Animals with different diets have different kinds of teeth. The predominant teeth in carnivores (meat eaters) are the canines, which tear flesh. Herbivores (plant eaters) need the wide surfaces of molars to grind away at the tough cell walls of plants. Omnivores (animals that eat both meat and plants) have both kinds of teeth—humans are omnivores.

Copyright © Pearson Education, Inc., or its affiliates. All Rights Reserved.

Name ______________________ Date __________ Class __________

Procedure *(continued)*

3. **Something is Missing** Examine this chart. It shows the kinds of teeth found in dinosaurs and some living animals. Pay particular attention to the sauropods. How are they different from other herbivores?

____

Animal	Food	Kinds of Teeth			
		chisel-shaped, for biting	pencil-like, for shredding	sharp, for tearing	wide, for grinding
sauropods	plants		✔		
theropods	meat			✔	
elephants	plants				✔
cattle	plants	✔			✔
horses	plants	✔			✔
tiger	meat			✔	
bears	meat and plants	✔			✔
raccoons	meat and plants	✔		✔	✔

Conclusion

Let's see what you learned about digestion.

1. In humans, the digestive process begins with chewing. How does chewing help digestion?

____

____

2. Why do different animals have different types of teeth?

____

3. What kind(s) of teeth did sauropods have? What was the purpose of those teeth?

____

4. Why do you think sauropods may have used gizzards to grind their food?

____

____

A controversy has broken out in your class. Some students think that since sauropods had teeth they didn't need gizzards or gastroliths. You are one of the students who understands that teeth were not enough. Your teacher has asked everyone who understands this idea to tutor someone who doesn't understand. First, you must put your ideas in writing. On an index card, write two reasons why you are convinced that sauropods needed gizzards with stomach stones. Write your reasons using complete sentences.

Copyright © Pearson Education, Inc., or its affiliates. All Rights Reserved.

Fantasy Zoo

Investigation Overview

- Gather enough materials for students to complete this investigation in pairs.
- Write the names of the major animal groups (sponges, cnidarians, flatworms, roundworms, segmented worms, mollusks, echinoderms, crustaceans, insects, centipedes, spiders, fish, amphibians, reptiles, birds, and mammals) on 16 pieces of paper and fold them so that it is impossible to see what is written on each piece.
- Have students read the Scenario and Procedure. While they are reading, place the folded papers in a box or other container, shuffle them, and allow each team to pull one from the box. Before proceeding, answer any questions.
- Students should not be expected to create real Latin names. However, a list of some real scientific names will help them see the kinds of endings that are common to Latin names. Some examples include *Mus musculus* (house mouse), *Ursus maritimus* (polar bear), *Hymenolepis diminuta* (tapeworm), and *Paralithodes camtschaticus* (king crab).

SCORING RUBRIC	
SCORE 4	Student team draws a full-color picture that accurately represents the assigned animal group and includes all appropriate labels and a list of characteristics common to the creature's group.
SCORE 3	The drawing meets all of the content requirements for a score of 4, but students did not contribute equally to the project.
SCORE 2	The picture of the creature is accurate, but some of the required information is missing.
SCORE 1	A large portion of the required information is missing or inaccurate.

Extension Activities

Assignment Have students identify a real animal that belongs to the same group as their fantasy animal. Have them use the library or Internet to research its scientific name and the characteristics that make it a typical member of its group. They should also try to find one characteristic that sets it apart from the group.

Cooperative Learning Have each student team join another team to create a 30-second radio advertisement for the new fantasy feature of the zoo. Give each person on the team a role to play: producer, director, sound-effects expert, and on-air talent. Everyone on the team is responsible for writing a clever script that will catch people's attention. The producer is responsible for obtaining and operating the recording equipment. The director will help the on-air talent and sound-effects expert rehearse their parts. The talent will read the script, and the sound-effects expert will make animal noises and other zoo-related sounds.

Field Trip Arrange a field trip to a local zoo or animal preserve and have students find one real representative of each of the animal groups investigated.

Copyright © Pearson Education, Inc., or its affiliates. All Rights Reserved.

Name ______________________ Date ____________ Class ____________

Fantasy Zoo

Purpose To investigate animal diversity

Materials
- markers or crayons
- blank paper

Scenario

As one of the keepers at your local zoo, your job depends on keeping the public happy and the attendance high. The new baby panda will keep people coming for a long time, but what happens when it grows up? What will be the zoo's next attraction?

You just finished reading a book that gave you an idea. The newest book in *The Adventures of Henry Porter* series by Curtis Larking is called *The Creepy Food Chain.*

The story is really weird—it takes place in a fantasy world filled with imaginary plants and animals. Besides Henry, the main characters in the book are an herbivore, a carnivore, and a scavenger. The organisms are fictional but scientifically accurate in the ways they relate to one another.

The book has given you an idea. You and the other zookeepers can create imaginary animals—one representing each of the major animal groups. Once your creations are ready, you can hide them in the exhibits with real animals of the same group so that people can hunt for the fantasy animals as they visit.

The zoo's director loves your idea and wants you to get started immediately by drawing a picture that shows what one of the fantasy animals will look like.

Procedure

1. **Fantasy Teams** For this project you will work in pairs. You will work together to design a fantasy animal that is scientifically accurate.
2. **Inventing a Mollusk (For Example)** Your teacher will ask you to pull one of 16 folded pieces of paper from a box. Each piece will identify a different animal group. The fantasy creature that your team designs has to fit with the group listed on your paper.
3. **Creating a Creature** Remember, the creature you are creating must be strange. After all, if we are going to attract more people to the zoo, the creatures have to be *very* interesting. Work together with your partner to create a creature that no one has ever seen before. Make sure your creature has all of the characteristics listed in your textbook for your particular animal group.
4. **What Not to Show** Also make sure that your fantasy creature does not have any characteristics that should not be found in the group. For example, reptiles cannot have feathers and fish cannot have feet.
5. **Drawing Your Creature** Draw a full-color picture of your creature. Make it big enough to almost fill a sheet of copier paper, but leave room for some labels.

Copyright © Pearson Education, Inc., or its affiliates. All Rights Reserved.

Name ______________________ Date ______________ Class ______________

Conclusion

Let's see what you learned about the animals in your group.

1. What animal group does your creature represent?

2. What kind of symmetry does your animal have?

3. Is your creature a vertebrate or an invertebrate?

4. Is it an ectotherm or an endotherm? Explain what that means.

The zoo director wants some labels on the drawing of your creature. Be sure to give it a common name and a scientific name. Use what you know about other creatures' scientific names to invent the scientific name. (Your teacher can give you a few examples.) List the group to which your creature belongs, and label all of the characteristics that are common to that group. If the creature has a particular symmetry or is a vertebrate, be sure to mention it on your poster.

Copyright © Pearson Education, Inc., or its affiliates. All Rights Reserved.

Mom's Car Must Be Alive

Investigation Overview

- Make sure that students bring their textbooks on the day of the investigation. Prior to the start of class, locate the page(s) in the Student Edition that describe the characteristics of living things. You will need to direct students to the appropriate textbook page(s).
- Begin by having students read the Scenario and Steps 1 and 2. Answer all questions, and have students work individually to complete the investigation.
- As students work, circulate among them, answering questions as they arise.

SCORING RUBRIC	
SCORE 4	Student writes a script that answers the question by including one characteristic only found in living things (cellular organization, growth and development, or reproduction), explaining the characteristic, and explaining how to tell that it is missing from cars and other nonliving things. The answer is short, simple, and understandable to a sixth grader.
SCORE 3	The script covers all content standards for a score of 4, but the wording is not appropriate for a sixth grader.
SCORE 2	The script does not explain how to tell that the characteristic is missing in nonliving things.
SCORE 1	The script provides an incorrect characteristic, or gives a correct characteristic but does not include an explanation.

Extension Activities

Assignment Some of the characteristics of living things are hard to see or measure without special equipment, and others are easy to see. Have students plant a bean seed against the inside of a clear plastic cup, observe it for two weeks, and record any observable evidence that the bean is alive. (They should see evidence of growth and development.)

Cooperative Learning The producers of a new science-fiction movie need an imaginary living creature. Have your students work together in teams of three to design the creature. They must account for how the creature grows and develops, how its cells are organized, and how it reproduces. Each student will be responsible for a different characteristic of the creature. Each student should work independently on their assigned characteristic, which should be strange or unique. They will then write a brief explanation and share their ideas with the rest of the team. Next, each team will work together to design and draw a picture of the outward appearance of their creature and place it on a poster along with the explanations they have written. The challenge is to make the outward appearance match the uniqueness of the characteristics described.

Field Trip Arrange a field trip to a local zoo or animal park. Have each student prepare a brief report on the growth and development of a different animal. This information is usually displayed at each animal exhibit. A representative from the zoo should be able to provide you with a list of animals in the exhibits so that you can assign each student a different animal before arriving. Such a list may also be found on the zoo's web site.

Copyright © Pearson Education, Inc., or its affiliates. All Rights Reserved.

Name ______________________________ Date______________ Class______________

Mom's Car Must Be Alive

Purpose To investigate the characteristics of living things

Materials
- Student Edition
- paper
- pen or pencil

Scenario

On your local radio station, you are known as *The Science Answer Person*. Your show has a simple format. The audience e-mails questions to you, and you answer them on the air.

You know your science, so most of the questions are easy to answer. Sometimes the answers are hard to put into words that very young children can understand. But today's question from a sixth grader should be easy:

Hi Science Answer Person,

Yesterday my science teacher told us about something she called "life processes." She said that all living things move, sense their environment, get energy from food, use oxygen, excrete waste products, grow, and reproduce.

Until she mentioned growing and reproducing, all I could think of was my mom's car. Her car moves, its headlights dim automatically when it sees another car at night, her car gets its energy from food (gasoline), it takes in oxygen, and excretes exhaust.

I know her car doesn't grow or reproduce, but it communicates (it has a talking GPS system). Surely that counts for something.

My mother's car must be alive ... right?

Signed: Confused Sixth Grader

This sixth grader is confused because the old list of life processes mentioned in the above letter isn't very useful today. Many nonliving things do the same things that living things do. It's much more useful to look at the characteristics that are common to all living things. These are the same characteristics that are discussed in your textbook.

You will need to answer this listener's question on your next show. To make your answer as simple (and entertaining) as possible, you must pick the one characteristic of living things that makes the point most clearly.

Copyright © Pearson Education, Inc., or its affiliates. All Rights Reserved.

Name ______________________ Date ____________ Class ____________

Procedure

1. **Read All About It** Your teacher will direct you to read the pages in your textbook about the characteristics of living things

2. **Pick One** Some of the characteristics described apply to both living things and some nonliving things. Other characteristics are unique to living things. Which one characteristic do you think makes it most clear that a car is not a living thing? Explain your choice.

____

____

____

Conclusion

Let's see what you learned about the characteristics of living things.

1. Which characteristics are only found in living things?

____

____

2. Which characteristics of living things can also be found in nonliving things?

____

____

3. How are growth and development different?

____

____

____

4. Organisms reproduce in two different ways. What are they called and how do they differ?

____

____

____

Now it's time to prepare the script for tomorrow's show. In the script, you must answer the question that Confused Sixth Grader asked. Answer it by stating the one characteristic that you believe makes it most clear that a car is not living, explain what the characteristic means, and then explain how you can tell that the characteristic is missing from cars and other nonliving things. Keep your explanation short, simple, and understandable to a sixth grader.

Copyright © Pearson Education, Inc., or its affiliates. All Rights Reserved.

Plants in Space

Investigation Overview

- In this investigation, students will recommend a plant that will help support the crew of a Mars colony.
- Begin by having students read the Scenario and Procedure.
- Discuss the Scenario as a class and answer any questions. Also, discuss the problems that humans will have living on Mars, based on the conditions listed in "Life on Mars."
- Review the characteristics of the different kinds of plants (nonvascular, seedless vascular, and vascular plants with seeds).
- Ask students to suggest food plants they can use and list them on the board or chart paper.
- Encourage students to think about advantages of growing a variety of food plants instead of just one crop. Answers may include: the risk of a disease wiping out the crop, the desire for variety in the diet, and the fact that each food provides a unique set of nutrients.

SCORING RUBRIC	
SCORE 4	Student prepares a recommendation for the best plant to use on the Mars colony, includes all required information about the plant, and discusses the importance of producing oxygen and removing carbon dioxide from the atmosphere.
SCORE 3	The letter contains all of the content required for a score of 4 but is not well written or contains minor errors.
SCORE 2	The letter fails to explain why the colony needs a plant to produce oxygen and reduce carbon dioxide or is missing one required piece of information about the recommended plant.
SCORE 1	The letter is missing more than one required piece of information about the plant, or the information given is incorrect.

Extension Activities

Assignment Have students investigate how the plant they have selected is pollinated (by wind, bird, or insect) and describe how they will make sure that it will be pollinated within the walls of the Mars colony. They should also discuss any possible problems caused by the pollination method. (For example, if bees are needed to pollinate the plant, what problems might the bees cause?)

Cooperative Learning Have students work in teams of three to design an enclosure to keep the residents of the Mars colony safe while providing them with everything they need to survive in an alien world. It may help to have students read about the Biosphere 2 project in Oracle, Arizona. The team should work together on their design, but each member should also have a different primary responsibility. One should design the human working area, one should design the human living space, and the third should design the agricultural area. The final product can be in the form of a poster, model, or formal presentation.

Field Trip Arrange a trip to a forest, botanical garden, or arboretum. The focus of the trip should be on the variety of plants and the roles that different plants play in their respective environments.

Copyright © Pearson Education, Inc., or its affiliates. All Rights Reserved.

Name ______________________ Date ____________ Class ____________

Plants in Space

Purpose To select the best plant for a space station on Mars

Materials
- Student Edition
- paper
- pen or pencil

Scenario

Each spring, farmers and gardeners begin planting seeds and tending their gardens. It's a tradition with a history that may be as many as 23,000 years old. Someday this annual gardening ritual could make the difference between life and death for the residents of a space station on the planet Mars.

Science-fiction novels often describe space colonies on alien planets. Often these fictional colonies contain Earth plants that support the people living in the colony. Plants are vital for human survival on another planet. The plants provide food for the colonists and make the air breathable and the water drinkable.

NASA scientists agree that colonizing another planet must include plants. They are figuring out what kind of plants to use for the planned Mars colony. You are a botanist. You have been asked to help. The fate of NASA's plans is in your hands.

Life on Mars

Although Mars is the planet in our solar system that most closely resembles Earth, life on Mars would be very different from what we are used to. Consider the environment on Mars:

- Average Temperature: −63°C (−81.4°F)
- Average Daily Temperature Range: −89 to −31°C (−128.2 to −23.8°F)
- Atmosphere: 95.32 percent carbon dioxide (CO_2); 2.7 percent nitrogen (N_2); 1.6 percent argon (Ar); 0.13 percent oxygen (O_2); 0.08 percent carbon monoxide (CO)

Procedure

1. **What Are the Choices?** There are three kinds of plants from which NASA can choose: nonvascular plants, seedless vascular plants, and vascular plants with seeds.
2. **Choosing the Best** NASA is looking for a kind of plant that will absorb carbon dioxide, release oxygen, and provide the space colonists with food to eat. Use your textbook to research the characteristics of the three different kinds of plants. Which kind do you believe will do the best job of supporting the Mars explorers? Explain your answer.

____

____

____

Copyright © Pearson Education, Inc., or its affiliates. All Rights Reserved.

Name ______________________ Date __________ Class __________

Procedure *(continued)*

3. **Selecting One Example** Once you have chosen the best type of plant, select one example that you believe will provide a good source of food for the crew. (You can use the examples in the chart below, or you can use your own.) Explain why your choice is a good one.

____

____

____

Plant Examples				
		Vascular with Seeds		
Nonvascular	Seedless Vascular	Gymnosperms	Angiosperms	
moss liverworts hornworts	ferns club mosses horsetails	cycads conifers ginkgoes gnetophytes	wheat rice beans apples tomatoes	corn rye potatoes oranges spinach

Conclusion

Let's see what you learned about plants and their benefits to humans living in space.

1. What is the name of the gas that plants absorb from the air and use to grow?

____

2. Plants release a different gas back into the air. What is the name of that gas?

____

3. What is the process by which plants use light to produce their food called?

____

4. Which of the three kinds of plants produce most of the foods that humans eat?

____

Prepare your recommendation for NASA in the form of a business letter. In your letter:

- name the plant you recommend
- give the name of the gas the plant will absorb and the gas it will release
- explain how this gas exchange will benefit the residents of the Mars colony

Use your textbook or the Internet to find the nutritional value of the food produced by the plant you recommend, and include that information in your report.

Copyright © Pearson Education, Inc., or its affiliates. All Rights Reserved.

How Could That Be?

Investigation Overview

- The Scenario for this investigation is based on statements by microbiologists Carolyn Bohach and Gary Huffnagle. For more information, see the November 30, 2007 issue of *Scientific American* magazine.
- Gather all materials listed on the student page several days before you plan to conduct this activity.
- On the day of the activity, have students read the Scenario and Steps 1–3. Answer all questions, distribute materials, and let students begin.
- You may want to point out to students that the Procedure instructs them to build cell models in the shape of cubes. This is easier than it would be to build spheres or other rounded shapes. You should emphasize, however, that real cells are usually rounded and can come in a variety of shapes (generally spherical or cylindrical).
- Monitor students' progress and answer questions as necessary.
- Encourage students to help each other. If Step 4 confuses most students, you should stop and have a class discussion about the use of beneficial bacteria in food production.
- Show students how to cut out the net of a cube, which looks like a lowercase "t," to minimize the number of seams that need glue.
- The investigation will be more accessible to student if you avoid using "μm" in reference to the unit of micrometers (1 micrometer = .000001 m).

SCORING RUBRIC	
SCORE 4	Student produces a display titled "Human and Bacterial Cells Compared" with neatly made models that accurately compare a human cell to a bacterial cell. Both cells are labeled, and the correct scale is reported. The weight of the bacteria in an average man is shown as 1.8 pounds, 1.6 pounds for the average woman.
SCORE 3	The display meets all of the content standards for a score of 4, but there are minor errors or the display is not neatly made.
SCORE 2	There are minor errors or omissions of the required content, but the majority of the display is accurate and well made, and the student understands the basic concepts.
SCORE 1	The display is lacking one or more major components or contains significant errors. The display indicates that the student did not make an effort or did not fully understand the concept.

Extension Activities

Assignment A typical virus particle measures 0.4 micrometers in length. Ask students to design a display that will show the relative sizes of human and bacterial cells as well as virus particles. (Since it will be impossible to build a model virus cube with sides that are only 0.4 mm in length, students should change their scale to 1 micrometer : 1 cm.)

Guest Speaker Arrange for a spokesperson from a local dairy or bakery to discuss the role that bacterial cultures play in the products they produce, such as yogurt, cheese, or sourdough bread. Alternatively, have a nutritionist or medical doctor talk to your students about the importance of probiotics in a healthy diet.

Copyright © Pearson Education, Inc., or its affiliates. All Rights Reserved.

Name ______________________ Date ____________ Class ____________

How Could That Be?

Purpose To investigate the relative sizes of human cells and bacterial cells

Materials

- metric ruler
- scissors
- colored construction paper
- all-purpose white glue

Scenario

Today your teacher told you about an interesting article featured in this month's issue of *American Science*. The article was about the bacteria that humans encounter in their everyday lives. In the article, there was a quote from a university scientist: "There are *ten times* as many bacterial cells in your body as there are human cells!" How could that be?

It might be true for people who don't take showers or brush their teeth, but you shower every day and brush your teeth twice a day. Certainly *your* body doesn't have more bacterial cells than human cells, does it?

The article also said that most of the bacteria inside your body are good for you, but how did they get inside you? You swallowed the bacteria in your mother's womb. You got more bacteria from your mother's skin and milk. You are still adding helpful bacteria today. They come from the food you eat and the water you drink.

Most of the bacteria live in your intestines, where they break down foods you couldn't otherwise digest. Bacteria also help grow intestinal blood vessels, make vitamin K and other vitamins, store energy, and remove damaged cells from the intestinal lining.

When you were a baby, bacteria helped teach your immune system which cells were part of your body and which cells belong to the outside world. Today they help keep your immune system healthy.

If there are ten times as many bacterial cells as human cells inside you, how much space do they take up? Your teacher has challenged the class to build models of a typical bacterial cell and a typical human body cell to compare their volumes.

Procedure

1. **Body Cells Are Small** If the cells that make up your body were cubes, each of their sides would be an average of 40 micrometers in length. (There are 1,000 micrometers in 1 millimeter.) Use the scale of 1 mm : 1 micrometer to build a model of a cube-shaped human cell from colored construction paper and white glue.
2. **Bacteria Are Smaller** Bacterial cells are about 1/10 the size of human cells. If they were cube-shaped, their sides would each be an average of 4 micrometers in length. Use the same material and scale to build a cube-shaped bacterial cell.
3. **Mounting Your Models** Use white glue to mount both models on another sheet of construction paper. Give a title to the sheet containing the models.

Copyright © Pearson Education, Inc., or its affiliates. All Rights Reserved.

Procedure *(continued)*

4. **Calculating Volumes** The volume of a cube is found by multiplying the length of one of its sides by itself three times (length × length × length).

   What is the volume of an average human cell? ____________________

   What is the volume of an average bacterial cell? ____________________

5. **How Many Times Larger?** How many times larger is a human cell than a bacterial cell? To figure this out, divide the volume of the human cell by the volume of the bacterial cell.

   ____

6. **How Much Smaller?** The volume of one bacterial cell is what fraction of the volume of a human cell?

   ____

Conclusion

Let's see what you learned about the helpful bacteria that live in your body.

1. Where do most bacteria live?

   ____

2. There are ten times as many bacterial cells in your body as your own human cells, but each bacterial cell is much smaller. How much of your volume is really bacteria? (*Hint:* multiply your answer to Step 6 by ten.)

   ____

3. Multiply your answer to Question 2 by your weight. How much do your bacteria weigh?

   ____

4. Name one food that contains helpful bacteria.

   ____

It turns out that the director of your local science museum read the same article as your teacher and wants to make an interesting display that illustrates the main points of the article. The director wants a display that shows models of a human cell and a bacterial cell. You have already built the models of the human and bacterial cells. You need to add the following information to your display:

- the scale used
- a label for each cell
- the weight of the bacteria in an average-sized adult (about 170 pounds)

Copyright © Pearson Education, Inc., or its affiliates. All Rights Reserved.

Muscle Fatigue

Investigation Overview

- Before the investigation, you will need to obtain one soft rubber ball and a stopwatch for each pair of students.
- Since students are the test subjects, and can subconsciously influence the results, avoid asking them to state a hypothesis.
- Begin by having students read the Scenario and Procedure. Answer any questions. You may want to demonstrate the technique of squeezing the ball and suggest ideas for warming up without squeezing the ball.
- Make sure students understand in Step 6 that only the warm-up changes. Students should still perform four trials squeezing the ball.
- If students are confused by percent change and percent decrease, show students a formula they can use to calculate percent change:

$$\text{percent change} = \frac{\text{new} - \text{original}}{\text{original}} \times 100$$

SCORING RUBRIC	
SCORE 4	Student suggests two clear strategies for preventing overuse injuries and cites data that effectively support the suggestions.
SCORE 3	Student meets the criteria for a score of 4, but the plan is not well presented or may contain minor errors.
SCORE 2	Student only suggests and supports one strategy, or makes two suggestions without providing support for either.
SCORE 1	The plan is largely incomplete, or the suggestions and support provided are mostly illogical or inaccurate.

Extension Activities

Assignment The heart is one muscle that never gets fatigued. Have students research the reason that the heart can keep beating without growing tired or suffering from overuse injuries, and then write a brief paragraph summarizing the reason(s) they find.

Cooperative Learning This investigation focused on the fatigue that occurs when small muscles are used rapidly and repeatedly. Does the same thing happen when they are contracted continuously (for example, holding the squeeze for a long period of time)? Do large muscles react the same way as small muscles if they are contracted rapidly and repeatedly? Have teams of four students design an experiment that can answer one of these questions. Have each team present their findings at a poster session. Have students suggest things that should be on the posters and develop a rubric for grading them.

Field Trip Arrange a field trip to a local youth or high school baseball game. Have each student tally all pitches made for each pitcher (including warm-up pitches). They should also record the results of each pitch (ball, strike, bat on ball, wild pitch). For homework, students should examine the data to see if the results change as the number of pitches increases. If possible, arrange for a team trainer or other spokesperson to talk to your students about the strategies they use to prevent overuse injuries.

Copyright © Pearson Education, Inc., or its affiliates. All Rights Reserved.

Name ______________________ Date ____________ Class ____________

Muscle Fatigue

Purpose To investigate the role that warming up before physical activity plays in muscle fatigue

Materials
- small rubber ball
- stopwatch

Scenario

Overuse causes 30 to 50 percent of all injuries seen in young teens. It starts when a repeated motion weakens a muscle or tendon. Little League elbow is an overuse injury that is very common in young baseball players. To prevent such an injury, teens should not throw more than 80 to 100 pitches in a week. Also, they should not throw more than 1,000 pitches in a year.

You have volunteered as the coach of a youth baseball team. Your best starting pitcher has a bad pain in his pitching arm, but he doesn't want to miss his next game. When you look at his pitch count for the week, you see that he has already thrown 85 pitches. You have no choice; he has to rest his arm.

You know that when muscles and tendons are tight and cold they are more likely to suffer overuse injury. Just as most teams do, your pitchers warm up at the beginning of each inning by throwing practice pitches before they face a batter. Does warming up muscles and tendons slow the process of muscle fatigue, or does it add to it? In other words, is it better to warm up by doing the same activity or warm up by doing a different but related activity? You will conduct an experiment to answer this question.

Procedure

1. **Squeeze and Release** With a partner acting as timekeeper, use your right hand to squeeze and release a soft rubber ball as many times as you can in 30 seconds.
2. **Record and Rest** Record this value below as the "Warm-Up," and then rest for 10 seconds.
3. **Squeeze, Release, Record, and Rest** Repeat Steps 1 and 2 four more times for a total of five trials. Make sure each trial lasts 30 seconds, and you take a break for 10 seconds between each trial. Record all your information in the table at the right.
4. **Swap Roles** Trade places with your partner and act as timekeeper as your partner performs Steps 1–3 and records his or her data.
5. **Now the Left Hand** Trade places with your partner again and repeat Steps 1–4 using your left hand. Record your data in the last column of the table.

Warming Up by Squeezing

Trial	Right-Hand Squeezes	Left-Hand Squeezes
Warm-Up		
1		
2		
3		
4		

Copyright © Pearson Education, Inc., or its affiliates. All Rights Reserved.

Name ______________________________ Date ____________ Class ____________

Procedure *(continued)*

6. Warming Up Without Squeezing Now you will repeat the entire experiment. This time, warm up the muscles and tendons in your hands and forearm another way. You and your partner should decide on an action that involves your hands and forearm but does not involve squeezing. (Note: You will still squeeze the ball in your trials. Only your warm-up is different.) Record your data in the table to the right.

Warming Up Without Squeezing		
Trial	**Right-Hand Squeezes**	**Left-Hand Squeezes**
Warm-Up		
1		
2		
3		
4		

7. Analyzing the Results Compare Trial 1 with Trial 4 for both hands with a squeezing warm-up. Because of muscle fatigue, you probably were not able to squeeze as many times in 30 seconds during Trial 4. By what percentage did your number of squeezes decrease in each hand between Trials 1 and 4?

Right ____________ Left ____________

Now compare Trial 1 with Trial 4 for both hands with a non-squeezing warm-up. By what percentage did your number of squeezes decrease in each hand?

Right ____________ Left ____________

Conclusion

Let's see what you learned about muscles and tendons.

1. What kind of muscles did you use to squeeze the ball? (*Hint*: They are named this because you have conscious control over them.) ____________

2. Which type of muscle tissue were you using to squeeze the ball? ____________

3. Muscles are attached to the bones they move by what connective tissue? ____________

4. What is an overuse injury, and how can you best prevent it?

As the coach of a youth baseball team, you want to protect your pitchers from the injuries caused by overusing muscles and tendons. Prepare a plan for your team that identifies two strategies for preventing overuse injuries. The plan must include data that support your strategies.

Copyright © Pearson Education, Inc., or its affiliates. All Rights Reserved.

Oh No! My Heart's Beating Too Fast!

Investigation Overview

- In this investigation, students will compare the average resting heart rates of adults and people in their age group.
- Remind students that heart rate is expressed as beats per minute (bpm), and resting heart rate varies greatly based on factors such as age, fitness, and diet. Young people tend to have relatively high heart rates.
- Prior to the investigation, obtain a sticky note for each student in the class. Use different colors for boys and girls.
- On the board or chart paper, vertically list the following tens' place values: 5, 6, 7, 8, 9, 10, 11, and 12. Each student will place his or her sticky note next to the appropriate pulse range, creating a stem-and-leaf plot of the class data. For example, if a student's heart rate is 84 bpm, he or she would write "4" on the sticky note and place it in the row next to the 8. You may want to demonstrate how you want the sticky notes placed using resting heart rate, but do not have students include that data point in their calculations.
- Have students read the Scenario and Steps 1 and 2. Answer any questions and make sure students can find their heart rates. Show students multiple pulse points if necessary.
- Arrange the sticky notes within each row in order of increasing value, making sure they are spaced evenly across rows to make the distribution clear.
- Help your students to visualize the trends shown by the plot. Point out that the median heart rate for the class is the middle number in the overall list, and have students calculate the mean heart rate for the whole class. You may need to review the difference between median and mean. Make sure students realize that "average" refers to mean rather than median.

SCORING RUBRIC	
SCORE 4	Student's letter correctly identifies the problem, effectively describes the class data, and suggests a way to present the information clearly to future classes.
SCORE 3	Student's letter identifies the problem, describes the class data, and suggests a way to present the information to future classes.
SCORE 2	The letter has two of the content requirements listed for a score of 4.
SCORE 1	The letter has one of the content requirements listed for a score of 4.

Extension Activities

Assignment Have students analyze the class data again, this time focusing on the difference between the average resting heart rates of boys and girls. Students should use the Internet to research why the numbers might differ.

Guest Speaker Have a spokesperson from a local fitness center speak to your students about the importance of aerobic exercise and the calculation of a target heart rate that is appropriate for their age.

Copyright © Pearson Education, Inc., or its affiliates. All Rights Reserved.

Name ______________________________ Date______________ Class______________

Oh No! My Heart's Beating Too Fast!

Purpose To calculate the average heart rate of middle school students

Materials
- stopwatch
- sticky note
- markers
- graph paper

Scenario

You learned in science class that a human heart beats 100,000 times every day. That's about 69 beats per minute (bpm). But when you and the other students in your class checked your heart rates, many of you found rates much higher than 69 bpm! You and your friends with rapid heart rates are worried. Are your hearts beating too fast? Is there something wrong with you?

Don't worry! According to medical experts, the heart rate for an "older child" is between 90 and 110. What do they mean by "older child?" Are you included in that category? Could the average for people your age be different? What could possibly cause that difference?

Your teacher thinks the best way to answer your questions is for you to investigate the average heart rates of the students in your class. If your results are different from what you learned in class, your teacher will be able to use those results next year. If your teacher can add this information to the lesson for next year's students, then they will not be alarmed the way that you were.

Procedure

1. **Finding Your Pulse** Every time your heart beats, you can feel a pulse anywhere that an artery is located close to the skin. To feel the pulse in your wrist, place your index and middle fingers on the underside of your opposite wrist, just below the base of the thumb. Press gently until you feel your pulse. (Don't use your thumb to find your pulse because your thumb has its own pulse.)

2. **Counting Your Pulse** Count your pulse for one full minute. This number is your resting heart rate in beats per minute (bpm).

3. **Reporting Your Pulse** Use a marker to write your pulse on a sticky note. You only need to write down the last digit (ones' place) of the number. Place the number on the class chart next to the appropriate tens' place number. (For example, if your resting heart rate is 81 bpm, write "1" on your sticky note, and place it in the row next to the "8."

4. **Graphing Class Results** Your teacher will rearrange the sticky notes so that they are in order of increasing value. This kind of arrangement is called a *stem-and-leaf plot*. Copy the finished plot on a sheet of graph paper.

Copyright © Pearson Education, Inc., or its affiliates. All Rights Reserved.

Name ______________________ Date __________ Class __________

Conclusion

Let's see what you learned about the heart.

1. What is the average heart rate for an adult?

____

2. What is the average heart rate for students in your class?

____

3. Explain why pulse rate and heart rate are the same.

____

____

____

4. What factors cause different people to have different resting heart rates? Which factor was the primary reason your answer to Question 1 does not match your answer to Question 2?

____

____

____

If your class's average pulse is higher than 69 beats per minute, write a letter to your teacher explaining how to present the information about human heart rates to future classes.

Begin your letter with this opening statement:

Dear ____________,

My classmates and I found your lesson on heart rate alarming because many of our resting heart rates were higher than the average heart rate.

Explain what you think your teacher should tell future students about the average human heart rate. Include the results of your study in your letter so that your teacher can explain to future students how normal heart rates for middle school students may be different.

Copyright © Pearson Education, Inc., or its affiliates. All Rights Reserved.

Eating for Success

Investigation Overview

- This investigation takes place over several days.
- Begin by having students read the Scenario and Procedure. Answer any questions.
- Explain that this investigation uses the word "diet" to refer to the kinds of food and drink we consume and how that relates to our health.
- Point out that the chart in Step 2 contains five different food groups. Discuss what foods belong to each group and what nutritional benefits we derive from each group. Show students sample portion sizes of cups and ounces for reference.
- Tell students they can get a personalized plan of what and how much to eat based on their age, gender, weight, height and level of physical activity using the My Pyramid Plan feature at the U.S. Department of Agriculture (USDA) web site: http://www.mypyramid.gov.
- Stress to students that they should not alter their eating habits during this investigation and must keep honest and accurate records. They will not be graded on how they eat but rather how well they reflect on their current eating habits.

SCORING RUBRIC	
SCORE 4	Student's contract states three dietary changes with a clear, correct benefit and an effective strategy for each.
SCORE 3	Contract states three dietary changes with a correct benefit and a strategy for each. The contract may contain a minor error.
SCORE 2	Contract only includes two dietary changes but gives a correct benefit and strategy for each, or contract includes three dietary changes, but one benefit or strategy is incorrect or questionable.
SCORE 1	Contract includes at most two dietary changes, or many benefits and strategies are incorrect or missing.

Extension Activities

Assignment Before class, prepare at least as many slips of paper as students, and write a different healthy food on each one. Let students choose a slip of paper out of a bowl and prepare a poster that promotes that healthy food. Have them include three reasons why that food is good for them and a graphic to illustrate each point.

Cooperative Learning Divide your class into teams, and have each team create a presentation listing the goal(s) they decide to work on to improve their eating habits. Have them identify and explain the negative characteristics of the food they will give up and what benefits exist for the food they will be eating instead.

Field Trip Arrange a trip to a local farmers' market. Discuss the benefits of eating foods that are in season and grown locally. You could also ask a local farmer to come to your class and speak to students about the same topics.

Copyright © Pearson Education, Inc., or its affiliates. All Rights Reserved.

Name ______________________ Date __________ Class __________

Eating for Success

Purpose To investigate foods that promote good health and help you perform at your best

Materials • small notebook

Scenario

The best player on your school's varsity basketball team this year is T. J. Warren. He is very strong and very athletic. Things were very different last year for T.J. He was in a slump and spent most of the basketball season sitting on the bench. During the off-season, however, T. J. changed his lifestyle. He ate smarter and began running and lifting weights every other day. His plan worked! He lost 12 pounds and started this season much leaner and quicker.

What about your diet and exercise? Even if you are not an athlete, you know that a healthy diet and exercise can help you perform at your best. Maintaining your health and fitness can help you live longer and may improve your mood or performance in school. You have decided to look at your diet to see if it can be improved.

Procedure

1. **A Food Log** Keep a food log for two days. Make a chart like the one below to carry around with you. Record everything you eat, the approximate size of each serving, and the food group to which it belongs. Include a check box at the end of each day to indicate whether or not you ate a balanced diet on that day (for information about a balanced diet, refer to Step 2).

Food Log

Day	Item	Amount	Food Group
1	mac & cheese	1 cup	grains/milk
1	grape juice	1 cup	fruits
1	graham crackers	2	grains
Did I eat a balanced diet today? ☐			

2. **Recommended Daily Nutrition** Look at the chart on the next page. It has the recommendations from the U.S. Department of Agriculture (USDA) for what boys and girls your age should eat each day based on their levels of activity. Compare these recommendations to the items you entered in your food log. Have you eaten a balanced diet? (A balanced diet requires you to eat enough from each food group without eating too much of any one group.) If so, check the box in your food log for that day.

3. **How Did You Do?** If you got a check mark for both days, that's great! You are doing a good job helping your body function at its full potential. If you did not check a day or only checked one, use the chart from Step 2 to analyze of which foods you ate too little or too much.

Copyright © Pearson Education, Inc., or its affiliates. All Rights Reserved.

Name ______________________ Date __________ Class __________

Procedure *(continued)*

Recommended Daily Nutrition for 13 Year Olds			
	Daily Activity Level		
	Less than 30 min/day	30–60 min/day	More than 60 min/day
Male	Grains 6 oz Vegetables 2.5 cups Fruits 2 cups Milk 3 cups Meat & Beans 5.5 oz	Grains 7 oz Vegetables 3 cups Fruits 2 cups Milk 3 cups Meat & Beans 6 oz	Grains 9 oz Vegetables 3.25 cups Fruits 2 cups Milk 3 cups Meat & Beans 6.5 oz
Female	Grains 5 oz Vegetables 2 cups Fruits 1.5 cups Milk 3 cups Meat & Beans 5 oz	Grains 6 oz Vegetables 2.5 cups Fruits 2 cups Milk 3 cups Meat & Beans 5.5 oz	Grains 7 oz Vegetables 3 cups Fruits 2 cups Milk 3 cups Meat & Beans 6 oz
Quantities above obtained from the USDA at http://www.MyPyramid.gov.			

Conclusion

Let's see what you learned about your eating habits.

1. When you compared your food log to the USDA recommendations, what food group(s) did you find you should eat more of? Why does your body need more of that food group?

   ____

2. Which food groups should you eat less of? Explain why you should eat less of these foods.

   ____

3. Why do more active people need to eat larger amounts of food?

   ____

4. Notice that foods like candy and ice cream are not in the chart above. Why do you think the USDA recommends that you restrict the amount of these foods that you eat?

   ____

Now use your answers to prepare a contract with yourself. Your contract should:

- list three ways you will change your food choices.
- support each statement with one benefit of the change.
- include a strategy that will make the change easier for you.

Example: *Goal:* I will eat more carrots.
Benefit: Carrots are low in fat and high in vitamins.
Strategy: I will dip the carrots in my favorite low-calorie salad dressing.

Copyright © Pearson Education, Inc., or its affiliates. All Rights Reserved.

Stay Calm if You Can

Investigation Overview

- Prior to the investigation, collect samples of pamphlets for students' reference as they design their pamphlets. For example, you can find pamphlets in doctor's offices, pharmacies, and hotel lobbies.
- Begin the investigation by having your students read the Scenario. When they are finished, point out that the pitcher had both physical and emotional reactions to the pressure of the situation. Ask students what they think the differences are between emotional and physical reactions to a stimulus.
- Because the two different kinds of reactions often occur together, students may need help in understanding the difference between physical and emotional reactions. Make sure they are clear about the difference before you proceed.
- Next, have students work in pairs to discuss and list some of the physical reactions that they have had when anxious, scared, embarrassed, or angry.
- Use students' answers to fill out a class chart listing common physical reactions to each of the four emotions.
- Ask: What actually causes these physical changes? (*Hormones*)
- Now have students read Steps 1–3. Answer any questions, and instruct them to begin the Procedure.

SCORING RUBRIC	
SCORE 4	Student fully participates in the creation of the pamphlet, contributing high-quality work, including a drawing or picture.
SCORE 3	Student makes an adequate contribution to the pamphlet, including a drawing or picture.
SCORE 2	Student does not fully participate, or the contribution contains minor errors or omissions.
SCORE 1	Student participates minimally, or the work contains significant errors and/or omissions.

Extension Activities

Assignment Have students design a quiz that requires other students to match the nine endocrine glands found in the Student Edition with one function of each gland. The student must also provide an answer key.

Guest Speaker Arrange a visit by a spokesperson from the office of a psychologist or a community health department where stress-management and/or anger-management services are provided. Have the spokesperson discuss the coping strategies they recommend to people who have issues with stress or anger.

Copyright © Pearson Education, Inc., or its affiliates. All Rights Reserved.

Name ______________________ Date ____________ Class ____________

Stay Calm if You Can

Purpose

To investigate how emotions stimulate the release of hormones that influence behavior

Materials

- small notebook

Scenario

As you sit on your couch watching TV, your favorite baseball team is still in the lead. The game is almost over and your team's young pitcher is on his way to earning his first win in the Major Leagues. Suddenly, his pitches start to miss the plate. The manager watching from the dugout can see the rookie pitcher begin to fidget and sweat. The more nervous the pitcher gets, the harder it is for him to hit the target.

The manager knows exactly what to do—he calls a time-out. He walks out to the young pitcher and gives him a short speech about how to throw a strike. Of course, the pitcher already knows how to throw a strike, but the manager's words are not the important part. The manager's confidence and joking style are exactly what a nervous pitcher needs. By the time the manager heads back to the dugout, the pitcher is smiling, relaxed, and ready to pitch again. He finishes the game with a strong performance, and gets his first win!

When was the last time you experienced nervousness, fear, or anger? Perhaps you can remember a test, a nightmare, or an argument that caused the emotion. Think about your body's physical reaction to the emotion.

- How did your body change?
- Did your heart race?
- Did your face and ears grow warm?
- Did you begin to breathe faster?
- Did you tremble all over?
- Did you sweat?

The glands in your endocrine system release certain hormones into your bloodstream, which cause these physical changes in your body. When you were angry or scared, did you stay calm and in control, or were you sloppy, careless, or forgetful? You will now conduct a survey to explore these issues.

Procedure

1. **The Fight or Flight Response** When you perceive a threat or danger, your emotion causes the release of certain hormones like adrenalin and cortisol. They increase the heart rate, slow digestion, and send blood to your muscles, giving your body a burst of energy and strength. This *fight or flight response* got its name because it prepares us to defend ourselves or run away when faced with danger.

2. **Lingering Effects** Sometimes, the fight or flight response is activated when neither fight nor flight is called for. Even the anxiety of taking a test can cause the release of those same hormones. When the stress is gone, the adrenalin and cortisol levels fall and our bodies return to normal. If you experience stress often, the hormones can cause damage to your body and interfere with your ability to think clearly.

Copyright © Pearson Education, Inc., or its affiliates. All Rights Reserved.

Name ______________________ Date ____________ Class ____________

Procedure *(continued)*

3. **Conducting a Survey** Work with your partners to write a set of questions for a survey. Your survey needs three kinds of questions:

- What kinds of things trigger these emotions: nervousness, fear, anger?
- How do their bodies respond when this happens?
- What strategies do they use to calm themselves back down?

4. **Interviewing** For homework, each member of your team will interview five people. Do not record their names. It is easier to get detailed, honest responses if you keep your surveys anonymous and let subjects fill out the surveys themselves.

Conclusion

Let's see what you learned about hormones and their effects on the body.

1. Anger is a response to what kind of stimulus? ______________________

2. When an angry person's heart rate increases, what kind of physical response occurs?

____

3. Fear, anger, and other negative emotions cause the release of adrenalin. What gland produces adrenalin? ______________________

4. Why do you think extended periods of stress are harmful to the body?

____

____

Based on the findings from your survey, work with your partners to make a pamphlet called "Dealing With Stress." Your pamphlet should contain the following four sections, with an illustration for each:

- Introduction: Explain what hormones are and name the hormone that causes the fight or flight response.
- Causes: List and explain the most common causes of stressful emotions such as anger, nervousness, or fear. (If someone tells you an interesting story, briefly retell it in this section.)
- How Your Body Reacts: List and explain the most common ways that people said their bodies respond to stress.
- Strategies For Managing Stress: List and explain any successful strategies that people use to deal with stress.

Copyright © Pearson Education, Inc., or its affiliates. All Rights Reserved.

Working Together Is the Key

Investigation Overview

- The class before this investigation, tell students to bring their textbooks to the next class.
- Begin by having students read the Scenario. Answer all questions. You may want to explain to students that "cardio" refers to the heart and "pulmonary" refers to the lungs.
- Give each student a card with a number from 1 to 6, and tell students to partner with another student with the same number.
- Be prepared to tell students where to look in their textbooks for descriptions of the functions of each organ system.
- If students cannot find partners with the same number, pair students and allow them to decide which number they will be.
- As students work on Step 3, remind them that each person in a team should focus on one of the two systems. Let students know that they will share their findings with their partner in Step 4.
- You may want to use the Internet to find more information about the first successful use of the machine referenced in the Scenario, the evolution of the machine since its invention, or the amazing story of a man who survived on the machine for 16 days.

SCORING RUBRIC	
SCORE 4	Student's description effectively demonstrates how organ systems work together to accomplish one goal or a set of related goals.
SCORE 3	The description is correct but may contain minor errors.
SCORE 2	The description contains one or two content errors but shows some understanding of the lesson's concepts.
SCORE 1	The description demonstrates minimal understanding of the lesson's concepts.

Extension Activities

Assignment Assign a pair of organ systems that work together but were not included in the list under Step 1. Have students think of what task(s) the two systems accomplish together. The easiest pairings are: circulatory with skeletal (blood cells are produced in bone marrow), and muscular with respiratory (the diaphragm and intercostal muscles are involved in breathing).

Cooperative Learning Have two teams that are working on the same organ-system pair join together to make up an advertisement for a new medicine that will increase the cooperation between the two organ systems. They should work together to give the new fictional medicine a clever name and create an advertising poster that exaggerates the benefits but accurately portrays the cooperation that occurs.

Field Trip Arrange a trip to a fitness center or gym where a trainer or other spokesperson can discuss the roles that different organ systems play in keeping a person healthy and fit. The muscular and skeletal system will immediately come to mind, but health and fitness involve much more than strong bones and muscles. They also involve maintaining a healthy weight, having a healthy heart, having good nutrition, keeping the skin clean and hydrated, and handling stress in healthy ways. Many of these areas of wellness will provide opportunities for you to emphasize the role of homeostasis.

Copyright © Pearson Education, Inc., or its affiliates. All Rights Reserved.

Name ______________________________ Date ______________ Class ______________

Working Together Is the Key

Purpose To investigate how organ systems work together to accomplish a goal

Materials
- Student Edition
- notebook
- pen or pencil
- numbered card

Scenario

Have you heard of open-heart surgery? In order to perform this procedure, the surgeon must stop the patient's heart! A mechanical pump acts in place of the heart to keep the patient's blood moving during the operation.

"Wait a minute," you say. "If the heart is stopped, doesn't the patient stop breathing?" Good question. The answer is yes! When the heart stops, the patient also stops breathing. It takes more than just a pump to keep the patient alive. Something also needs to add oxygen to the patient's blood and remove the carbon dioxide. The machine that does all three of these jobs is called a *heart-lung machine.*

Notice that the heart-lung machine does the work of two organs from two different organ systems. The heart is part of the circulatory system, and the lungs are part of the respiratory system. Even though these two systems have unique functions, they also work together. The circulatory system is responsible for transporting oxygen to the cells of the body and carrying away the carbon dioxide that the cells produce. The respiratory system is responsible for removing carbon dioxide from the blood and giving the blood oxygen to carry.

This two-system partnership is not unique. It's not unusual for two different organ systems to work together to accomplish a goal that neither can accomplish alone. In this investigation, you will examine two organ systems and explore how they work together.

An Amazing Machine

The first successful use of a heart-lung machine (also known as a cardiopulmonary bypass pump) on a human was on May 6, 1953. The patient was an 18-year-old woman with a hole between two chambers of her heart. Her heart was stopped for 26 minutes while Dr. John Gibbon opened her heart and repaired the hole. For those 26 minutes, the young woman's life depended on a machine.

Procedure

1. **Other Systems that Cooperate** You now know how the circulatory and respiratory systems work together. Here is a list of some other organ-system pairs that work together:

Organ Systems that Work Together			
1	skeletal and muscular	4	circulatory and integumentary
2	circulatory and digestive	5	muscular and nervous
3	circulatory and excretory	6	nervous and endocrine

Copyright © Pearson Education, Inc., or its affiliates. All Rights Reserved.

Procedure (continued)

2. **Find a Partner** As you entered class today, your teacher handed you a card with a number on it. Find someone who has a card with the same number. That person will be your partner. Let your teacher know if you cannot find a partner with a matching number.

3. **Working Together** Now that you have a partner, look at the list of organ-system pairs and find your number. That is the pair of organ systems you will study. Each of you should investigate one organ system from the assigned pair. Decide which partner will research which organ system. Use your textbook to research your organ system. Take notes on the organ system's functions.

4. **Comparing and Contrasting** Next, work with your partner to compare and contrast the functions of the two systems you are investigating. You are looking for any function(s) they have in common. (The functions do not have to be identical but must be closely related, just as the circulatory and respiratory systems work together to supply oxygen to the body.)

5. **A Function in Common** Make a chart that lists the names of your assigned organ systems, the function(s) they share, and how each system contributes to the function(s).

Conclusion

Let's see what you learned about interactions among organ systems.

1. An organ system is a group of organs that work together to perform a major function. Name the organ system you investigated and three major organs in that organ system.

____

____

2. What is the *primary* function of your organ system?

____

____

3. Name another organ system that cooperates with yours to achieve a goal different from the one above.

____

4. What is that goal? Explain your system's role in this task.

____

____

Now work with your partner to write a description in your notebook of how the two organ systems you investigated work together to accomplish one goal or a set of related goals. You and your partner are working together to share what you found, but you each will write your own description.

Copyright © Pearson Education, Inc., or its affiliates. All Rights Reserved.

Name ______________________________ Date__________ Class______________

Procedure *(continued)*

4. **You'll Need This Number Later** After you have exchanged liquids with the other person, record his or her cup number in your table under "Exchange 1."

5. **Spreading Your Germs Around** When your teacher tells you to, repeat Steps 2 through 4. Never exchange with the same person twice. Once you have completed "Exchange 4," return to your seat.

6. **Are You Sick Yet?** Your teacher will now add a special test chemical to see if you have the disease. If your liquid turns pink, you are infected!

Conclusion

Let's see what you learned about the spread of disease.

1. Can you catch the flu from a person who does not appear sick? Explain.

____

____

2. A virus causes the flu. Name a microorganism that can cause disease and a disease that it causes.

____

3. Explain how a flu shot can keep you from catching the flu.

____

____

____

4. If you do catch the flu, will antibiotics help you? Explain your reasoning.

____

____

____

____

A real disease can spread from person to person in the same way the simulated disease spread. To control the spread of disease, epidemiologists try to trace an infection back to its source. To figure out which cups had the infection first and how the disease spread, you will need to back-track. Share your ideas with the rest of the class and work with your teacher to solve the mystery.

Once you are sure which cups were the first to have the disease, prepare a report describing the results of your simulation for the director of your town health department. The report should identify the students (cup numbers) that were originally infected. It should also include how many and what percentage of the students were infected at the start of the simulation, and how many and what percentage of the students were infected at the end.

Copyright © Pearson Education, Inc., or its affiliates. All Rights Reserved.

Hit the Ball or You're Out!

Investigation Overview

- Gather all materials prior to the start of the activity.
- Begin by having students read the Scenario, Step 1, and "How to Measure Reaction Time."
- Answer all questions and demonstrate how to measure reaction time with the help of a student volunteer.
- Provide students with copies of the "Reaction Time Chart."
- Encourage students to identify variables that could skew their results.
- After all teams have determined their baseline reaction times and brainstormed strategies for improving reaction times, ask for ideas and list all of them on the board or chart paper. Have students vote on the strategies they think will work best for improving reaction time.
- Select the top four strategies, and then divide the class into four equal groups. Assign each group a strategy to test.

SCORING RUBRIC	
SCORE 4	The card provides one tip and evidence for the effectiveness of the strategy. It defines reaction time and tells which parts of the nervous system are working together during the act of batting. The card includes appropriate diagrams.
SCORE 3	The card provides one tip that meets the content standards for a score of 4, but may have minor errors, or may show lack of creativity in presentation.
SCORE 2	The card provides one tip but demonstrates one or two incorrect understandings about reaction time and/or how the parts of the nervous system work together.
SCORE 1	The card provides one tip but does not demonstrate adequate understanding of reaction time or how the parts of the nervous system work together.

Extension Activities

Assignment Once you determine the strategy most effective in improving reaction times, have all students test this strategy. Does it work for everyone?

Cooperative Learning Reaction time is important in many sports and other activities. Have students work together in teams of four to investigate an activity for which reaction time is important. Have each team produce a poster that shows the reaction pathway in the nervous system that leads to success in the activity. Make sure each team has one good artist and one person with neat handwriting. The other two students will help with brainstorming and research.

Guest speaker Arrange for a batting coach or other representative from a local minor-league, high-school, or little-league baseball team to explain any training drills he or she conducts to help batters improve at hitting fastballs.

Copyright © Pearson Education, Inc., or its affiliates. All Rights Reserved.

Name ______________________________ Date______________ Class______________

Hit the Ball or You're Out!

Purpose To investigate strategies that a baseball batter can use to improve reaction time

Materials
- metric ruler
- notebook
- index card

Scenario

Some major-league baseball pitchers can throw a fastball 95 miles per hour or faster. At 95 mph, the ball takes about 0.43 second to travel the 60.5 feet from the pitcher's mound to home plate.

By the time the ball has gone only 12 feet, the batter's eyes have seen the ball, and the brain has analyzed its speed and spin. The brain has automatically calculated whether the pitch is a fastball, curveball, slider, knuckleball, screwball, or changeup.

If the batter decides to swing, the bat must start moving when the ball is about 25 to 30 feet away. At that point, the ball will arrive at the plate in another 0.25 second. If the batter makes a timing error as small as a few thousandths of a second, the swing will result in a strike or a foul ball.

That's not the only problem! Hitting the ball a few millimeters above its center of gravity means a grounder; hitting it a few millimeters below the center of gravity causes a pop-up. No wonder your team is doing so poorly!

You are the batting coach for the worst-hitting team in the league. You must find ways to improve your batters' reaction times or you will be fired. But before you can experiment with strategies for improving your batters' reaction times, you need some baseline data. What is a normal reaction time?

Procedure

1. **Establishing a Baseline** Measuring very short intervals of time is difficult. It takes expensive equipment that you don't have. But there is a way to estimate reaction times. You can convert the distance an object falls into an accurate estimate of the time the object was falling. Work with your partner to determine your personal baseline. One of you will play the role of batter and the other will be the pitcher. After you have one partner's baseline, switch roles and calculate the other's.

How to Measure Reaction Time

1. The batter sits in a chair beside a desk or table, with his or her forearm laying flat on the desk and the fingers and thumb extending straight out over the edge. (The wrist and palm must stay on the table to prevent downward motion of the hand.)
2. The pitcher stands in front of the batter, holding the ruler by its 30-cm end and dangling the 0-cm end so that it is even with the top of the batter's thumb and index finger.
3. Without warning, the pitcher releases the ruler and the batter tries to catch it as quickly as possible. (If the batter misses catching the ruler, it does not count.)
4. The pitcher checks the ruler just above the batter's index finger to see how many centimeters it fell. The pitcher uses the chart to convert centimeters to seconds and records the seconds in a notebook.
5. The pitcher and batter repeat this procedure three times. When finished, the batter calculates and records his or her average reaction time. This is the baseline.

Copyright © Pearson Education, Inc., or its affiliates. All Rights Reserved.

Name ______________________ Date __________ Class __________

Procedure (continued)

Reaction Time Chart	
Distance (cm)	**Time (seconds)**
1	0.045
2	0.064
3	0.078
4	0.090
5	0.101
6	0.111
7	0.120
8	0.128
9	0.136
10	0.143
11	0.150
12	0.156
13	0.163
14	0.169
15	0.175
16	0.181
17	0.186

2. **Brainstorming** Work with your partner to make a list of things you could do that might improve your reaction time.

3. **List All Strategies** Your teacher will make a list of all the ideas that your class comes up with.

4. **Test One Strategy** Your teacher will divide your class into groups. Each group will test one strategy for improving reaction time. You and your partner will test the strategy assigned to your group five times on each of you. Calculate the average and record it in your notebook. Find the difference between your baseline average and your strategy average. (Baseline Average – Test Strategy Average = Change Score).

5. **Bigger Is Better** Post your change score for all to see. (A positive change score means that your strategy produced a better reaction time.)

Conclusion

Let's see what you learned about your reaction time.

1. How did the strategy you tested change your score?

____

2. What part(s) of your nervous system are involved in catching a falling object? Explain.

____

____

3. Are the same nervous system parts involved when a batter hits a baseball? Explain.

____

4. Is your reaction time fixed at birth? If not, what can you do to improve it?

____

Your team's advertising department has a deal with a cereal company. Prepare a strategy card to put in a cereal box. The card should explain what reaction time is, include a tip for how batters can improve their reaction times, and describe evidence that the strategy is effective. It should also explain how the parts of the nervous system work together during batting. Use diagrams to make your points clear.

Copyright © Pearson Education, Inc., or its affiliates. All Rights Reserved.

Dialysis Works, Too

Investigation Overview

- For this investigation, you will perform a demonstration of how kidneys filter blood. You will need to purchase an appropriate kit from a science supply company. Examples of these kits include the Modeling Kidney Function Lab Investigation (www.enasco.com) and the Kidney Dialysis Simulation Lab Activity (wardsci.com). Use the information in your kit to supplement the directions provided here.
- Before class, set up microscope stations where students can view wet-mount slides.
- Begin by having students read the Scenario and Step 1. Explain that you will perform a demonstration, and they should observe you, take notes, and record results.
- First use salt test strips to test for salt in a sample of distilled water and a sample of simulated blood.
- Use a piece of dialysis tubing to create a model of a blood vessel entering the kidney. Tie a knot in one end of the tubing, fill it with about 15 mL of blood, and tie the other end. Gently rinse any blood off the surface of the tube.
- Place the tube in a cup of distilled water and have students observe the initial colors of the water and the blood in the tube. After 20 minutes, remove the bag and have students again observe the colors of the water and the blood.
- Test the water for the presence of salt. Open the tube and test the blood for the presence of salt. Ask students what represents urine in this model (the water that has absorbed salt from the blood).
- Create wet-mount slides of the simulated urine and blood, and direct your students to the microscope stations so that they can complete Step 4. Red blood cells should be visible at 400x total magnification.

SCORING RUBRIC	
SCORE 4	Student's summary of the steps of the demonstration includes an accurate and complete explanation of each result. It also explains how the dialysis tubing worked and correctly states that kidneys return glucose and water to the blood.
SCORE 3	The summary includes all content required for a score of 4 but may contain minor errors.
SCORE 2	The summary misses or incorrectly states one major point or a few minor points.
SCORE 1	The summary is largely incorrect or incomplete.

Extension Activities

Cooperative Learning Have students work in pairs to write a kidney quiz and answer key. Two pairs should then exchange their quizzes and take the other pair's quiz. When both teams are finished, have students hand the quizzes to their creators, who will use the answer key to grade the other pair's answers.

Field Trip Arrange a tour of a dialysis center in your community, and have a spokesperson describe the process of dialysis and answer students' questions.

Copyright © Pearson Education, Inc., or its affiliates. All Rights Reserved.

Name ______________________ Date __________ Class __________

Dialysis Works, Too

Purpose To investigate the processes by which kidneys clean the blood

Materials

- simulated blood
- dialysis tubing
- clear cup
- salt test strip
- pipette
- microscope slides
- coverslips
- disposable gloves
- compound microscope

Scenario

The Kidney

Kidneys are important organs in your excretory system. When your kidneys work correctly, they filter about 50 gallons of blood every day. They remove about half a gallon of urea and other waste products, along with extra water. Urine is the mixture of the extra water and waste filtered out of your blood.

In 1938, a young Dutch doctor named Willem Kolff watched helplessly as a 22-year-old patient suffered through the final stages of kidney failure. At the time, kidney failure was an untreatable condition. Before death, as the wastes that the kidneys normally filtered out of the blood continued to build up, patients with kidney failure experienced symptoms such as fatigue, weakness, shortness of breath, and blindness.

Dr. Kolff searched for a cure for kidney failure, and his research led him to an article by John Abel, a scientist at Johns Hopkins University in Baltimore, Maryland. In 1913, Dr. Abel had described a process for cleaning blood that he had used successfully on animals. Dr. Kolff was determined to create a similar process for humans.

In the early 1940s, the Netherlands was in the middle of World War II. Dr. Kolff worked under difficult conditions and with limited supplies. Using sausage skins, orange-juice cans, a washing machine, and other ordinary items, Dr. Kolff built a machine that could remove wastes from the blood. In 1945, Dr. Kolff had his first success. After 11 hours attached to the machine, a 67-year-old woman in kidney failure awoke from her coma. She lived seven more years before she died from an unrelated cause.

Today, thanks to Dr. Kolff, doctors use dialysis machines to filter the blood of patients waiting for kidney transplants.

Procedure

1. **Dialysis in Action** Your teacher will use a model to demonstrate how your kidneys work. It involves simulated blood (a red liquid containing salt and tiny particles that represent red blood cells), plain water, and dialysis tubing. This special tubing is made from a material with tiny holes that allow small particles to pass through, but not water or large particles.

Copyright © Pearson Education, Inc., or its affiliates. All Rights Reserved.

Name ______________________ Date __________ Class __________

Procedure *(continued)*

2. Before and After Use this chart to record your observations for Steps 3-5.

	Presence of Salt		Color		Looking for "Red Cells"	
	Simulated Blood	**Water**	**Simulated Blood**	**Water**	**Simulated Blood**	**Urine**
Before						
After						

3. Testing for Salt At each stage of the demonstration, your teacher will use a special strip that changes color in the presence of salt. Record results as positive (color change) or negative (no color change).

4. The Color of Things Observe and record the color of each liquid at each stage of the demonstration.

5. Under the Microscope Use a microscope to examine samples of the blood and urine used in the demonstration. Look to see if any blood cells leaked into the water as the urine formed.

Conclusion

Let's see what you learned about how blood is cleaned.

1. The kidneys are part of what organ system? What is their primary goal?

____

2. Your kidneys remove a mixture of wastes and water that your body doesn't need. What is this mixture called, and what is the primary waste in this mixture?

____

3. What happens when the kidneys fail to work properly?

____

Summarize how the model used in this demonstration simulates kidney function. Discuss the following points:

- What happened to the material in the dialysis tube when it was surrounded by plain water?
- What happened to the water?
- Did blood cells appear in the urine?
- What property of the dialysis tube allowed for the changes that took place?
- The materials in the demonstration moved in one direction. In our bodies, however, kidneys remove some beneficial things from the blood along with the waste, and then later return them. Name the two things the kidneys take out and return to the blood.

Copyright © Pearson Education, Inc., or its affiliates. All Rights Reserved.

No Shoes in This Box

Investigation Overview

- In this investigation, students will work in groups to use indirect evidence to try and identify the contents of a "mystery box."
- Prior to the investigation, prepare a mystery box for each group by gluing a variety of items inside of a shoe box. Arrange the items so that they form partitions, ramps, and barriers. Add a small ball such as a marble to the box and seal the box with tape. NOTE: Make all of the boxes identical.
- Begin the investigation by asking students to raise their hands if they think it is possible to know what Earth's interior is like without actually visiting it. Record the results of the vote on the board.
- Next, hold up a mystery box and ask students to raise their hands if they think it's possible to know what's inside the box without opening it. Record the votes on the board. Now, tilt the box so the ball rolls around. Walk around the classroom so that students hear the sounds made by the ball. Ask students to read Steps 1 and 2 and record their answers.
- Distribute the boxes. Give students 10 minutes to explore the box and draw a picture of the interior by listening to the sounds made by the ball rolling around inside.
- Have students report their results by drawing the insides of their boxes on the board. As a class, discuss the differences and similarities of the drawings.
- If students ask whether their drawings are correct, remind them that scientists cannot check their answers. That's why scientific theories are always subject to change. New tests sometimes produce results that cannot be explained by the current theory, and scientists must come up with a new theory.
- At the end of the investigation, ask students again to raise their hands if they think it is possible to know what Earth's interior is like without actually visiting it. Record the votes on the board.

SCORING RUBRIC	
SCORE 4	Student paragraph summarizes the findings, including voting results, and uses them to make a well-supported recommendation for the use or exclusion of the activity.
SCORE 3	Paragraph meets content requirements for a score of 4 but may contain minor errors.
SCORE 2	One piece of required information is incorrect or incomplete.
SCORE 1	Most of the required information is incorrect or incomplete.

Extension Activities

Assignment Have students use the Internet to research how scientists use the behavior of P-waves and S-waves to study the internal structure of Earth.

Field Trip Since much of what we know about the inside of Earth is based on earthquakes, arrange a field trip to a seismic monitoring station near your school. If there is no such station nearby, arrange to visit a site where an engineering company is using explosives to create artificial earthquakes as it searches for deposits of oil or minerals under the surface (seismic exploration).

Copyright © Pearson Education, Inc., or its affiliates. All Rights Reserved.

Name ______________________ Date ____________ Class ____________

No Shoes in This Box

Purpose To investigate how scientists develop theories when they cannot observe data directly

Materials
- mystery box
- blank paper
- pen or pencil

Scenario

Once you have a misconception, it's hard to get rid of it. One common misconception is that Earth's crust is solid, and its interior is molten, which means hot and liquid. The truth is that much of Earth's interior is solid. Only the outer core is molten.

One reason that so many people misunderstand the nature of Earth's interior is that no one has ever seen it. So, how can you really know what's there? How can anyone know what Earth's interior is like?

Scientists are able to describe Earth's internal structure based on measurements they have taken from the planet's surface. Scientists call these types of observations *indirect evidence* because they have to use the information from the measurements to figure out what they are observing. It is not as simple as looking directly at Earth's interior, but the information is still valid and useful.

Although surface observations and measurements support the current theory that most of Earth's interior is solid, many people still cling to the misconception that it is molten. To them, indirect evidence is not convincing. The publishers of a new science textbook want to find a way to convince those with this misconception that it is truly possible to know what Earth's interior is like, even though we can't actually visit. The publishing company has designed an activity that uses a "mystery box" to show students that it is possible to know what is inside of an object without looking inside.

You are an educational researcher for the publishing company. You and your partners are studying whether the mystery box activity can convince students that it is possible to determine the contents of something without peeking.

Procedure

1. **Before You Start** Your teacher will show you a sealed mystery box. The box has walls, ramps, and barriers glued inside. It also contains a ball that can roll around freely. It will be your job to determine the internal structure of the box just by listening to the ball as it rolls around. Do you think you can to do it?

____

2. **How About the Others?** Every group's mystery box is the same inside as your box. Do you think everyone in your class will come up with the same design at the end of this activity? What percentage of the groups in your class do you predict will come up with the same design as your group?

____

Copyright © Pearson Education, Inc., or its affiliates. All Rights Reserved.

Name ______ Date ______ Class ______

Procedure *(continued)*

3. **The Rubber Meets the Road** When your teacher gives your group your mystery box, do not open it! Just explore the interior by listening to the sounds the ball makes.
4. **Roll, Listen, and Draw** As you listen try to imagine what the inside of the box looks like. Discuss your ideas with your group and work together to draw the inside of the box.
5. **Post Your Results** When you are satisfied with your drawing, copy it onto the board. Be sure to include your names with the drawing.
6. **Peer Review** Compare your drawing to those of the other groups. Are there similarities? Are there differences? ______
7. **Agreement?** Are more than half of the diagrams similar to each other? ______
8. **Refining Your Theory** Find a group whose diagram is different from yours and work together to refine your theory. Post changes on the board.
9. **How About Now?** Are more than half of the diagrams similar now? ______

Conclusion

Let's see what you learned about using indirect observations to explore the interior of an object.

1. How many diagrams were almost identical? ______
2. Is it possible to know what's in the box without opening it? Explain.
3. Is it possible to know what Earth's interior is like without actually going there? Explain.

Remember, you want to know whether the mystery box activity can convince students that it is possible to determine the contents of something without peeking inside. To answer the question look at the number of students who thought it was possible *before* exploring the box, and the number who thought it was possible *after* exploring the box. Use the results of your study to write a letter to the publisher explaining whether or not the new textbook should include this activity.

Copyright © Pearson Education, Inc., or its affiliates. All Rights Reserved.

High-Priority Earthquake Zones

Investigation Overview

- On the morning of the investigation, visit the U.S. Geological Survey's web site (http://earthquake.usgs.gov/earthquakes/recenteqsus) for records of earthquakes that have occurred in the past seven days. Print the map showing recent earthquakes and their magnitudes. Make enough copies so that each pair of students will have a map to use during the activity. You should also have a large map showing the names of the states.
- Refer your students to the map of the United States in the lesson about monitoring earthquakes in their Student Edition. Ask them to examine the map and tell you what it shows. (It shows which areas of the U.S. are at the highest risk for earthquakes and which are at the lowest risk based on the location of past earthquakes across the U.S.)
- Distribute the earthquake maps. Ask your students to examine the map and explain how it differs from the map in their textbook.
- Review the Scenario and Procedure with your students. Explain that in Step 2, when they are ranking the states, they may choose any method for deciding the rank as long as they can justify it logically. Students may need to modify their method when ranking the next ten states in Step 3.

SCORING RUBRIC	
SCORE 4	The PSA script identifies the student as an emergency-preparedness expert, announces the availability of the pamphlet, and explains why it is important for everyone in the state to have a copy. It specifically mentions the number of earthquakes that occurred in the past seven days. The script closes by telling the audience how they can get a copy of the pamphlet.
SCORE 3	The script gives the most critical information only. It tells the audience that the pamphlet is available, why everyone needs it, and where to get it.
SCORE 2	The script meet the criteria for a score of 3, but the reasons for why people need the pamphlet are unclear or weak.
SCORE 1	The script does not include all of the critical information required for a score of 2 or 3.

Extension Activities

Assignment One week after completing the investigation, have your students examine a new seven-day earthquake map from the same web site. Have them compare and contrast the two maps and explain whether they would change either of their lists and why.

Cooperative Learning Have students work in pairs to create posters that focus on one of the items from the "What to Do …" pamphlet. Each pair of students should choose a different piece of advice to feature on their poster and illustrate in some way.

Field Trip Arrange a field trip to a local college or university that is actively monitoring earthquake activity. Your state's geological survey will be able to tell you whether there are seismographs in operation near your school.

Copyright © Pearson Education, Inc., or its affiliates. All Rights Reserved.

Name ______________________ Date ____________ Class ____________

High-Priority Earthquake Zones

Purpose To investigate which states have experienced earthquakes during the last seven days and rank them based on future risk

Materials
- map of earthquakes during the past seven days
- small notebook
- pencil or pen
- Student Edition

Scenario

As emergency-preparedness planners with the U.S. government, you and your partner have a new assignment. You have already created a pamphlet with a list of things people should do to protect themselves in an earthquake. You only have enough money to send the pamphlets to the preparedness offices in 10 states. You must decide which states need the pamphlets the most.

WHAT TO DO DURING AN EARTHQUAKE

Stay as safe as possible during an earthquake. Know that some earthquakes are actually foreshocks and a larger earthquake might follow. Get to a safe place as quickly as possible and stay indoors until the shaking has stopped.

IF INDOORS

- **DROP** to the floor, take **COVER** by getting under a sturdy table or other piece of furniture, and **HOLD ON** until the shaking stops. If there isn't a table or desk near you, cover your face and head with your arms and crouch in an inside corner of the building.
- Stay away from glass, windows, outside doors and walls, and anything that could fall, such as lighting fixtures or furniture.
- Stay in bed if you are there when the earthquake strikes unless you are under a heavy light fixture that could fall. Hold on and protect your head with a pillow.
- Use a doorway for shelter only if it is in close proximity to you and you know it is a strongly supported, load-bearing doorway.
- Stay inside until the shaking stops and it is safe to go outside. Research has shown that most injuries occur when people inside buildings attempt to move to a different location inside the building or try to leave.
- Be aware that the electricity may go out or the sprinkler systems or fire alarms may turn on.
- **DO NOT** use the elevators.

IF OUTDOORS

- Stay there. Move away from buildings, streetlights, and utility wires.
- Once in the open, stay there until the shaking stops. The greatest danger exists directly outside buildings, at exits, and alongside exterior walls. Many of the 120 fatalities from the 1933 Long Beach, California, earthquake occurred when people ran outside of buildings only to be killed by falling debris from collapsing walls. Ground movement during an earthquake is seldom the direct cause of death or injury. Most earthquake-related casualties result from collapsing walls, flying glass, and falling objects.

IF IN A MOVING VEHICLE

- Stop as quickly as safety permits and stay in the vehicle. Avoid stopping near or under buildings, trees, overpasses, and utility wires.
- Proceed cautiously once the earthquake has stopped. Avoid roads, bridges, or ramps that might have been damaged by the earthquake.

IF TRAPPED UNDER DEBRIS

- Do not light a match.
- Do not move about or kick up dust.
- Cover your mouth with a handkerchief or clothing.
- Tap on a pipe or wall so rescuers can locate you. Use a whistle if one is available. Shout only as a last resort. Shouting can cause you to inhale dangerous amounts of dust.

Based on a Preparedness list from FEMA

Copyright © Pearson Education, Inc., or its affiliates. All Rights Reserved.

Name ______________________ Date____________ Class__________

Procedure

1. **Analyzing the Data** Your department head (played by your teacher) will give you a map that shows all earthquakes that have struck in the U.S. during the past week. Examine the map and make a list in your notebook of all states that experienced an earthquake in the last seven days.
2. **Ranking the States** Some states have a higher earthquake risk than other states. It is important to first send "What to Do During an Earthquake" to the 10 states with the highest risk. Create a new list in your notebook with the states arranged in order from most likely to least likely to have an earthquake. Describe in your notebook how you determined the order.
3. **Where to go next?** If your office gets more money to print and send the pamphlet to 10 more states, which ones should be next? List the next 10 states in order. (Use the map in your textbook for help if necessary.) If you have to change your ranking procedure to select the next 10 states, explain your new method in your notebook.

Conclusion

Let's see what you learned about where earthquakes happen in the United States. Answer the following questions.

1. Compare the earthquakes that happened during the last seven days with the earthquake risk map in your textbook. How do the two maps compare?

   ____

2. Did any lowest-risk areas experience earthquakes? If so, which ones?

   ____

3. Did any earthquakes occur in your state in the last seven days? If so, where did they occur?

   ____

4. Some states have very high numbers of earthquakes. Explain why this is true.

   ____

   ____

Now use your answers to prepare the script for a Public Service Announcement (PSA). Radio stations in a high-risk state near the top of your list will broadcast your PSA. In the script, identify yourself as an emergency-preparedness expert, and then tell the audience about the "What to Do During an Earthquake" pamphlet and why it is important for everyone to have a copy. Be sure to mention the level of risk in their state and the number of recent earthquakes. Close by telling the audience how they can get copies of the pamphlet.

Copyright © Pearson Education, Inc., or its affiliates. All Rights Reserved.

My Rock Tells a Story

Investigation Overview

- The day before the investigation, gather enough pens, pencils, paper, and colored pencils or markers for the class.
- Begin the investigation by having students read the Scenario and Procedure. Answer all questions and let them begin.
- As students work, move around the room checking on their progress. You can guide them by asking questions such as: "What kind of rock are you writing about?" "How did your rock form?" "What useful purpose does your rock serve now?"
- It is possible to conduct this investigation in small pieces over the course of a week. Be sure to let students know what steps they should work on at the start of each class.
- Consider playing the role of the publisher in this investigation. Collect each group's draft each day and give feedback to make the process more realistic.

SCORING RUBRIC	
SCORE 4	Student writes a logical short story about a rock and its adventures. The story has a beginning, middle, and end. All scientific statements are correct, and the use described is realistic. At least one picture is used to illustrate each part of the story.
SCORE 3	The story is not logical or may contain minor errors, or it is not sufficiently illustrated.
SCORE 2	One part of the story is missing or contains incorrect information.
SCORE 1	More than one part of the story is missing or contains incorrect information.

Extension Activities

Assignment Have students write a paragraph describing how the rock cycle could turn their rock into another kind of rock. Challenge students to write a sequel in which their rock undergoes a transformation to another type of rock.

Field Trip Arrange a field trip that focuses on the uses of rocks. Visit a quarry, stone dealer, or cement and gravel business near your school. Have a spokesperson talk about the kind of rock they work with, how it formed, and what uses it serves. Alternatively, invite the spokesperson to your class as a guest speaker.

Copyright © Pearson Education, Inc., or its affiliates. All Rights Reserved.

Name ____________________ Date ____________ Class ____________

My Rock Tells a Story

Purpose
To explore the types, origins, and uses of different types of rock

Materials
- Student Edition
- lined and blank paper
- pencil or pen
- colored pencils or markers

Scenario

You are a successful author of children's books. The stories you write are usually about fluffy little animals and their wild adventures. Your books are popular with elementary school children and their parents. Science organizations and elementary schools love your books because they are always scientifically accurate.

Your publisher has given you a new challenge: Write a short story about a rock and its adventures. The story will be for third graders, so you should avoid big words and use plenty of pictures.

The beginning of this story should tell where the rock came from and how it formed. Is it sedimentary, igneous, or metamorphic? The middle of the story is where the adventure takes place. How did the rock get from the place where it formed to the place where it's being used? Did the rock encounter any dangers? Did it travel with any other rocks? What happened to them? The end of the story should tell how the rock is used to help people.

Procedure

1. **Starting At the End** Since your story must end with your rock being used in some way, the end is a good place to begin. Select a rock with a use that is familiar to you and your readers. That way, when you get to the end of your story, you will have a rock that is sure to have a use that you can write about.
2. **A Rock Is Born** Give your rock a clever name that matches the kind of character you want your rock to have, and then start your story with a description of your rock's formation. Where was it formed? What minerals is it made of? What is its texture? Are its crystals large or small? (If you have to use vocabulary that a third grader would not understand, be sure to explain what the words mean.)
3. **The Adventure** This is where you get to be creative. Make up a story about how your rock traveled to where it is used today. What happened along the way? Did humans cut it and polish it? Did they grind it up? Did they mix it with other things? Make this part of your story as exciting and interesting as you can.
4. **Scientific Accuracy** Most of your story (such as the rock's formation and use) will be scientifically accurate. But, in order to build an adventure story around a rock, some parts cannot be scientifically accurate. For example, you can pretend the rock has feelings just like a person. Did the cutting and grinding hurt? Did your rock leave its friends behind? Did the trip to its new home make it carsick?
5. **The Joy Of Helping Others** You started your work by selecting a rock that serves a useful purpose. End your story by talking about how happy the rock is in its new job.

Copyright © Pearson Education, Inc., or its affiliates. All Rights Reserved.

Name ______________________ Date __________ Class __________

Procedure *(continued)*

6. **Rough Draft** Once you have your ideas, begin writing your first draft by putting the ideas together in a story.

7. **Second Draft** Once you finish your first draft, read it out loud. Are there words you can leave out? Are there big words you can replace with simpler words? Are your sentences in the best order? Is there a better way of saying the same thing?

8. **A Second Set of Eyes** The best stories are the ones that receive feedback from another person. Have a partner read your story and give you any suggestions for making your story the best it can be.

9. **Adding Pictures** Now draw a picture to illustrate each section of your story. You must have at least three illustrations. (One or two for each section of the story is best.)

Conclusion

Let's see what you learned about rocks.

1. Which kind of rock did you write about in your story? ______________________

2. How does this kind of rock form? ______________________

____

____

3. Where does this kind of rock form?

____

4. Describe how the rock's texture tells the story of its origins.

____

____

Check your story one more time before sending it to your publisher.

- Are the story and its pictures neatly presented?
- Does your story have a beginning, middle, and end?
- Are all scientific statements correct?
- Is the use you describe for the rock a real use?
- Do you have at least three pictures?
- Is the grammar correct and are the words spelled correctly?

If your answer to all of these questions is "Yes!", then your story is ready! If you answered "No" to any of them, go back and make any necessary changes before sending it off to the publisher.

Copyright © Pearson Education, Inc., or its affiliates. All Rights Reserved.

Flight 7084 to Barcelona

Investigation Overview

- Each student will need a copy of the Student Edition. Be ready to tell students where to look in their textbooks to find information on seafloor spreading.
- Begin by having students read the Scenario and Steps 1 and 2.
- Answer all procedural questions, then let students begin. (Although this is an individual investigation, you may want to encourage students to work together to help one another, or you can use the "Cooperative Learning" strategy described below.)
- If your students are unfamiliar with the word "terrain," substitute "landscape" or "topography" and discuss the meaning before students begin.

SCORING RUBRIC	
SCORE 4	Student paragraph correctly describes the Mid-Atlantic Ridge and how it was formed, and shows understanding of what feature may have caused the loss of the RLB.
SCORE 3	The paragraph contains all required elements but may contain minor errors.
SCORE 2	The paragraph contains one or two inaccuracies or omissions of the required information.
SCORE 1	The paragraph contains significant inaccuracies or omissions and shows a minimal understanding of the Mid-Atlantic Ridge and seafloor spreading.

Extension Activities

Assignment Have students identify the site of the Flight 7084 incident on a map of the world that shows the Mid-Atlantic Ridge. You can find a map for this assignment on the Internet.

Cooperative Learning Have students work in pairs to write the report for the Central Intelligence Agency. Although students will write the paragraph for the report together, one student can edit the paragraph, and the other student can provide a drawing of the mountainous terrain of the Mid-Atlantic Ridge to accompany the paragraph.

Field Trip If your school is near the site of any geologic evidence that supports the theory of plate tectonics, arrange a trip to the site with an expert speaker who can explain the relevance of the formations found there.

Copyright © Pearson Education, Inc., or its affiliates. All Rights Reserved.

Name ______________________ Date __________ Class __________

Flight 7084 to Barcelona

Purpose To investigate the Atlantic Ocean floor near the Mid-Atlantic Ridge

Materials
- Student Edition
- paper
- pen or pencil

Scenario

Dirk wasn't the least bit nervous about the flight he was boarding. He had flown the same route on the same plane five times in the last four weeks. Sure, the plane (a model DC-8-32) was old, and Barcelona was pretty close to the maximum distance this particular plane could fly, but that's not why Dirk Conn was nervous. Dirk was nervous because he was on a top-secret mission to deliver a metal case full of classified files and surveillance equipment to an undercover agent in Spain.

At 7:03 p.m., on June 1, Spanish Air Flight 7084 finally took off from Miami International Airport. The 5:05 p.m. departure was delayed by a problem with the right-side cargo door.

About three and a half hours into the flight, the crew made their last voice contact with Miami air-traffic control. Everything was normal. One hour later, Captain Sergio Rivera radioed his company: "Getting warning codes. Putting down in the Azores." These troubling codes flashed red across the plane's computer screen:

```
221002006CARG PRESS LOW
341040006RT SD CARG DR DISAGREE
34220006ISIS 1,,,,,,,,ISIS (22FN
34123406IR2 1,EFCS1X,IR1,IR3,
213100206ADVISORY
```

The coded messages told a frightening story. The first message indicates the pressure in the cargo bay was low. The second tells that the right-side cargo door was not closed. The third and fourth together say that the seals that keep the passenger cabin pressurized were leaking. And the last message—213100206ADVISORY—says that cabin pressure was lost!

What the computer didn't say was that the right-side cargo door was gone! It had blown open, leaving a gaping hole in the side of the plane. The door and all checked baggage were gone, including the top-secret metal case Dirk Conn was guarding. As soon as Flight 7084 was safely on the ground, Dirk called his bosses at the CIA to report the possible security breach.

It's been two years since the top-secret cargo was lost over the Atlantic Ocean west of the Azores. The CIA is preparing its final report for the President of the United States. The President is furious and wants to know why the case was never recovered—after all, it had a radio locator beacon (RLB). How could it be lost? The President is especially disturbed because the items in the case were worth over $200 million. Based on the rugged landscape of the seafloor where they believe the case landed, CIA officials think the case and its contents are lost forever.

Is that possible? Does seafloor ruggedness help to explain why the case was never found? You are an oceanographer who studies ocean-floor structures. The director of the CIA has asked you to provide a brief description of the Mid-Atlantic Ridge in order to explain the loss of the case and the RLB.

Copyright © Pearson Education, Inc., or its affiliates. All Rights Reserved.

Name ______________________ Date __________ Class __________

Procedure

1. **RLB Facts** A radio locator beacon (RLB) is a device used to track the location of an item. The RLB emits radio signals that can be traced to a specific location, making it possible to recover objects (or even people) in extreme cases such as an avalanche or a plane crash. The RLB used in the top-secret metal case was very strong, made to withstand the force of a crash, the heat of a fire, and the pressures of being lost below thousands of feet of water. As strong as the RLB was, the search could only last 30 days. After that time, the batteries died and the radio signals ceased.
2. **Seafloor Spreading** Read the passage in your textbook that discusses seafloor spreading. Review it carefully, paying particular attention to the kind of terrain or landscape that is found along mid-ocean ridges.

Conclusion

Let's see what you learned about the ocean floor around the Mid-Atlantic Ridge.

1. What is a mid-ocean ridge?

   ____

2. What theory did the discovery of mid-ocean ridges support?

   ____

3. How would you describe the terrain along mid-ocean ridges?

   ____

4. Name a feature of the Mid-Atlantic Ridge that may have made it impossible to ever find the secret case's RLB.

   ____

The CIA director needs a paragraph about the Mid-Atlantic Ridge to use in the report to the President. In that paragraph you must explain how the Mid-Atlantic Ridge formed, what the landscape is like around the ridge, and a special feature of the ridge that could explain the loss of the secret case.

Begin your paragraph with this opening:

On June 1, the right-side cargo door of Spanish Air Flight 7084 opened at 38° 25′ N Latitude, 30° 22′ W Longitude, directly over the Mid-Atlantic Ridge. The Mid-Atlantic Ridge formed when …

Copyright © Pearson Education, Inc., or its affiliates. All Rights Reserved.

Jane Versus the Volcano

Investigation Overview

- For this investigation, provide maps of the United States marked only with latitude and longitude for students' reference. Such maps are available at various web sites. You may need to briefly review the use of latitude and longitude with your class.
- Prior to the investigation, determine the latitudes, longitudes, and names of currently active volcanoes in the United States. The U.S. Geological Survey provides this information on its web site (http://volcanoes.usgs.gov/activity). Post the coordinates for each volcano on the board. Provide the names of the volcanoes if students do not have Internet access.
- Have students read the Scenario and Procedure. Answer any questions.
- Your students may need help with Questions 1 and 2. Volcanoes are located either near a tectonic plate boundary or over a hot spot. You may wish to have a map of tectonic plate boundaries and hot spots available for students' reference.
- If students do not have Internet access, you will need to provide them with information about the different volcanoes.

SCORING RUBRIC	
SCORE 4	Student prepares an e-mail containing the name of an active volcano, its classification, its longitude and latitude, and the name of the city and state where it is located. The e-mail also states whether the volcano is located near a plate boundary or over a hot spot, and demonstrates understanding of the locations of volcano formation.
SCORE 3	The e-mail includes all information required for a score of 4 but may contain a minor error.
SCORE 2	The e-mail is missing one of the pieces of information required for a score of 4, or one of the pieces is incorrect.
SCORE 1	More than one piece of required information is incorrect or missing from the email, and it shows minimal understanding of where volcanoes form.

Extension Activities

Cooperative Learning Depending on a number of factors, the closest volcano to the studios may not actually be the cheapest trip. Have students work in groups to research the travel cost for the cast and crew. Assign each group one of the volcanoes nearest to the studio. The group should find the cost of a flight from Los Angeles, California, to the airport nearest the volcano, and the cost of an overnight stay at a hotel near the site. Have groups compare costs to see which film location would be the cheapest option for the producers.

Field Trip Reserve your school's computer lab for a virtual field trip. Some educational web sites offer virtual volcano trips. You may either select one location for all students to explore or assign student teams to different destinations.

Copyright © Pearson Education, Inc., or its affiliates. All Rights Reserved.

Name ____________________ Date ____________ Class ____________

Jane Versus the Volcano

Purpose To investigate the locations of erupting volcanoes

Materials
- map of the United States
- locations of active volcanoes

Scenario

A small film studio is ready to start production of a new movie called *Jane Versus the Volcano*. The story is about an adventurous young volcanologist who travels to a remote Pacific island to study an active volcano. Once she arrives at the site of the volcano, she discovers a world trapped in the past. Throughout the rest of the movie, Jane must find a way out of this prehistoric nightmare, all while trying to escape the many dangers surrounding the volcano.

The special-effects crew has been hard at work building a life-size robotic *Tyrannosaurus rex* that will terrorize Jane throughout the movie. The dinosaur is impressive, but the studio spent so much money on it that they don't have enough left to fly the entire cast and crew to the Pacific island where they originally planned to shoot the film.

To save money, the producers have decided to film at an active volcano within the United States. You are a volcanologist who studies volcanoes throughout the Pacific. When the producers originally consulted you for a filming location, you were able to tell them where to find the most exciting active volcano for their film shoot. Now that they want a new location, they have come to you again for a more affordable recommendation.

As soon as you find the producers an active volcano within the United States, they can start to relocate the set, equipment, cast, and crew. They want the information right away. Time is money!

Procedure

1. **Plotting Active Volcanoes** Your teacher has posted latitudes and longitudes for all volcanoes in the United States that are currently active. Carefully plot the volcanoes on a U.S. map.
2. **Picking the Location** Once you have plotted all active volcanoes on your map, select the one closest to the studio's headquarters in Los Angeles, California. That is the volcano you will recommend to the producers.
3. **What's the Name?** The studio travel department wants to know the name of the volcano you select as soon as possible. Once you have chosen a volcano, perform an Internet search of its coordinates, along with the word "volcano," to find the volcano's name and the nearest city.

Copyright © Pearson Education, Inc., or its affiliates. All Rights Reserved.

Name ______________________________ Date______________ Class______________

Conclusion

Let's see what you learned about volcanoes.

1. Where are most volcanoes located in Earth's crust?

____

2. What is a hot spot? Where are they found?

____

____

3. What are three kinds of volcanoes?

____

____

____

4. Which two kinds of volcanoes are made of lava? What is the third kind made of?

____

____

The producers are in a big hurry. As soon as you have picked a volcano, prepare an e-mail response with the following information:

- the name of the volcano
- the latitude and longitude of the volcano
- the name of the city and state where the volcano is located.

The scriptwriters also need some facts about the volcano to include in their script. Answer these questions in your e-mail, too.

- Why has a volcano formed at that location?
- What kind of volcano is it?
- When was the last time the volcano erupted?

Either write your e-mail on a piece of paper, or send your e-mail to your teacher.

Copyright © Pearson Education, Inc., or its affiliates. All Rights Reserved.

Dunwich Is Done

Investigation Overview

- Prior to this investigation, collect one paint tray for each group. An alternative to a paint tray is a disposable 9" × 12" × 2" baking pan with one end elevated 5 cm. Each group will also need play sand, which is available anywhere that sells children's sandboxes.
- To begin the investigation, have students read the Scenario and Procedure.
- This experiment can create a mess if students are not careful. Caution them not to be overly aggressive as they generate waves. Answer all procedural questions and let them begin.
- When students reach Step 5, they may need help with ideas for preventing erosion. Common solutions include structures such as groins, jetties, seawalls, and breakwaters. You may wish to have information about these structures available in the classroom.

SCORING RUBRIC	
SCORE 4	Student takes a lead in creating a poster that contains both sets of before-and-after diagrams. One set effectively shows erosion without protection, and the other correctly shows how a protective structure prevented erosion. The poster has a title, labels for natural and man-made features, and a conclusion.
SCORE 3	The poster contains all information required for a score of 4, and the student adequately participated in the group.
SCORE 2	The poster contains most of the necessary information, and the student played an adequate role in the group.
SCORE 1	The poster lacks significant content, and the student did not work well with the group.

Extension Activities

Assignment Have students use the Internet to identify and research a beach town in the United States that is threatened by erosion. They should use their models to test different strategies for saving the town.

Cooperative Learning Although this investigation provides a cooperative learning setting, it also provides an excellent opportunity to add the Jigsaw strategy. Instruct each team to decide on one erosion-prevention strategy for each student on the team to investigate (groins, jetties, seawalls, and breakwaters). Form four expert groups based on these techniques and have each group investigate the selected strategy. When the experts return to their teams to conduct Step 5 of the investigation, the decision of what strategy to test will now be informed by "expert" opinions as they debate the pros and cons of the different techniques.

Field Trip Arrange a field trip to a beach near your school where students can observe groins, jetties, seawalls, and breakwaters firsthand and evaluate their effectiveness. While there, have students identify erosion and deposition features associated with these structures. If your school is too far from the ocean or a large lake, visit a meandering river or creek instead.

Copyright © Pearson Education, Inc., or its affiliates. All Rights Reserved.

Name ______________________ Date ____________ Class ____________

Dunwich Is Done

Purpose To investigate beach erosion caused by waves

Materials

- paint tray
- 500 mL of moist play sand
- 1 L of water
- wave stick (half of a 30-cm ruler or half of a paint stir stick)
- tongue depressor or craft stick
- small pebbles or rocks
- 10 cm × 10 cm corrugated board
- scissors
- notebook
- poster board or construction paper
- pen, pencil, and markers

Scenario

Your room at the quaint inn on St. James Street in Dunwich, England, was comfortable and very quiet. It had a fantastic view looking out over the marsh, and the sunrises were spectacular. Even the food was good. While exploring Dunwich on your bicycle, you discovered some very interesting facts about the town's history—facts that were especially interesting to a coastal-erosion expert like you.

Dunwich, England, was once a thriving seaport. By the middle of the 13th century, Dunwich had eight churches, two hospitals, and a population of about 3,000 people. The main exports from Dunwich were wool and grain. Its imports were cloth, fish, furs, timber, and wine. Today, however, Dunwich is just a tiny fishing village with a population of only 80 people. It sits on the edge of a cliff that was once over a mile from the coast. What happened to the old Dunwich?

In the year 1286, the people of Dunwich had no idea that their thriving town was doomed. That year, a violent storm struck the English coast—a storm so fierce that it carried parts of Dunwich away into the North Sea. When the storm cleared, the people banded together. They worked hard to rebuild their harbor. Then, in 1328, the harbor was wiped out. The village of Newton, a few miles up the coast, was also swept away.

In 1347, another storm swept 400 houses into the sea, and all attempts to save Dunwich ended forever. Today, its eight churches and other original buildings are gone. Their ruins have been deep beneath the waves for hundreds of years. Even the land between the new Dunwich and old Dunwich is gone. The long-shore drift slowly ate away at the low-lying land.

You were especially interested to hear this story because you and your partners are studying how different structures can stop or slow the erosion that long-shore drift causes.

Procedure

1. **Building a Beach** Make a model beach by spreading 500 mL of wet play sand across the shallow end of a paint tray. Shape your model beach any way you like.
2. **Adding a Harbor Town** Make a small crater in the sand to represent the harbor. The crater should be about 8 cm wide and expose the bottom of the container. Use little pieces of corrugated board to build a town (like Dunwich) next to the harbor.
3. **Filling the Ocean** Add approximately 1 L of water to the deep part of the tray where there is no sand. The water represents the ocean. (Make sure that the water fills the harbor.) In your notebook, draw a diagram of your model beach, harbor, and town.

Copyright © Pearson Education, Inc., or its affiliates. All Rights Reserved.

Name ______________________ Date ______________ Class ______________

Procedure *(continued)*

4. **Making Waves** You and your partners should each take a turn creating small waves in the ocean. Hold the wave stick vertically and use quick but short pushing motions to make a wave at an angle to the beach. Each of you will make 20 waves at the same angle. After everyone has had a turn, make a second diagram. Label any special features caused by the erosion. Compare the before-and-after diagrams and describe how the shape of the coastline has changed.

____

____

____

5. **Saving Dunwich** Brainstorm ways that you can use the rocks and/or tongue depressor (or craft stick) to keep your beach, harbor, and town from eroding away. Seawalls, groins, jetties, and other barriers can prevent beach erosion. Decide on a strategy and test it by rebuilding your beach, harbor, and town, and then repeating the wave-making procedure described in Step 4. Again, try to make the waves at the same angle to the beach as before. In your notebook, draw another set of before-and-after diagrams and describe how your plan to prevent beach erosion turned out.

Conclusion

Let's see what you learned about the erosion caused by wave action.

1. When waves strike a beach at an angle, the sand is carried along the beach in the direction of the current. What is this process called?

____

2. This process can cause special land features to form. Name three such features and briefly describe how waves form each feature. ______________________

____

____

3. Waves cause both erosion and deposition. Identify one erosion feature and one deposition feature caused by wave action.

____

____

You and your partners must create a poster to present at a scientific conference. The poster will show the results of your experiments about protecting a beach, harbor, and town from the eroding forces of waves hitting the beach at an angle. Your poster needs two pairs of before-and-after diagrams. The first pair will show the erosion caused by wave action without protection. The second pair of diagrams will show how well the protective feature you tested worked. Be sure to include a title, labels for all features shown, and a conclusion.

Copyright © Pearson Education, Inc., or its affiliates. All Rights Reserved.

Goodbye, Columbus

Investigation Overview

- To prepare for this investigation, each student will need the Student Edition and several sheets of graph paper.
- Begin by having students read the Scenario. Review the concept of carbon-14 dating with the class. If students ask where carbon-14 comes from, tell them that it is created when cosmic rays interact with the upper atmosphere.
- *For your information only*: The interaction causes a single neutron to be formed. That neutron reacts with nitrogen to form a carbon-14 atom and a hydrogen atom. The reaction is: $^{1}n + ^{14}N \rightarrow ^{14}C + ^{1}H$
- Next, have students read and answer the questions in Steps 1 and 2. Discuss their answers and make sure students understand that carbon-14 dating only works on things that were alive within the last 50,000 years. Both the parchment and the ink at one time had living components.
- For Steps 4 and 5, suggest that students plot a point on either side of the measurements obtained. (Place the "Years-Before-Present" data on the *x*-axis with a range from 550 to 600. On the *y*-axis, place the "% Carbon-14 Remaining" data with a range from 92.999 to 93.563. The larger the graph, the easier it will be to correctly estimate the age of the parchment and the ink.
- The correct answer was determined in 2010 to be 570 years old (±5 years). Since students are assuming a linear relationship, their answers should fall between 565 and 575.

SCORING RUBRIC	
SCORE 4	Student correctly records all information in the provided form and writes a convincing conclusion.
SCORE 3	Student records all information in the provided form and writes a conclusion.
SCORE 2	Student reports one or two incorrect results, or the conclusion is incomplete.
SCORE 1	Significant portions of the form are missing or incorrect.

Extension Activities

Cooperative Learning Have your class design a museum exhibit showing the geologic history of Earth. Create three teams and assign each team a different era of Earth's history: Paleozoic, Mesozoic, Cenozoic. Each member of the team will make a different poster for display in the museum. Poster topics must include climate, tectonics (the location of the modern continents at the time), and one poster for each of six to eight significant organisms that lived during the era.

Field Trip Arrange a field trip to a museum that has a collection of ancient artifacts and/or fossils. Have a curator from the museum explain to your students how relative and absolute dating techniques were used to establish the ages of the different items in the museum.

Copyright © Pearson Education, Inc., or its affiliates. All Rights Reserved.

Name ______________________ Date ____________ Class ____________

Goodbye, Columbus

Purpose To understand how carbon-14 dating can be used to find the age of ancient objects

Materials
- Student Edition
- graph paper

Scenario

Many people in the United States learn that Christopher Columbus discovered the New World in 1492, but he might not have been the first European to set foot on American soil! Vikings might have been here first. In the 1950s, a Swiss art dealer revealed a very old-looking map drawn on parchment. He called it the "Vinland" map. It showed an island west of Greenland that had features similar to the east coast of Newfoundland, Canada. The art dealer claimed that the map was redrawn in 1440 from the 13th-century original. That's 52 years before Columbus "discovered" America! For years, the map has sat in the Yale University Map Collection as experts argued over whether or not it was real.

You are a carbon-14 dating expert working for the world's largest radiocarbon dating service. The map's owners have hired your company to date the map using the carbon-14 method. A small sample of the map has just arrived, and you have to determine the age of the parchment and the ink.

Procedure

1. **When Does Carbon Dating Work?** Carbon-14 dating can only determine the age of things that were alive within the last 50,000 years. Parchment is a thin paper-like material made from the skin of goats, sheep, or calves. Was parchment ever alive? Explain.

   ____

   ____

2. **Now, The Ink** Hundreds of years ago, people made ink from plant materials, such as a mixture of wine and extracts of tree bark. Was the ink ever alive? Explain.

   ____

   ____

3. **Here Come the Readings** Everyone in your laboratory is excited to see the results:

Parchment:	93.321
Ink:	93.340

Both samples contain about 93 percent of the carbon-14 they originally contained.

Copyright © Pearson Education, Inc., or its affiliates. All Rights Reserved.

Name ______________________ Date __________ Class __________

Procedure *(continued)*

4. How Old Is the Parchment? Use the table of carbon-14 data to the right to determine the age of the parchment. The exact percentage and/or age will not be on the table. You need to estimate.

5. **How Old Is the Ink?** Now determine the age of the ink. ______________________

Carbon-14 Analysis Table	
Years Before Present	**% Carbon-14 Remaining**
0	100.000
50	99.397
100	98.798
150	98.202
200	97.610
250	97.021
300	96.436
350	95.854
400	95.276
450	94.702
500	94.131
550	93.563
600	92.999
650	92.438

Conclusion

Let's see what you learned about using carbon-14 dating:

1. What is the half-life of carbon-14? ______________________

2. Why does carbon-14 dating only work for objects that were once alive and are less than 50,000 years old?

____

____

____

3. If an artifact is thought to be about 200,000 years old, carbon-14 dating will not work. What radioactive isotope can be used instead? ______________________

The director of The Yale Map Collection is anxious to see the results. Prepare a report by filling in the blanks on your company's form:

CARBON DATING LABS, INC.
MIAMI, FL

Client: The Yale Map Collection, Sterling Library, Yale University, New Haven, CT		Specimen: Vinland Map	
Tested Specimen	% Carbon-14 Remaining	Estimated Age of Specimen	Estimated Date that Specimen Was Created
parchment			
ink			

Conclusion: Explain whether the Vinland Map was created before Columbus discovered the New World in 1492.

____
Carbon-14 expert signature

Copyright © Pearson Education, Inc., or its affiliates. All Rights Reserved.

The Fire Trucks Are Coming!

Investigation Overview

- Before you begin this investigation, you must capture a satellite image of your school and the surrounding neighborhood. Use the Internet to find a satellite image of your neighborhood on a map site. Make sure that the map is large enough to show the location of both your school and the nearest firehouse. Enter the addresses of your school and the firehouse on the map site. (You may prefer to manually mark each location on the printed images.)
- Copy the image or capture it with the *Print Screen* key (or similar key), and paste it into a word-processing document. Make any adjustments necessary to optimize the image. For example, crop or enlarge the image, change the page orientation or margins, or adjust brightness and contrast.
- Make a color copy of this image for each student to use. NOTE: Students will mark routes directly on their copy of the image. If you want to reuse the color images, you may want to laminate them and have students use washable markers.
- Have students read the Scenario and the Procedure. Instead of simply answering students' questions, lead them in the right direction by asking your own questions. Encourage students to ask each other for help.
- Distribute a satellite image and all other materials to each student.
- Display some professionally prepared maps so that students can see examples of legends.

SCORING RUBRIC	
SCORE 4	The student's map shows the fastest route from the firehouse to the school highlighted in green and at least one alternate route highlighted in yellow. The map includes the scale used and a legend with all symbols. The map is neatly made, and all streets and cross streets on the route are labeled. The map has a title that includes the name of the school.
SCORE 3	The route highlighted in green is a good route but is not the fastest one available. The map meets all of the other standards for a score of 4.
SCORE 2	The map fails to meet two or more of the standards described for a score of 4. The route highlighted in green may not be a fast route, or there may not be alternative routes shown.
SCORE 1	The map only shows one route, and most items are incomplete or demonstrate minimal understanding.

Extension Activities

Assignment Have students make a map that shows the routes from the firehouse to their homes.

Field Trip Arrange a field trip to the firehouse that is on students' maps. While there, present the maps to the fire chief and tour the firehouse. On the trip back, follow the route selected by the students and time the trip with a stopwatch. If there are traffic lights or stop signs on the route, run a separate stopwatch to measure the time spent stopped. At the end of the trip, subtract stopped time from total time to produce an estimate of the emergency-response time.

Copyright © Pearson Education, Inc., or its affiliates. All Rights Reserved.

Name ______________________ Date ____________ Class ____________

The Fire Trucks Are Coming!

Purpose To use a satellite image of the school and its neighborhood to create a map that shows the best path for fire engines to follow

Materials
- satellite image of the school and its neighborhood
- tracing paper
- masking tape
- dark-colored marker (nonpermanent)
- pencil
- fine pointed felt-tip pen (black)
- green and yellow highlighters

Scenario

In the past, mapmaking meant carefully measuring distances and elevations and using geometry. Mapmaking was hard work. Today it's much easier.

You are a modern-day mapmaker. You use aerial photographs and satellite images to make maps. Your clients range from small towns to large businesses. Today, your client is a school in your community. The principal needs a map for the local fire department.

The fire chief wants a map showing two things: the fastest route between the firehouse and the school, and at least one alternate route that emergency vehicles can use in case of traffic. The chief wants you to highlight the best route in green and alternate routes in yellow. The chief also wants the map to show the scale used, a legend that only uses symbols, and the names of all of the streets and cross streets on each route.

The principal wants the map to have a title that includes the name of the school.

Procedure

1. **Mounting the Satellite Image** Your teacher will give you a copy of a satellite image that shows your school and the closest firehouse. Tape the image to your desk with north at the top.
2. **Selecting the Route** Before you begin making the map, you must first decide on the best route. Remember, a fire engine on an emergency call can ignore stop signs, traffic lights, and one-way streets. Also look for alternate routes for emergency vehicles to use if the main route is blocked.
3. **Marking the Route** Use a dark-colored marker to trace all of the roads you want the fire engines to follow. Mark the best route and one or two alternate routes. Marking the routes will help you see them through the tracing paper in the next step.

A satellite image is not exactly a photograph.

A photograph is an image recorded on light-sensitive material. A satellite image is a composite that is recreated from the digital information (ones and zeros) that are collected by satellite-based sensors as they orbit high above Earth. Even when they look almost real, the colors are called *false colors,* because they are generated by digital image-processing techniques.

Copyright © Pearson Education, Inc., or its affiliates. All Rights Reserved.

Name ______________________ Date __________ Class __________

In Memory of Winifred

Purpose To investigate the weathering of a gravestone

Materials
- Student Edition
- notebook
- pen or pencil

Scenario

The last gravestone rubbing you made had these words on it: "In Loving Memory of Winifred." The words were hard to make out, and the rest of the writing on the gravestone was completely gone. There was no date of birth or death. Most of the writing on the marble headstone over Winifred's grave had weathered away. Nothing was left but smooth stone.

You are the local expert on gravestones. It's not your job; it's just a hobby. You've been making rubbings of gravestones for so long that you know from observation what happens to them after years of contact with wind, rain, and other weather factors. The lettering becomes harder and harder to read until, one day, it's gone!

Recently, the local historical society asked you to write an article for their monthly newsletter. The purpose of the article is to inform readers of the reasons local gravestones have become harder to read over time. What an honor! You are a bit nervous, though. Your experience has taught you what happens to gravestones but not *why* it happens.

Procedure

1. **Before You Panic** Don't panic! The information you need is at your fingertips. Your textbook explains two types of weathering: mechanical and chemical. Both can cause gravestone weathering.

2. **Two Types, Many Causes** Each type of weathering has several causes. Look over the causes and sort them into two columns based on logic and your own experience. In one column, place the causes of weathering that you predict change gravestones. In the other column, place the causes of weathering you think are unlikely to change gravestones.

Gravestone Weathering

Cause	Not a Cause

Copyright © Pearson Education, Inc., or its affiliates. All Rights Reserved.

Name ______________________ Date ____________ Class ____________

Procedure *(continued)*

3. **How Confident Are You?** Which items in each list are you most sure of? Circle all of the causes of weathering in each column that you are confident belong there. If you are not sure about an item, do not circle it.

4. **Creating a Master List** Your teacher will create a master class list of the causes of gravestone weathering by calling on students at random. When you are called, identify an item from your list that is not already on the master list. Or, if your ideas are already listed, you may need to pass.

Conclusion

Let's see what you learned about weathering.

1. What are the two types of weathering called?

____

____

2. Which of the several causes of weathering is most likely to damage gravestones in your area? Explain.

____

____

____

3. Which of the several causes of weathering is least likely to damage gravestones in your area? Explain.

____

____

____

4. What happens to the small particles of stone that are weathered away from the surface of a gravestone?

____

____

The historical society wants you to select two causes of weathering from the master list and write a paragraph about each. Each paragraph must explain how the cause of weathering actually destroys a gravestone.

Copyright © Pearson Education, Inc., or its affiliates. All Rights Reserved.

Mile-High Baseball

Investigation Overview

- To prepare for this investigation, cut two 6 inch × 6 inch squares of aluminum foil for each student group. Each group will also need two sheets of copier paper and a stopwatch.
- Begin by having students read the Scenario and Procedure. Answer any questions, and allow students time to discuss how a change in altitude may affect gravity and air density.
- Once students have discussed their ideas with classmates, ask how they think air density and gravity change from sea level to an altitude such as Denver's.
- Reveal to students that, at Denver's altitude of one mile, air density and gravity both decrease compared to sea level. Air density decreases by 14.5 percent, and gravity decreases by 0.06 percent.
- Once students understand the effect of the stadium's altitude on air pressure and gravity, allow them to proceed with the investigation. Make sure that students do not throw their objects to the ground during testing. They must simply release the objects and let them fall.
- There are a number of ways to eliminate or counteract the batting advantage in the stadium. Options include increasing the distance to the fence so that balls have to travel farther to become home runs, adding a pressurized dome to the stadium so that there is the same amount of air resistance as at sea level, and using a baseball with a larger surface area in order to create more resistance.

SCORING RUBRIC	
SCORE 4	Student's letter clearly and accurately explains why there are more home runs in Denver, and provides a logical solution for eliminating the advantage. The solution is justified using sound scientific reasoning.
SCORE 3	Student's letter explains Denver's home run advantage and gives a justified, scientific solution. The letter may contain minor errors.
SCORE 2	Student's letter explains the advantage and gives a justified solution. There may be a significant error, or the reason for the solution may not be scientific.
SCORE 1	Student's letter contains significant errors or shows a minimal understanding of air density.

Extension Activities

Assignment Have students use the Internet to investigate whether or not baseball statisticians take into account stadium location for calculating home runs. Write a report arguing whether or not they should consider it.

Cooperative Learning Have students work in groups to brainstorm other factors that could affect the number of home runs hit in different cities. For example, a wind may often blow from home plate toward the outfield. Have students write a letter to the commissioner of Major League Baseball explaining their ideas and suggesting a way to make stadium conditions more consistent throughout the league.

Guest Speaker Arrange for a local baseball coach to speak to your class about the different fields where the team plays. Ask whether any of the fields seem to give players an advantage or disadvantage, and what features of the field create that condition.

Copyright © Pearson Education, Inc., or its affiliates. All Rights Reserved.

Name ______________________ Date ____________ Class ____________

Mile-High Baseball

Purpose

To investigate the effect of air density on the flight of an object

Materials

- two 6 inch × 6 inch aluminum foil squares
- stopwatch
- two sheets of plain copier paper

Scenario

Denver, Colorado, is called "The Mile-High City" because it sits about one mile above sea level. Denver is the highest city in the United States with a Major League Baseball team, the Colorado Rockies.

The Rockies hit many more home runs during home games than during away games. You might say the Rockies have the ultimate home-field advantage. The stadium where the Rockies play has been called "the greatest hitter's park in baseball history." Home runs hit there travel farther than home runs hit in other ballparks. There are even players who can hit home runs in Denver but nowhere else.

The commissioner of Major League Baseball wants to know why it is so much easier to hit home runs in Denver. Is it the result of gravity or air resistance? Is there anything that the league can do to take away what some consider an unfair advantage? As a physicist and a baseball fan, you have volunteered to answer the commissioner's questions.

The Effect of Altitude on Baseball Flight

Initial speed of ball (m/s)	Distance traveled at sea level (m) (elevation 0 m)	Distance traveled in Denver (m) (elevation 1,609 m)	Distance traveled in Mount Everest (m) (elevation 8,848 m)	Distance traveled in a vacuum (m)
35	72.9	77.2	94.5	123.1
40	85.3	91.0	115.2	160.8
45	96.9	104.2	135.7	203.5
50	107.7	116.5	155.8	251.2

Procedure

1. **Gravity or Friction** Discuss with your partners how both gravity and air density change as you go higher in the atmosphere. Which do you think changes more? Explain.

   ____

2. **Share Your Ideas** After discussing this with your group, share your answer with another team and compare your reasons. When your teacher asks, share your ideas with the class.

3. **Lessening the Impact** As a baseball moves through the air, it pushes air molecules out of the way, but the air also pushes back. The faster the ball moves, the greater the air pushes back. This is called air resistance. Since Denver is a mile above sea level, its air is less dense, meaning there is less air resistance. How can you decrease air resistance? Work with your team to think of some possibilities.

Copyright © Pearson Education, Inc., or its affiliates. All Rights Reserved.

Name ______________________ Date____________ Class____________

Procedure *(continued)*

4. **Test Your Ideas** Time how long it takes for a sheet of paper to fall to the floor. Record the time in the table provided. Next, change the shape of the paper in a way that you think will make it fall faster. You cannot change the mass of the paper. Drop the paper from the same height as before, and record the new fall time.

Object	Fall Time
paper	
altered paper	
foil	
altered foil	

5. **Does the Material Make a Difference?** Repeat Step 5 using a sheet of aluminum foil and record your results.

Conclusion

Let's see what you learned about how air density affects an object's flight.

1. Which is more likely to affect a baseball hit in Denver: decreased gravity or decreased air density? Explain.

2. Why is the air less dense in Denver?

3. Why do you think less air density causes the baseballs to travel further?

4. How do you think home runs would be affected at a baseball stadium that was located below sea level? (*Hint:* Below sea level means the altitude is lower than the altitude of the surface of the ocean.)

Write a letter to the baseball commissioner explaining why there are more home runs in Denver than in other cities. Include one suggestion for counteracting the effect of air density at Denver's altitude. Explain why you think your idea will work. Make sure to discuss the science behind your idea.

Copyright © Pearson Education, Inc., or its affiliates. All Rights Reserved.

What Causes Our Climate?

Investigation Overview

- To complete this investigation, students will need to know the prevailing wind direction for your town. Show them local weather maps spanning several days. Help students determine the prevailing wind direction by following the movement of highs, lows, and fronts across the map.
- Prior to the investigation, gather the materials and information your students will need. Make each student a copy of a blank map of the United States (available on the Internet). Students will need to mark and label your town's location on the maps. You will need to find your town's altitude and latitude (available on the Internet) for students' reference.
- Begin the investigation by having students read the Scenario and Procedure. Answer any questions, distribute the maps and other materials, and tell the students your town's altitude and latitude.

SCORING RUBRIC	
SCORE 4	Student creates a map with all required factors clearly marked and labeled. The e-mail includes a well-written introduction and shows an understanding of each factor's effects on local temperature and precipitation.
SCORE 3	The map or e-mail contains a minor error or is not sufficiently supported by fact.
SCORE 2	Both the map and e-mail contain errors or omissions.
SCORE 1	A large portion of the map or e-mail is largely incorrect or missing.

Extension Activities

Assignment Have students identify a city or town at the same latitude somewhere else in the U.S. or the world. The city should be in a different climate region (use the map of climate regions in the Student Edition in the chapter about climate and climate change). Have students explain why that city's climate is different from your climate.

Cooperative Learning Instead of having students complete the activity individually and write an e-mail, have them work in groups to prepare a poster session. Each student should contribute information about one of the factors that influence your local climate.

Field Trip Arrange a field trip to an assisted-living facility in your community. While there, have your students interview residents who have lived in your community for 50 years or more. Questions should focus on changes in the weather that the residents have noticed during their lifetimes. Note: Changes in climate tend to be more gradual than one human lifetime. Nevertheless, the results of the interviews can lead to a class discussion of the difference between climate and weather.

Copyright © Pearson Education, Inc., or its affiliates. All Rights Reserved.

Name ______________________ Date ____________ Class ____________

What Causes Our Climate?

Purpose To investigate factors affecting your local climate

Materials

- map of the United States
- pen or pencil
- colored pencils
- Student Edition

Scenario

As a climatologist, a person who studies climate, you often receive calls from newspaper reporters asking for your thoughts on each new claim about global climate change.

Today's phone call was different. The reporter who called is writing an article about the climate in your town. The reporter is interested in the roles that six different factors (latitude, prevailing wind direction, nearby bodies of water, mountain ranges, ocean currents, and altitude) play in determining the climate.

By tomorrow, you have promised to send the reporter a map with all the factors marked on it and one paragraph for each factor explaining how that factor contributes to your local climate. Your teacher will provide you with latitude and altitude information, and it's up to you to find out about the prevailing wind direction, important bodies of water, and mountains.

Procedure

1. **Put Your Town on the Map** Your teacher will provide you with a map of the United States. Neatly mark your town and write the name of your town on the map.
2. **Latitude Attitude** Draw a horizontal line through your town and write the latitude on the line.
3. **Which Way Is the Wind Blowing** Draw a red arrow to indicate the prevailing wind direction. Make the arrow long enough so that it passes over water and/or mountains that influence your climate.
4. **Water and Currents** Before the wind reaches your town, does it blow across a large body of water? If so, draw and write the name of the body of water on your map. Is there an ocean current that warms or cools the air? If so, draw a blue arrow to show the direction of the current.
5. **Mountains in the Way?** If the prevailing winds flow over mountains, that will affect the moisture content of the air. On your map, draw and write the names of any mountains that influence your town's climate.
6. **How High Are We?** Finally, the reporter wants the town's altitude. Once your teacher tells you the town's altitude, write it on your map near the name of your town.

Copyright © Pearson Education, Inc., or its affiliates. All Rights Reserved.

Name ______________________ Date ____________ Class ____________

Conclusion

Let's see what you learned about the factors that contribute to your town's climate.

1. Which factor(s) is most responsible for your average temperature? Explain.

____

____

____

2. Which factor(s) is most responsible for the amount of precipitation your town gets? Explain.

____

____

____

3. In what climate region is your town located? How do you know?

____

____

____

On a piece of paper, write what you will say in your e-mail to the reporter. Include an introduction that summarizes what your map shows, and two or three sentences for each factor (latitude, prevailing wind direction, water, mountains, ocean currents, and altitude) describing how it affects your town's climate. Be sure to explain how each factor affects the temperature and/or precipitation for your town. Refer to information on the map in your descriptions. Use your textbook to check your facts.

Copyright © Pearson Education, Inc., or its affiliates. All Rights Reserved.

My Water Smells Like Gasoline!

Investigation Overview

- Several weeks before conducting this investigation, dig several pails of soil from a flower bed or vegetable garden. Spread the soil on newspapers in a place where it will remain undisturbed for at least two weeks so that it will dry out. (The drying time will depend on the humidity in the area.) You can purchase sand at a hardware store or garden center, and art supply stores sell potter's clay.
- Before you conduct this investigation, assemble all materials listed on the student page. Since the sand, clay, and garden soil will become wet during the investigation, be sure to have enough so that each class can begin with dry material.
- Have your students read the Scenario and Procedure. Encourage students to work without much guidance. This experiment is very flexible; students are likely to make mistakes, especially if this is their first time designing an experiment by themselves. It is best to let students use trial and error and repeat their experiment if needed.
- If it is necessary for you to explain porosity to your students, a simple demonstration can be performed using colored water, marbles, and a graduated cylinder. Fill a large beaker with marbles and ask if the beaker is full. Most students will say yes. Now slowly add the colored water from a graduated cylinder until the level of water in the beaker matches the level of marbles in the beaker.

SCORING RUBRIC	
SCORE 4	The student fully participated in the investigation. The script defines permeability and porosity, and it correctly explains how each makes it possible for clay to protect the water below. The poster contains diagrams describing the experiments, results of permeability and porosity calculations, and a diagram showing how a clay layer protects the water beneath it. All information and calculations are correct.
SCORE 3	The poster and script meet all content requirements for a score of 4, but the student did not fully participate in the investigation.
SCORE 2	The student helps with the investigation but was not engaged, or either the poster or script did not meet all of the content requirements for a score of 3 or 4.
SCORE 1	The student did not participate, or content is missing from both the script and poster.

Extension Activities

Assignment Many chemicals can contaminate groundwater. Have your students research other chemicals found in groundwater and write a report about one of them.

Cooperative Learning Separate students into groups and assign each group one groundwater contaminant. The main inorganic contaminants of groundwater include antimony, arsenic, asbestos, barium, beryllium, cadmium, chromium, copper, cyanide, fluoride, lead, mercury, nickel, nitrate, nitrite, selenium, and thallium. Have each group research its contaminant and present its findings to the class using presentation software.

Copyright © Pearson Education, Inc., or its affiliates. All Rights Reserved.

Name ______________________ Date __________ Class __________

My Water Smells Like Gasoline!

Purpose To investigate permeability and porosity of soils

Materials

- water
- sand
- clay
- dry garden soil
- two 100-ml beakers
- 100-ml graduated cylinder
- funnels
- coffee filters
- tape
- rubber bands
- scissors
- stopwatch
- notebook

Scenario

TOWN MEETING

Where: Town Hall
When: Tonight, 7:30 P.M.

Due to the recent discovery of a leaking gasoline storage tank at one of our local gas stations, authorities have warned that well water in the area may be contaminated. They say that only residents with shallow wells need to avoid drinking their water, and that the water in deep wells is safe because a layer of clay protects it. Is your drinking water safe? Find out at tonight's town meeting. Hear local experts explain how clay in the ground protects the water in deep wells. Ask them your questions and decide for yourself. Don't drink the water until you know it is safe!

You are a science student in a class that has been learning about groundwater. Your teacher needs to send two students to a town meeting to explain permeability and porosity to the townspeople and demonstrate how a clay layer can protect the groundwater below it.

Your teacher has issued a challenge to your class: work in pairs to develop a demonstration of permeability and porosity to show at the town meeting. Be prepared to explain how clay can keep water in a deep aquifer safe from the leaking gasoline. Your teacher will give you a collection of materials to use for your demonstration. It is up to you to decide what to do next.

Porosity

Porosity is a measure of the space between particles. The more porous a material, the more space there is between its particles. Porosity is expressed as a percentage of the amount of space in a known volume of material. Water is often used to measure porosity.

Permeability

Permeability is a measure of the speed with which a liquid or gas passes through a substance. The faster it moves, the greater the permeability. Permeability is expressed in liters per minute.

Copyright © Pearson Education, Inc., or its affiliates. All Rights Reserved.

Name ______________________ Date ____________ Class ____________

Procedure

1. **Where to Start?** In your demonstration at the town meeting, you must be able to show that sand, garden soil, and clay each have a different porosity and permeability. But how do you do that? Start by thinking about the definitions of porosity and permeability. Then, examine the list of materials together and brainstorm how you can use the materials to measure porosity and permeability.

2. **Things to Consider** As you measure porosity and permeability, consider these questions: How does grain size affect porosity and/or permeability? Is the amount of material tested important?

3. **Making the Measurements** Set up everything according to your plan and conduct your investigation. Think about the definitions of porosity and permeability. What measurements do you need to take to determine porosity and permeability?

4. **Keeping Records** Record all procedures and all measurements in your notebook.

5. **Calculating the Answers** Use your measurements to calculate the porosity and permeability of each of the materials you tested.

Sizes of Soil Particles

Name of Particle	Median diameter (mm)
boulder	256–129
cobble	128–65
gravel	64–2.1
sand	2.0–0.126
silt	0.125–0.008
clay	0.004 or smaller

Conclusion

Let's see what you learned about porosity and permeability.

1. What is porosity? ______________________
2. What is permeability? ______________________
3. Which is most porous: sand, garden soil, or clay? ______________________
4. Which is most permeable: sand, garden soil, or clay? ______________________
5. How can a layer of clay protect a deep aquifer from contamination by gasoline?

____

Now prepare the poster you will use at the town meeting and write a script of exactly what you will say to the townspeople. Make sure your poster has the following information on it: two labeled diagrams to show how the experiments were done; the porosity and permeability calculated for sand, clay, and garden soil; and a diagram showing how a clay layer can protect water lying beneath it.

Copyright © Pearson Education, Inc., or its affiliates. All Rights Reserved.

Cutting Corners Doesn't Always Save

Investigation Overview

- For this investigation, your students will work in groups. Each group will need a model of the floor of a harbor and a wooden skewer with one pointed end and one dull end.
- To make each model harbor, securely attach rocks or other solid objects to the bottom of the inside of a shoe box. Randomly arrange rocks of various sizes so that they form a row down the center of the shoe box. You can attach the rocks with a hot-glue gun, clay, or Plaster of Paris.
- Do not put a lid on the box. Instead, tape graph paper over the opening. Make sure the paper is secure; students will be poking through the paper with the skewers.
- Begin the investigation by assigning groups and having them read the Scenario and Procedure.
- Make sure that students understand the Procedure. Demonstrate the technique if necessary, and then let students begin.
- Students may need help plotting points below the x-axis in Step 4. Direct students to draw the x-axis near the top of the page. Demonstrate how to plot points, if necessary.

SCORING RUBRIC	
SCORE 4	Student's report to the harbormaster follows the correct format and contains all required elements. All findings and the recommendation are logically supported by evidence.
SCORE 3	Student's report to the harbormaster follows the correct format, contains all required elements, and is mostly supported by evidence.
SCORE 2	Two of the three portions of the report are logical and complete.
SCORE 1	The report is largely incomplete, or the opinions and facts presented are illogical and/or incorrect.

Extension Activities

Assignment Have students research and write a report explaining the phenomenon known as the squat effect and how it causes problems in harbors.

Cooperative Learning You can make this investigation more structured by assigning specific roles to the students in each group. Examples of roles include: the oceanographer (supervises the investigation and edits the final report), ship captain (makes the soundings), chart maker (plots the points on a graph and draws the chart), and pilot (observes the sounding probe to make sure it is vertical).

Field Trip If you live near a harbor, arrange a field trip so that your students can observe large ships entering and leaving the harbor. Arrange for a spokesperson from the harbormaster's office to describe to your students the strategies they use to ensure the safety of the ships.

Copyright © Pearson Education, Inc., or its affiliates. All Rights Reserved.

Name ______________________________ Date ______________ Class ______________

Cutting Corners Doesn't Always Save

Purpose To investigate the relationship between sounding interval and mapping accuracy

Materials
- model harbor
- graph paper
- long stick with a pointed end
- pencil
- metric ruler

Scenario

As an oceanographer, you know that there are many important and interesting reasons for mapping the seafloor. For example, mapping the seafloor along ancient trade routes can reveal sunken treasure ships. The most valuable seafloor maps, however, are made near the shore, at the harbors where huge ships dock. An accurate harbor map (or chart) is vital to the safe movement of ships into and out of a harbor.

Making harbor charts involves a process called "sounding." For thousands of years people used sounding to measure the depth of the water and chart the seafloor. Sounding used to involve lowering a weight on the end of a chain until it hit the harbor bottom. Modern soundings are usually made with sonar, a device similar to radar that uses the reflection of sound to measure the distance to an object under water.

Today the harbormaster called you with an interesting question: "If you are going to use the weight-and-chain method to make soundings, how close together do the weight drops need to be?" Soundings are normally taken every meter, but this is very costly and may not be necessary. The harbormaster wants to know how far apart the soundings can be without losing accuracy. You and your partners will try to answer that question with a scientific experiment.

Procedure

1. **Shoe Box Harbor** Your teacher has made a model harbor for you to test. It has objects on the bottom to represent the bumps, dips, and deep channels on a harbor floor. It has a cover made of graph paper to represent the water's surface. Instead of a weight on a chain, you will use a long stick to measure the distance from the water's surface to the harbor floor.
2. **Costly Interval** Taking a sounding every meter will cost the harbor master $10,000. Since he doesn't have that much money to spend, he wants to know if an interval of two meters will produce the same chart. How about a three-meter interval? To test the most costly interval first, make a harbor chart by pushing a long stick through the graph paper every centimeter along a line down the center of the shoe box.
3. **Measuring a Sounding** Make sure the stick is perfectly straight up and down and mark it with a pencil where the surface of the "water" hits it. Remove the stick and measure from the tip to the mark in centimeters. Record the depth in your notebook and number it. Erase the mark, and then repeat this procedure for each of the soundings.

Copyright © Pearson Education, Inc., or its affiliates. All Rights Reserved.

Procedure *(continued)*

4. **Drawing a Chart** Once you have made a sounding for every centimeter across the harbor, it's time to make a chart of the bottom. Make the chart on graph paper so that the *x*-axis represents the water's surface. Treat each of your sounding measurements as negative numbers, since you were measuring the depth *below* the surface. Therefore, you should plot your sounding results *below* the *x*-axis. Once you are finished plotting your soundings, draw lines to connect the dots. The line is a chart of the harbor that represents the most costly way to make a harbor chart.

5. **Is Cheaper Good Enough?** Now repeat Steps 2–4 using intervals of 2 centimeters, and then using intervals of 3 centimeters. Use a separate piece of graph paper for each chart.

Conclusion

Let's see what you learned about mapping the ocean floor. Define each formation below and identify whether you found one in your box. Explain your reasoning.

1. Abyssal plain ______________________________

2. Seamount ______________________________

3. Continental slope ______________________________

4. Channel ______________________________

Assume that the harbor chart you made at 1-cm intervals is accurate and compare it to the other two charts. Does the 2-cm chart look the same? Does it show every hazard? How about the 3-cm chart? Write a report of your findings to the harbormaster. Begin with this opening statement:

"My colleagues and I used a model of your harbor to test the accuracy of soundings made at three different intervals. We used a 1-cm interval to represent the one meter standard interval. Then we tested intervals at 2 cm and 3 cm. We found that … "

Complete the sentence by stating your findings. In the next paragraph, state the evidence that supports your findings. In the third and final paragraph, tell the harbormaster which sounding interval you recommend based on your results. Remember, you want the least expensive interval that will still provide enough information to keep ships safe.

Copyright © Pearson Education, Inc., or its affiliates. All Rights Reserved.

Predicting the Weather Is No Sport

Investigation Overview

- This investigation begins on a Monday and ends the following Monday. You need to provide your students with weather maps from your local newspaper for one full week. Be sure the maps include temperatures and the positions of highs, lows, fronts, and areas of precipitation. If your class does not meet every day, assign the appropriate steps as homework.
- Begin on a Monday by having students read the Scenario and Steps 1 and 2. Answer all questions. Distribute copies of the day's weather map and tell students to begin.
- On Tuesday, distribute copies of the weather map and tell students to complete Step 3, focusing on how the weather has changed since yesterday and where certain features might be tomorrow. Repeat this process for Wednesday (Step 4) and Thursday (Step 5).
- On Friday, provide each student with the daily weather map, and two blank maps of the United States. Have them complete the Conclusion. Remind students to include keys on their weather maps.
- On Saturday and Sunday, record the actual positions of all highs, lows, and fronts on two blank weather maps. Also record the actual high and low temperatures for your town and whether or not there was precipitation. On Monday morning, make copies of the Saturday and Sunday weather maps for your students.
- On Monday, show students the maps of the actual weather from Saturday and Sunday. Also show the actual weather for your town and discuss the accuracy of their predictions.

SCORING RUBRIC	
SCORE 4	Student prepares a weekend weather forecast for your town that includes weather maps showing the positions of highs and lows, fronts, and precipitation. The map has a key for all symbols used. All aspects of the forecast are logical and indicate an excellent understanding of related weather concepts.
SCORE 3	The forecast is adequate but may contain one or two minor errors.
SCORE 2	The forecast contains some errors or is missing one or two required pieces of information.
SCORE 1	The forecast is largely incorrect or incomplete, or the forecast is not logical.

Extension Activities

Cooperative Learning Have students work in teams to write and perform a weather forecast skit for a television news program. Assign each team a different kind of severe weather event (hurricane, tornado, blizzard, flash flood, and tsunami) for them to dramatize. Assign the roles of camera operator, weather forecaster, anchor, and director. The teams should research their assigned weather event and write a script for the anchor and weather forecaster. The producer is responsible for all graphics used and the camera operator for videotaping and editing a three-minute production. Since some of these severe weather events only occur in certain places, students should set their skits in appropriate cities.

Field Trip Arrange a field trip to the closest U.S. Weather Service forecast office (find locations at www.weather.gov).

Copyright © Pearson Education, Inc., or its affiliates. All Rights Reserved.

Name ______________________ Date__________ Class__________

Predicting the Weather Is No Sport

Purpose

To predict weekend weather by following the movement of weather systems across the United States

Materials

- daily weather maps for one week (Monday–Friday)
- tracing paper
- two blank maps of the United States

Scenario

You are the sports reporter for the newspaper in your town. The paper's weather forecaster is going on vacation this Friday, and it's your turn to forecast the weekend weather. This is a real problem because you're not a meteorologist! You can't even forecast the winner of your town's high school football games.

The forecaster tries to calm you: "Don't worry. A few days of weather maps will show you what's coming. Watch the low- and high-pressure systems and fronts as they move across the United States." The forecaster also recommends that you ask yourself the following questions:

- What direction do the fronts move?
- How fast do they move?
- Is colder or warmer weather coming?
- Is rain moving your way?

The forecaster's last piece of advice is "Just pay attention, and forecasting is easy."

Procedure

1. **Five Days of Maps** Each day for the next five days your teacher will give you a copy of the day's weather map from the local newspaper.
2. **Panic on Monday** Don't panic yet. All you can do today is examine the map and make a copy of it. Notice the position of high- and low-pressure systems and fronts, the daily high temperatures, and the type and amount of precipitation. Pay attention to anything you think might be helpful in predicting your weekend weather. Trace the map onto tracing paper.
3. **Tuesday** Trace Tuesday's map and compare it to Monday's map. Notice that the weather moves. Pay close attention to the direction and speed of that movement. Based on movement alone, try to predict tomorrow's high temperature and precipitation for your town.

____

____

Copyright © Pearson Education, Inc., or its affiliates. All Rights Reserved.

Name ______________________ Date __________ Class __________

Procedure *(continued)*

4. **Wednesday** Trace Wednesday's map. Was your prediction right? Is it raining? How hot will it be today? Is the weather still moving the same direction? Is it still moving at the same speed? Take what you learn and use Wednesday's map to predict Thursday's weather.

____

____

5. **Thursday** Trace Thursday's map. Ask yourself the same questions from Step 4 and use Thursday's map to predict Friday's weather.

____

____

Conclusion

Let's see what you learned about the movement of weather across the country.

1. According to the weather maps, does precipitation seem to come with high pressure or low pressure?

____

2. In what direction does weather usually move across the United States? What causes weather to move in this direction?

____

____

____

3. If a front passed through your town during the week, name the type of front, the day it came through, and tell how the weather changed. If a front didn't pass through your town, choose another city and answer the questions.

____

____

____

Friday is the big day. Time has run out, and you have learned everything you could. Your paper's regular weather forecaster left for vacation. It's time for you to write the weather forecast for the weekend edition of the paper. What will the weather be on Saturday and Sunday? Use two blank maps of the United States to show where you think the pressure systems and fronts will be this weekend. Where will it be raining or snowing? Provide a key for any symbols you use.

Prepare a more detailed forecast for the weather in your town for each day. Predict the high and low temperatures. Will it rain or snow where you live? Will it be cloudy or sunny? You can present your forecast in a chart or in complete sentences. Over the weekend, pay attention to the weather to see how you did.

Copyright © Pearson Education, Inc., or its affiliates. All Rights Reserved.

Smearing Causes Seasons

Investigation Overview

- A common misconception is that the seasons are the result of changes in the distance between Earth and the sun. This investigation shows that seasons actually result from Earth's tilt on its axis, which determines whether a constant amount of solar energy spreads over a larger or smaller part of Earth's surface.
- To complete this investigation, you will need an overhead projector, a screen that can be tilted to an angle of approximately 23.5°, a piece of paper with a 2 cm × 2 cm square cut into its center, and three index cards for each student. Make sure that when you tilt the screen, the area of light on the screen is noticeably larger than when the screen is vertical.
- Begin by having your students read the Scenario and Step 1. When everyone has finished reading, answer any questions and proceed.
- Project the 2 cm × 2 cm square onto the screen and ask a volunteer to measure the square and announce the measurements. Have students complete Steps 2 and 3. Provide help as needed.
- Next, complete Step 4 by tilting the screen to an angle of 23.5°. Ask another volunteer to measure the light area and have students complete the remainder of the investigation.

SCORING RUBRIC	
SCORE 4	Student outlines a presentation correctly explaining the cause of the seasons, using language appropriate for young children.
SCORE 3	Student outline is correct but does not target young children, or it is not sufficiently clear.
SCORE 2	Outline contains some incorrect information, indicating that the student does not fully understand the cause of the seasons.
SCORE 1	Outline indicates that the student has a minimal understanding of the cause of the seasons.

Extension Activities

Assignment People living near the equator have similar weather throughout the year. People living closer to the poles have drastically different weather in the summer and winter. Have your students account for these differences using the smearing of energy concept.

Cooperative Learning The relative positions of Earth, the moon, and the sun account for Earth's tides, lunar phases, solar and lunar eclipses, and seasons. Using the Jigsaw strategy, divide your class into four expert groups. Assign each group one of these four phenomena to investigate. They should explore how the relative positions of the three objects account for the phenomenon they are investigating. Reassign students to groups containing one of each type of expert, and have groups create posters explaining each phenomenon.

Field Trip Plan a trip to a local planetarium so that your students can see how the relative positions of Earth, the moon, and the sun explain the tides, lunar phases, and solar and lunar eclipses.

Copyright © Pearson Education, Inc., or its affiliates. All Rights Reserved.

Asteroid Smasher

Investigation Overview

- This investigation is adapted from a classroom activity featured on the NASA web site. The basic instructions for building the launch pad and pencil rockets are available at http://www.grc.nasa.gov/WWW/K-12/TRC/Rockets/pencil_rocket.html. You will need to build this launch pad for the investigation, making the modifications described at the right.
- Before constructing the launch pad, obtain all of the materials listed on the web site, plus one piece of wood (1/4" × 3/4" × 12"), two 3/4" butt hinges, two 1/4" flat washers, one 1" #10 sheet-metal screw, one 1" #12 wood screw, and a protractor.
- Obtain enough of the materials listed on the student page for each team to build a pencil rocket. Print copies of the NASA instructions for each team.
- Divide students into teams and have them read the Scenario and Steps 1–3. Show the class the launch pad and demonstrate how to vary the launch angle and amount of thrust. Answer any questions and have students begin.
- Allow teams to conduct ten experimental launches as they modify their designs. When testing is complete, conduct the final presentation for the President (your principal or another teacher).

Launch Pad Modification

- Build the launch pad according to the instructions on the NASA site, but mount the vertical panel with two hinges in order to make the launch angle adjustable.
- The vertical panel is now adjustable and needs a variable support arm. Use the sheet-metal screw and washers to permanently attach one end of the long piece of wood to one side of the launch platform base. The support arm is permanently attached, but it should swing freely.
- To create an angle-locking hole where the support arm will meet the vertical panel, drill a 5/32" hole 3/4" into the side of the top end of the vertical panel (about 1/2" below the cup hooks).
- Finally, you need to drill holes in the support arm to set the vertical panel to varying angles. Use a protractor to position the vertical panel at launch angles of 30°, 35°, 40°, 45°, and 50°. For each angle, use a 5/16" bit to drill a hole in the support arm where it aligns with the angle-locking hole on the side of the vertical panel.
- Use the 1" #12 wood screw to fasten the support arm at the desired angle.

SCORING RUBRIC	
SCORE 4	Student's report thoroughly and accurately describes the results and uses the results to justify a recommendation to the President.
SCORE 3	Report meets the content criteria for a score of 4 but contains minor errors.
SCORE 2	Report adequately describes results but does not logically justify the recommendation.
SCORE 1	Report is incomplete, or conveys limited understanding of the investigation.

Extension Activities

Assignment Have students diagram all forces acting on their pencil rockets. Label the action force and the reaction force, and explain how this causes the rocket to fly.

Cooperative Learning Have students work in teams to create a poster about rockets. The poster should include the history of rockets, how they work, and diagrams and pictures.

Copyright © Pearson Education, Inc., or its affiliates. All Rights Reserved.

Name _______________________ Date ___________ Class ___________

Asteroid Smasher

Purpose To examine how thrust and launch angle affect a rocket's course

Materials

- wooden pencil (unsharpened)
- pencil cap eraser
- piece of wire or paper clip
- tape (adhesive or masking)
- small pieces of poster board for fins
- coping saw or mat knife
- flat file
- pliers
- rubber bands
- target, 1 foot in diameter

Scenario

Suppose you woke up tomorrow to find this article on the front page of your newspaper:

GIANT ASTEROID HEADED STRAIGHT FOR EARTH!

White House to Build Rocket

WASHINGTON, D.C. — In an early-morning press conference, the President confirmed reports that NASA scientists have discovered a large asteroid headed for Earth. Experts believe that the asteroid, called 2045DD, will collide with our planet in about six months.

The President reassured the panicked nation that plans are underway to build a rocket that will deliver a bomb to the asteroid. The explosion should break the asteroid apart, or at least change its course so that it misses Earth.

A team of engineers was seen entering the Oval Office shortly after the President's announcement. A source close to the President was overheard saying that the Commander in Chief isn't sure that the plan will work, but others speculate that, if designed correctly,

(story continued on page A2)

As aerospace engineers (rocket scientists), you and your partners know that a rocket carrying a bomb could destroy or change the direction of the asteroid. The President of the United States is skeptical. Therefore the White House has asked your team to build an inexpensive model of the rocket to demonstrate its accuracy and reliability. Your final objective is to stop the asteroid before it strikes Earth, but first you must convince the President and Congress to fund the project.

You and your partners will work together to build and test a model rocket. You may find building the model easy, but the hard part is making sure your rocket can hit its target every time. You must test several variables, including the speed of the rocket, angle of launch, and distance to the target. You know that you should only test one variable at a time and keep all other variables constant. Your rocket would only get one chance to destroy an approaching asteroid, so the President is only going to watch one demonstration. You have to hit your target! If you fail, Earth may be doomed!

Copyright © Pearson Education, Inc., or its affiliates. All Rights Reserved.

Name ______________________ Date ____________ Class ____________

Procedure

1. **Building a Rocket** Follow the directions from NASA to build a pencil rocket.
2. **The Best Combination** A rocket's course is influenced by the angle of launch, the amount of thrust (number of rubber bands), and the distance to the target. The distance to the target is set. The other variables are not. Use the launch pad provided by your teacher to test one variable at a time and record all trials in a data table. Your goal is to find the best combination of launch angle and thrust so that your rocket hits a one-foot diameter target at a distance of 30 feet every time it's launched.
3. **Plan Well** Because you are sharing the launch pad with other companies, you will only be allowed ten launches to test the variables.
4. **The Big Day** You will only get one chance to impress the President of the United States. Use the best combination of angle and thrust you found during your tests. Give it your best shot!

Conclusion

Let's see what you have learned about rockets.

1. Rubber bands provided the thrust to get your rocket going. Why did the rocket keep moving after it left the launch pad and the rubber bands were no longer pushing it?

   ____

   ____

2. How did the launch angle affect the distance the rocket traveled?

   ____

   ____

3. What happens when a rocket reaches escape velocity?

   ____

   ____

4. Is the pencil rocket really a rocket? Explain.

   ____

   ____

Whether or not you hit the target on the final test day, the White House officials want your written report. In it, they want the results of your tests. You should address the following questions:

- What different thrust forces (number of rubber bands) did you test?
- What different launch angles did you test?
- What combination worked best, and did it work every time?
- What type of design do you suggest engineers use when they build the rocket?

Copyright © Pearson Education, Inc., or its affiliates. All Rights Reserved.

Do Planets Float?

Investigation Overview

- Although students should work individually to conduct the investigation, encourage them to help each other as needed.
- Begin the investigation by having your students read the Scenario and Steps 1-3.
- Lead students through the example of how to use scientific notation. Answer any questions, and have students proceed with the investigation.
- Note: When students calculate the density of Mercury, they will get an answer of 0.5428×10^1. This may appear to be a density less than one, *but it is not*. Students must write the answer in correct scientific notation form by moving the decimal point one place to the right. The correct answer is 5.428×10^0, or 5.428 g/cm^3.
- Students are likely to be skeptical that a large object like the planet Saturn could actually float. Be prepared to have a large (but low-density) object with which to demonstrate that size and density are not related.

SCORING RUBRIC	
SCORE 4	Student's e-mail correctly lists all densities, identifies which planets will float, and clearly explains how to calculate density to determine which planets will float.
SCORE 3	E-mail contains all content required for a score of 4 but contains minor errors.
SCORE 2	E-mail incorrectly identifies which planets will float, or the explanation of how to determine which planets will float is incorrect or incomplete.
SCORE 1	E-mail is largely incomplete or demonstrates a minimal understanding of density and scientific notation.

Extension Activities

Cooperative Learning Have students break into groups, and have each student choose the name of a planet or moon from a hat. Assign groups to create a travel brochure that involves a two-week vacation to three or four exotic locations. Each student is responsible for creating one panel of the brochure about the planet or moon that the student chose. You can also assign specific tasks for each student: editors/writers, fact checker, and artist.

Field Trip Plan a trip to a local planetarium so that students can observe the movement of planets against the background of stars.

Copyright © Pearson Education, Inc., or its affiliates. All Rights Reserved.

Name ________________________ Date ____________ Class ____________

Do Planets Float?

Purpose To investigate the densities of the planets

Materials
- pen or pencil
- calculator

Scenario

As an employee in NASA's public relations office, one of your jobs is to answer the e-mails sent to NASA's address with general questions. One of today's e-mails came from a middle school science teacher whose classes are studying the planets in our solar system. A student asked if any of the planets would float, and the teacher wants to know what to tell the student.

That seemed like a silly question at first. Planets are enormous! Then you realized that if a planet has a density of less than 1.0 g/cm^3 (the density of water), it would actually float. Therefore, you can predict if any planets will float by calculating their densities. You replied to the teacher saying that you would send an e-mail with the information tomorrow.

Procedure

1. **A Problem with the Data** You called the National Space Science Data Center to get the information you need. The center gave you the masses of the planets in scientific notation, but the volumes are in standard notation. This is a problem! Before you can calculate the density of each planet, you need to put the volumes into scientific notation, too.
2. **The Conversion** Scientific notation is a way to write really big and really small numbers in a shorter form that you can use to make simpler calculations. Use the following steps to convert the volume of each planet into scientific notation. Record your results in the table on the next page.

- Move the decimal point to the left until there is only one digit before the decimal.
- Count the number of places you moved the decimal point. That number is the exponent of 10.
- Drop all unnecessary zeros and state the answer as a multiplication of the new number times 10 raised to the power you counted.

Example: The volume of Earth is 1,083,210,000,000,000,000,000,000,000 cm^3.
Number: 1.08321
Exponent: 10^{27}

The answer is 1.08321×10^{27}.

Copyright © Pearson Education, Inc., or its affiliates. All Rights Reserved.

Name ______________________ Date ____________ Class ____________

Planetary Mass and Volume Data				
Planet	**Mass (g)**	**Volume (cm^3)**	**Volume (cm^3)**	**Density (g/cm^3)**
Earth	5.9736×10^{27}	1,083,210,000,000,000,000,000,000,000		
Mercury	3.302×10^{26}	60,830,000,000,000,000,000,000,000		
Venus	4.8685×10^{27}	928,430,000,000,000,000,000,000,000		
Mars	6.4185×10^{26}	163,180,000,000,000,000,000,000,000		
Jupiter	1.8986×10^{30}	1,431,280,000,000,000,000,000,000,000,000		
Saturn	5.6846×10^{29}	827,130,000,000,000,000,000,000,000,000		
Uranus	8.6832×10^{28}	68,330,000,000,000,000,000,000,000,000		
Neptune	1.0243×10^{29}	62,540,000,000,000,000,000,000,000,000		
Data provided by the National Space Science Data Center, NASA				

3. Calculating the Density To calculate the density of each planet, divide its mass by its volume. First, divide the numbers themselves. To divide the exponents, subtract them.

Calculate the density of each planet and record your results in the table.

The density of Earth is $\dfrac{5.9736 \times 10^{27}\ g}{1.08321 \times 10^{27}\ cm^3}$, or $5.5147 \times 10^0\ g/cm^3$

NOTE: $10^0 = 1$. The simplest answer for the density of Earth is $5.5147 g/cm^3$.

Conclusion

Let's see what you learned about the densities of the planets.

1. Which planets have a density greater than $1.0\ g/cm^3$?

____

2. Which planets have a density less than $1.0\ g/cm^3$?

____

3. Which, if any, of the planets will float in water?

____

4. What is the relationship between volume and density? Explain.

____

On a separate sheet of paper, write the e-mail you would send to the teacher. Include the densities of all of the planets. Then identify which planets will float in water and explain your answer.

Copyright © Pearson Education, Inc., or its affiliates. All Rights Reserved.

Name ____________________ Date ____________ Class ____________

Procedure

1. **Background** Use the information in your textbook to answer the questions in the Scenario. Record the answers in your notebook.

2. **Deeper Digging (Optional)** If you have access to a computer, you may wish to investigate the life cycle of the sun for more specific information. Several reliable videos about the life cycle of the sun exist on the Internet.

Conclusion

Let's see what you learned about the life cycle of a star like the sun.

1. What kind of star is the sun?

____

2. What are the different phases in the life of stars similar to our sun?

____

____

____

3. How old is the sun?

____

4. How much longer will the sun burn in the sky before it becomes a red giant?

____

Now, prepare an e-mail to send to your publisher in which you state the science facts you will use, as well as what's going to happen to your heroes as the story unfolds. In other words, will there be a happy ending or not? If you are planning a happy ending, how will your heroes be able to survive? Before you send the e-mail, make sure your facts are accurate.

Copyright © Pearson Education, Inc., or its affiliates. All Rights Reserved.

Ice Cream, You Scream

Investigation Overview

- In this investigation, students will learn the effects of solutes on freezing points. Students will make ice cream without a freezer and will learn that adding ice is not enough to freeze the ice cream. It is not until they add salt to the ice (thereby lowering the freezing point of the ice) that the ice cream freezes.
- Prior to the investigation, gather and measure the ingredients for each group. For the ice cream mix, each group will need 1/2 cup of milk, 1 tablespoon of sugar, 1/4 teaspoon of vanilla extract, and 2 one-quart resealable bags. For the ice mixture, each group will need 1/2 cup of rock salt, 4 cups of ice (crushed is best), and a 1-gallon resealable bag.
- As the ice cream forms, the outer bag will get extremely cold. Have students bring winter gloves to class or provide hand towels.
- Begin the investigation by having students read the Scenario and Procedure.

SCORING RUBRIC	
SCORE 4	Student correctly explains how salt causes ice cream to freeze and uses wording appropriate for a third-grader.
SCORE 3	Student explains the role of salt but the explanation contains minor errors or is not at a third-grade level.
SCORE 2	Student's explanation contains some content errors.
SCORE 1	Student's explanation indicates only minimal understanding of the role of salt in making ice cream.

Extension Activities

Assignment Have students research and write a description of why people put ice on roads during snow and ice storms.

Cooperative Learning Have students work together in groups to create an advertising poster for an ice cream company from the time of George Washington. The poster should have:

- a clever name for the company,
- a list of at least 10 flavors,
- pictures of ice cream cones and sundaes, and
- a description or illustration of how the ice cream is made, with a focus on the role of salt.

Guest Speaker If you live in an area that experiences winter temperatures below freezing, arrange for someone from your local department of public works to come to your class and explain what products they use to prevent and treat icy roads. If they use salt, have the speaker explain how the salt helps in icy conditions. If they do not use salt, have the speaker explain why not and what they use instead.

Copyright © Pearson Education, Inc., or its affiliates. All Rights Reserved.

Name ______________________ Date __________ Class __________

Ice Cream, You Scream

Purpose To investigate the effect of solutes on freezing points

Materials

- ½ cup whole milk
- ½ teaspoon vanilla
- 1 tablespoon sugar
- 4 cups ice
- ½ cup rock salt
- 2 one-quart resealable plastic bags
- one-gallon resealable freezer bag
- hand towel or winter gloves
- thermometer
- spoons for tasting

Scenario

According to legend, ice cream as we know it was invented in the 1600's by a chef of King Charles I of England. The king loved the treat so much that he ordered its recipe kept secret. However, once Charles I was beheaded, the chef was free to share his recipe, and soon wealthy people throughout Europe enjoyed what they called "crème ice." By the 18th century, ice cream was in America. Presidents George Washington, Thomas Jefferson, and James Madison served ice cream to their guests.

At the time, making ice cream was difficult. It took two large bowls, lots of ice and salt, and 40 minutes of shaking one bowl while stirring the other. Eventually, a variety of inventions such as the hand-cranked ice cream maker and electric freezers made producing and selling large amounts of ice cream easier.

Did you notice the recipe called for "lots of ice and salt" to make ice cream? Have you ever tasted salty ice cream? Probably not! Why, then, do you need salt to make ice cream?

Procedure

1. **Making the Mix** To make your ice cream mixture, combine the milk, vanilla, and sugar in a one-quart resealable plastic bag. Squeeze out most of the air and seal the bag tightly. (Make sure the bag is sealed! If it opens during mixing, the ice cream will be ruined.)
2. **Double Bag for Safety** Place the first bag inside another one-quart bag. Again, squeeze out as much air as possible and seal this bag, too. (The second bag lowers the risk of ruining your ice cream.)
3. **Building a Freezer** To make a freezer, place the double-sealed bag of ice cream mix into a one-gallon resealable bag. Fill the outer bag with ice. Squeeze out the air and seal it tightly.
4. **Shake and Massage** Wrap the bag in the towel or wear gloves as you shake and massage the bag for three minutes.

Making Ice Cream with Salt

In order for ice to melt, it must absorb energy (heat) from its surroundings. When you make ice cream, the ice melting in the outer bag absorbs heat from the ice cream mixture in the inner bag, leaving it cold. However, the ice does not absorb enough energy to cause the ice cream to freeze. By adding salt to the ice, you lower the ice's freezing point. Therefore, it takes more energy to melt the ice. Ice with salt absorbs enough energy from the ice cream to cause the ice cream mixture to freeze.

Copyright © Pearson Education, Inc., or its affiliates. All Rights Reserved.

Name ______________________ Date __________ Class __________

Procedure *(continued)*

5. **Is It Ice Cream Yet?** Open the outer bag and examine the inner bags (don't open them).

   Has the ice cream mix started to freeze? ______________________

6. **How Cold Is It Anyway?** Before you close the outer bag, take the temperature of the ice water that has formed and record it here: ______________________

7. **Add Salt and Try Again** Add salt to the ice, squeeze out the air, and shake and massage the bag again. You can stop when the ice cream mix has frozen.

8. **How Cold Is It Now?** Once the ice cream has frozen, open the outer bag and record the temperature of the salt/ice mixture. ______________________

9. **It's Time to Eat** Now carefully remove the inner bags and taste your homemade ice cream!

Conclusion

Let's see what you learned about how salt affects freezing point.

1. What happens to the freezing point of water when you add salt to it? ______________________

____

____

2. For ice to melt, it must absorb energy from its surroundings. Where do you think the energy needed to melt the ice came from? What effect did the loss of energy have on the ice cream mixture? ______________________

____

____

3. In a saltwater solution, what is the solvent and what is the solute?

____

____

What a coincidence! When you got home today, your little sister said her teacher told the class that President Thomas Jefferson served ice cream in the White House. "How could that be?" she asked. "They didn't have refrigerators back then, did they?" When you replied, "They used salt," she looked at you as if you were crazy.

You know how ice cream was made without freezers because you did it in class, but you need a good way to explain what you learned to your sister. Write down how you will explain to your sister how ice and salt can freeze ice cream. Make sure you explain it in a way that a third-grader could understand. You may find it helpful to use pictures with your written explanation.

Copyright © Pearson Education, Inc., or its affiliates. All Rights Reserved.

Bonding Super Heroes

Investigation Overview

- The day before you conduct this investigation, tell your students that their homework is to bring colored pencils and/or colored markers to your next class. You may also ask them to bring a comic book that features a superhero, if they have one.
- Prepare a set of index cards on which you write either W (for writing) or D (for drawing). Make enough cards for each student in your class to have one card. The cards should be split evenly between W and D.
- Begin the investigation by having students decide whether they are better at writing or drawing, and give each student an appropriate index card. Have each W student find a D student to work with.
- Now have the writer/illustrator teams read the Scenario and Step 1. Discuss the Scenario and ask about students' experiences with superheroes and superheroines. Answer all questions, and then tell students to complete Step 1.
- After a few minutes, call on each team and ask them to contribute one idea to list on a master chart. Keep calling on new teams until all ideas have been listed.
- Now have students read Steps 2-4. Answer any questions, and then let everyone begin. You will be needed throughout this investigation to give advice and answer questions. If some students don't know where to begin, suggest that they observe others for a while.

SCORING RUBRIC	
SCORE 4	Student pair produces two cartoons that are neatly drawn on white paper. The characters are large and colorful. Words and actions correctly demonstrate the difference between the two kinds of bonds. Drawings and words are neat and professionally presented.
SCORE 3	The student pair meets the content requirements for a score of 4, but the drawings and words are not neat and presented well.
SCORE 2	The student pair meets all the requirements for a score of 3, but there are a few errors.
SCORE 1	The student pair meets all requirements for a score of 3, but the work is messy and/or there are a number of significant errors.

Extension Activities

Assignment Give students a list of chemical compounds, giving either the correct name or formula. Have students classify each compound as either ionic or covalent, using these general rules:

- Ionic compounds form when a metal bonds with a nonmetal.
- Covalent compounds form when two nonmetals join.

Cooperative Learning Have two pairs join together to form a team consisting of two writers and two illustrators. Have this four-member team produce a newspaper comic strip featuring both sets of characters. This will require students to develop a story line that carries through several frames.

Copyright © Pearson Education, Inc., or its affiliates. All Rights Reserved.

Name ____________________ Date ____________ Class ____________

Bonding Super Heroes

Purpose To create cartoon characters to illustrate ionic and covalent bonds

Materials
- index card
- unlined paper
- colored pencils or colored markers

Scenario

LARGER-THAN-LIFE SUPERHEROES

A comic-book writer named Lee Falk created a cartoon character he called The Phantom in 1936. The Phantom wasn't the first cartoon crime fighter, and he didn't have any superpowers, but he was the first hero to wear a skintight costume and a mask to keep readers from seeing his face. His skintight costume and mask became features common to the comic book superheroes that followed him.

Superman is the first comic-book character whose powers went far beyond those of a normal human being. Bullets bounce off Superman's chest. He can run faster than a train and jump over tall buildings. American writer Jerry Siegel and Canadian artist Joe Shuster invented Superman. Superman appeared for the first time on June 30, 1938. He was shown in a skintight red, white, and blue costume as he lifted a car over his head.

In 1941, American psychologist and inventor William Moulton Marston created the first superheroine. He called her Wonder Woman.

The Phantom, Superman, and Wonder Woman are larger-than-life characters. Perhaps now it's time for a smaller-than-life superhero.

Atoms join to make molecules by forming either ionic bonds or covalent bonds. It's easy to memorize this fact and give the right answer when asked for it. But getting it right on a test doesn't mean you really understand the difference. Your teacher has a great idea to help you understand the difference. Why not create cartoon characters that can make atoms join together? One of the tiny (atom-sized) superheroes can only make ionic bonds. The other can only make covalent bonds.

You and your partner are perfect for this assignment! One of you is an illustrator and the other one is a writer.

Procedure

1. **Listing Characteristics** Before you can draw the two new microheroes, you need to know their characteristics. Since one of them makes ionic bonds, and the other makes covalent bonds, you should begin by thinking about the differences between those two kinds of bonds. Work with your partner to brainstorm the characteristics and list them here. Continue on a separate sheet of paper if you need more space.

Properties of Ionic Bonds	Properties of Covalent Bonds

Copyright © Pearson Education, Inc., or its affiliates. All Rights Reserved.

Name ______________________ Date ______________ Class ______________

The Pipeline Is Burning

Purpose To balance combustion equations

Materials • pencil or pen • paper

Scenario

MASSIVE FIREBALL IN DOWNTOWN MEDUSA

U.S. Department of Energy Investigating Cause

MEDUSA, OH – Shortly before noon on Friday, a massive fireball caused widespread panic in downtown Medusa. The incident occurred when road workers accidentally struck an underground pipe. A small spark ignited the contents of the pipe, creating flames that shot nearly 70 feet into the air.

Although no one was injured, the entire neighborhood lost power, and the hospital was forced to send patients to other nearby hospitals. A large portion of East Main Street was temporarily closed, creating traffic problems for the rest of the day. Federal inspectors from the U.S. Department of Energy are now at the scene to investigate the exact cause of the fire, and to determine if construction workers could have been

(Story continued on page A8)

It's not unusual to have all sorts of pipes, wires, and fiber-optic cables running under our feet without our even knowing it. The wires and cables carry electricity, telephone conversations, and Internet service. The pipes carry crude oil, natural gas, and water (both clean and dirty). Leaks in gas pipes create potential hazards, because even the smallest spark can ignite the gas and cause an explosion like the one in Medusa.

Federal inspectors from the U.S. Department of Energy are investigating the cause of the Medusa fire, and they need your help to complete their report. Part of their report includes a description of the possible chemical reactions that could have caused the explosion. The inspectors have come to you, a chemist, because they need balanced equations showing the combustion of natural gas and some other fuels that could have been in the pipe that the workers struck.

Procedure

1. **What Was Burning?** It turns out that the substance we call natural gas is mainly methane—a simple compound that has a single carbon atom surrounded by four hydrogen atoms. The formula for methane is CH_4. Methane is a highly flammable and odorless gas. The reaction of methane with oxygen leaves behind no ash and very little air pollution. Methane reacts with oxygen to produce heat, light, carbon dioxide, and water vapor. The chemical equation for this reaction is:

$$CH_4 + O_2 \rightarrow CO_2 + H_2O$$

Copyright © Pearson Education, Inc., or its affiliates. All Rights Reserved.

Name ______________________ Date __________ Class __________

Procedure (continued)

2. A Balancing Act Use the method described in your textbook to balance this equation. Write the balanced equation here.

____

3. One Equation Is Not Enough The inspectors are not certain that the pipe contained methane, so they want to compare the combustion of methane with the combustion of several other fuels. Use the same strategy to balance the following equations:

Gas	Reaction	Balanced Equation
Methanol	$CH_3OH + O_2 \rightarrow CO_2 + H_2O$	
Gasoline	$C_8H_{18} + O_2 \rightarrow CO_2 + H_2O$	
Hydrogen	$H_2 + O_2 \rightarrow H_2O$	

Conclusion

Let's see what you learned about balancing chemical equations.

1. One molecule of methanol (CH_3OH) has how many hydrogen atoms?

____

2. For each molecule of propane (C_3H_8) that burns, three molecules of carbon dioxide are produced ($3CO_2$). How many total oxygen atoms are in those molecules?

____

3. Is the reaction between methane and oxygen endothermic or exothermic? Explain why we burn fossil fuels, such as natural gas.

____

____

4. What principle requires that a chemical equation be balanced?

____

Write a paragraph for the investigators to add to their report. In the paragraph, write the balanced equations for the reaction of methane and oxygen, as well as the reactions for the three gases in your table above. Predict whether you think each reaction is exothermic or endothermic, and explain your reasoning. Classify each reaction as synthesis, decomposition, or replacement.

Copyright © Pearson Education, Inc., or its affiliates. All Rights Reserved.

The Element Museum

Investigation Overview

- Prior to the investigation, obtain plain white paper (heavy stock is best) and markers for each student.
- There are 35 well-known elements listed on the student page. On the day of the investigation, draw each student's name from a hat. When you call a student's name, allow him or her to choose an element. Continue the process until each student has a unique element to study.
- Have students read the Scenario. Review the list of requirements for the posters and, as a class, decide on the layout everyone will use.
- Remind students that the atomic number is the same as the number of protons and electrons, and the number of neutrons is calculated by subtracting the atomic number from the atomic mass.
- Step 4 requires students to think of extra details to add to their posters. This requires additional information and may be omitted or added as a homework assignment. You may wish to have the class brainstorm a list of possible details to include and decide which ones are acceptable.

SCORING RUBRIC	
SCORE 4	Student's poster features all required information and includes multiple attention-grabbing features.
SCORE 3	The poster includes all required information and one extra feature. There may be minor errors.
SCORE 2	The poster includes all required information, but there are some errors or there are no extra features.
SCORE 1	The poster is largely incorrect or incomplete and shows minimal understanding of the periodic table.

Extension Activities

Assignment Have each student use the Internet to research the history of his or her element and write a brief report that includes the circumstances of its discovery and the history of its uses.

Cooperative Learning Group students in teams to brainstorm ideas on how best to organize the element posters within the museum's element room. Have each team contribute an idea to the class discussion. Let the class vote on an idea and work together to display the posters in your classroom.

Copyright © Pearson Education, Inc., or its affiliates. All Rights Reserved.

Name ______________________ Date ____________ Class ____________

The Element Museum

Purpose To use the periodic table to investigate an element

Materials
- blank white paper
- markers of assorted colors

Scenario

Some people have all the luck! Your town is building a science museum with an Element Room. You are excited because the room will feature the most popular chemical elements. What is most exciting is that you and the other chemists at your company have been asked to help.

You will each pick an element from "The World's Best-Known Elements" list below and create a poster about the element to display in the museum. The museum's directors want certain parts of every poster to be the same, but they want you to show some creativity, too. They also want every poster to have the same layout because the posters will all be displayed in the same exhibit. Finally, the posters have to grab the attention of the museum visitors.

Procedure

1. **Selecting an Element** When it's your turn, your teacher will ask you to select an element from the list that has not already been chosen. You can choose an element you already know something about, or you can choose an element you're interested in learning about.

2. **The Chemical Symbol** Of course, the directors want the name of the element on the poster, but they also want its symbol. Every element has a symbol called the chemical symbol. Sometimes the symbol is a single capital letter. Sometimes it is a capital letter followed by a lowercase letter.

Element	Symbol
Tungsten	W
Cadmium	Cd

The museum wants the chemical symbol of your element to be the largest thing on the poster.

The World's Best-Known Elements

hydrogen	phosphorus
helium	sulfur
lithium	chlorine
boron	silver
carbon	tin
nitrogen	iodine
oxygen	platinum
fluorine	gold
nickel	argon
copper	potassium
zinc	calcium
bromine	titanium
krypton	chromium
neon	iron
sodium	mercury
magnesium	lead
aluminum	uranium
silicon	

Copyright © Pearson Education, Inc., or its affiliates. All Rights Reserved.

Name ______________________ Date ____________ Class ____________

Procedure (continued)

3. **Other Information** In addition to the symbol, the museum wants other information about each element that can be found on a periodic table of the elements:

- Atomic number
- Atomic mass
- The number of protons, electrons, and neutrons in an atom of the element (*Hint*: Use the atomic number and atomic mass.)
- Whether the element is a metal, nonmetal, or metalloid
  - If the element is a metal, include the kind of metal (alkali, alkaline earth, or transition)
  - If the element is a nonmetal, include the family name

4. **Being Creative** Finally, the museum directors want something that makes each element stand out when visitors tour the exhibit. Before you add these items, discuss what features might appeal to museum visitors and where you might be able to find this information.

Conclusion

Let's see what you learned about using the periodic table. Answer the following questions for the element germanium.

1. Complete the following chart about one atom of germanium.

Chemical symbol	Atomic number	Atomic mass	Number of protons	Number of neutrons	Number of electrons

2. What kind of element is germanium? ______________________

3. What elements have the same characteristics as germanium? Where are these elements located on the periodic table?

____

____

Prepare your poster for the museum. Follow the format your class has established. The poster must include the name of your element and its chemical symbol. The poster also must include all the information listed in Step 3. Finally, add something of interest to attract attention to the poster.

Copyright © Pearson Education, Inc., or its affiliates. All Rights Reserved.

What a Mass

Investigation Overview

- In this investigation, students will determine the densities of several objects. If you have not discussed density in class, you may wish to avoid introducing the term until the end of the investigation, when students have a clear understanding of the relationship between mass and volume.
- Prior to the investigation, obtain supplies for each group of students. Ideally, students should work in pairs. Each pair will need a balance and graduated cylinder as well as samples of steel, copper, brass, and aluminum. Samples should be small enough to fit in the graduated cylinders but large enough to obtain accurate measurements of mass and volume.
- Begin the investigation by having students read the Scenario and Step 1.
- Briefly review the concepts of mass and volume and ways to measure them. Make sure students understand how to use water displacement to measure the volume of an irregular object.
- Students' calculated densities may vary from the answers shown in the rubric below. Make sure you calculate your own figures using the materials from this investigation. Also, decide on a margin of error for students' calculations (5% is a reasonable margin of error).

SCORING RUBRIC	
SCORE 4	Student correctly lists the constants in order of increasing size, and with the correct calculated densities. Answers: aluminum (2.7 g/cm^3), steel (7.9 g/cm^3), brass (8.6 g/cm^3), copper (8.9 g/cm^3)
SCORE 3	Student lists the correct order of the constants, but one calculated density falls outside the allowed margin of error.
SCORE 2	One constant is listed incorrectly or some calculations are incorrect.
SCORE 1	The list and calculations contain multiple errors and demonstrate a minimal understanding of the concept of density.

Extension Activities

Assignment Have students identify unknown samples of aluminum, brass, copper, and steel by calculating their densities. You may want to paint the samples so that students cannot identify the objects by sight.

Cooperative Learning Have students work together in teams to develop density tables for a variety of common solids. Include different woods and plastics, rubber, paper, and additional metals. Assign each student one of the following roles: Volume Measurer, Mass Measurer, Calculator, and Recorder.

Guest Speaker Invite a forensic scientist to speak to your class about his or her work, the education required to enter the field, and the kinds of lab tests forensic scientists routinely perform. If density is one of his or her routine tests, have the scientist explain the techniques he or she uses.

Copyright © Pearson Education, Inc., or its affiliates. All Rights Reserved.

Name ______________________ Date ____________ Class ____________

What a Mass

Purpose To determine the relationship between mass and volume for different metals

Materials

- balance
- 100-mL graduated cylinder
- water
- metal samples (copper, aluminum, brass, steel)

Scenario

Last night there was a shooting at the corner of Elm and Main. Evidence from the scene includes metal fragments. It's up to you to find out what they are. You are a technician in a forensics lab.

Every lab technician knows that for every substance there is a relationship between its mass and its volume. In fact, this relationship is constant for each substance. No matter how much or how little of the substance you have, the relationship stays the same—it's a property of that substance. Forensic scientists often use this constant to help them identify unknown substances found at crime scenes. Wait, where is your list of these mass/volume constants?

You've searched the lab, but no one can find it. Your lab handbook has the constants for the relationships for metals, woods, common liquids, and many other substances. It has all the tables and charts anyone in your job could ever need.

Time is running out! You have no choice. You must develop your own table of constants. This will require very precise measurements of the mass and volume of all the metals in your lab.

Procedure

1. **What do we need?** For this investigation, you will need three pieces of information: the mass of each metal, the volume of each metal, and the formula for calculating the constant for a substance. You already know the formula: mass divided by volume.

$$\text{constant} = \frac{\text{mass}}{\text{volume}}$$

2. **Measuring the Mass** Use a balance to carefully measure the mass of each of the different metal samples. Record your measurements in the table provided.

Metal	Mass (g)	Volume (cm^3)	Constant (g/cm^3)
Aluminum			
Brass			
Copper			
Steel			

Copyright © Pearson Education, Inc., or its affiliates. All Rights Reserved.

Name ______________________ Date ____________ Class ____________

Procedure *(continued)*

3. **Measuring the Volume** Use a graduated cylinder and water to measure the volume of each of the different metal samples. Record your results in the table.

4. **Calculating the Constant** Finally, divide the mass of each metal by its volume, and record your results in the table.

Conclusion

Let's see what you learned about the relationship between mass and volume.

1. If the mass/volume constant for a substance is 2.0 g/cm^3, what will be the mass of 4 cm^3 of the substance?

   ____

2. The mass/volume constant for water is 1.0 g/cm^3. If a substance floats in water, is its constant less than 1 or greater than 1? Explain. (*Hint:* Do the metals above float?)

   ____

   ____

   ____

3. A scrap of metal has a mass/volume constant close to 8 g/cm^3. Based on your chart, what is the metal? Explain your answer.

   ____

   ____

   ____

4. What term describes the constant ratio between mass and volume?

   ____

Make a new chart for your lab that shows the constants for the metals you tested. List the constants in order from the metal with the smallest mass/volume constant to the one with the largest constant.

Copyright © Pearson Education, Inc., or its affiliates. All Rights Reserved.

My Glass Is Leaking!

Investigation Overview

- Prior to the investigation, obtain enough materials for students to work in small groups. Examples of suitable glass containers include beakers, canning jars, or tumblers. In addition to the materials listed on the student page, you will need to set out a glass of iced tea for students to examine.
- Have students read the Scenario. When they have finished reading, draw their attention to the glass of iced tea. Ask the class where they think the water on the outside of the glass is coming from. Make a list of students' ideas on the board.
- If your students use the words "evaporation" and "condensation," be ready to provide examples (clothes drying, rain puddles shrinking, breath condensing on windows, breath looking like clouds of smoke on a cold day). Discuss the role of energy in each of these processes. For example, if you heat water, its molecules move faster and it evaporates more quickly. As the water cools, its molecules slow down and return to a liquid state.
- Have students complete the Procedure. After they have finished, discuss what they observed. Tell your students that the temperature at which droplets first appear on the glass is called the dew point. Discuss where the water came from and explain that this process is condensation.

SCORING RUBRIC	
SCORE 4	Student's script correctly explains how water appears on the glass. The answer is complete, and the words used are appropriate for a third-grader.
SCORE 3	Script explains the appearance of water on the glass but is not written for a third-grade audience, or contains minor errors.
SCORE 2	Script explains the appearance of water on the glass but with a significant error.
SCORE 1	Script conveys a minimal understanding of condensation.

Extension Activities

Assignment Have students keep a diary in which they list examples they actually see of water condensing on a cold surface. If students have trouble finding examples, ask how they think humidity may relate to their problem.

Cooperative Learning Have students work in teams to investigate the relative cooling effects as water, vegetable oil, and rubbing alcohol evaporate from their skin. Ask students to determine which liquid evaporates most quickly, and which feels coldest as it evaporates. Challenge students to explain why evaporation makes the skin feel cold.

Guest Speaker Heat is absorbed during evaporation and released during condensation. Air conditioning system and heat pump designs are based on this principle. Arrange for an HVAC technician to speak to your class about how evaporation and condensation relate to the functioning of air conditioning systems and heat pumps.

Copyright © Pearson Education, Inc., or its affiliates. All Rights Reserved.

Name ______________________ Date ____________ Class ____________

My Glass is Leaking!

Purpose To investigate evaporation and condensation of water

Materials

- glass container
- magnifying glass
- thermometer
- water
- ice
- notebook

Scenario

On your local radio station you are known as "The Science Answer Person." Your show has a simple format: the audience e-mails questions to you, and you answer them on the air. That sounds easy, doesn't it?

Most of the questions are easy to answer, but sometimes it's hard to answer the questions in words that young children will understand. Today the mother of a third-grader sent you the following question:

> Hi, Science Answer Person,
>
> My daughter saw water droplets on the outside of a glass of iced tea the other day. She said, "Look, Mom, the glass is leaking!"
>
> I know our glasses do not leak. How do I explain to my daughter what is really happening? What should I say?
>
> Signed, Mrs. Confused

Of course, Mrs. Confused is right—the glass is not leaking. To help her with her question, you need to find the right words to explain to a third-grader what really is happening.

Procedure

1. **An Experiment May Help** Conducting an experiment will help you think of a good way to explain what's happening to the iced-tea glass. First, measure the temperature inside of an empty glass (any glass container should work). Use a magnifying glass to see if there is any water on the outside of the glass. Record all measurements and observations in the table provided.

2. **Adding Cold Water** Add cold water until the glass is half full and measure the temperature inside of the glass (above the water). Is the outside of the glass wet? Record your observations.

3. **One Cube at a Time** Next, add ice cubes to the water, one cube at a time. After you add each cube, measure the temperature and note whether there is water on the outside of the glass. When the water first appears, it will only look like a cloudy coating. Once water appears on the glass, stop adding ice. Record all of your observations.

Copyright © Pearson Education, Inc., or its affiliates. All Rights Reserved.

Procedure *(continued)*

4. **Note the Temperature** Record the exact temperature at which water droplets begin to appear on the jar.

Trial	Number of Ice Cubes	Temperature (°C)	Condensation? (yes/no)
empty glass	0		
1	0		
2	1		
3	2		

Conclusion

Let's see what you learned about evaporation and condensation.

1. During what process does liquid water turn into water vapor?

____

2. During what process does water vapor turn into liquid water?

____

3. During what process is heat absorbed from the surrounding environment?

____

4. What do you call the temperature at which water begins to form on a cold surface?

____

Now write the script for tomorrow's show. In the script, you must answer the question that Mrs. Confused's third-grade daughter asked. Explain why water appears on the outside of the iced-tea glass without leaking through the glass itself. Remember, your answer is for a third-grader, so choose your words carefully. If you use scientific words, remember to define them for your audience.

Copyright © Pearson Education, Inc., or its affiliates. All Rights Reserved.

My House Is Wired!

Investigation Overview

- Students should work in small groups for this investigation about electric circuits. Each group will require a piece of heavy cardboard (no more than 25 cm × 25 cm) and a kit containing three 1.5-V (D) batteries with holders, three flashlight bulbs (2.47 volts, 0.3 amps) with sockets, wire leads with alligator clips, and masking tape to connect the holders and sockets to the cardboard.
- Do not tell students how to connect the various components, but caution them that if any of the batteries or wires becomes hot to the touch, they should disconnect the circuit immediately.
- Many students will immediately try connecting the bulbs in series. After the investigation, you may want to discuss with students how strings of holiday lights used to be wired in series. Every time one bulb burned out, the entire string would go out, and there was no way to know which bulb needed replacing.
- To avoid repeating ideas, students should draw each arrangement that they try.
- As students work on the investigation, their findings will confirm that electric circuits in homes and offices are parallel circuits. Only in a parallel circuit can one bulb be removed without causing other bulbs to go out.
- Remind students not to take apart their setup until after they have completed the conclusion. Students may need to test what happens to the brightness of the bulbs when connected in series versus parallel.

SCORING RUBRIC	
SCORE 4	Student writes a letter describing what they liked and did not like about the kit, and creates a new, clearer set of instructions that explains the difference between series and parallel circuits and features a diagram of the correct circuit.
SCORE 3	Student letter and instructions include all required information but contain minor errors.
SCORE 2	Letter or instructions contain a significant error or omission, or is extremely similar to the original instructions.
SCORE 1	Letter and instructions are incomplete or convey only a minimal understanding of the investigation.

Extension Activities

Assignment Have each student investigate the electrical outlets in his or her home and then make a list of the rooms and the number of outlets in each. If he or she identifies outlets that are overloaded with high-wattage appliances, he or she should work with an adult to move some of the appliances to other outlets. (Remind students that as more and more lamps and appliances are plugged into a parallel circuit, the total resistance of the circuit becomes less and less.)

Field Trip Arrange a field trip to your local power company. Ask a company representative to discuss the variety of jobs performed in a typical power plant.

Copyright © Pearson Education, Inc., or its affiliates. All Rights Reserved.

Name ______________________ Date ____________ Class ____________

My House Is Wired!

Purpose To explore two types of electrical circuits

Materials

- three 1.5-V (D) batteries with holders
- three flashlight bulbs (2.47 volts, 0.3 amps) with sockets
- wire leads with alligator clips
- masking tape
- heavy cardboard

Scenario

Because of the recent focus on energy conservation, many people want to learn more about electricity. A toy company called That's My Toy (TMT) has made an electricity kit for use in elementary schools. TMT wants experts from your power company to check that the kits work. You and your partners at the power company will test the kits by following the directions written by TMT, and then provide feedback about how to improve the kits and simplify the directions to help fourth-graders understand them.

Procedure

1. **I Can't Make This Work** Obtain a kit from your teacher. Read and follow the instructions provided by TMT. Do your best to make everything work, but remember that your job is to rewrite the instructions so that fourth-graders will understand them and be successful.

INSTRUCTIONS FOR WIRING A HOME

On the cardboard base, build a circuit that works just like the circuit in your house or apartment. You must obey the following guidelines:

(a) make two flashlight bulbs light;
(b) connect the wires so that when you remove one bulb the other bulb stays lit; and
(c) after you succeed with goals (a) and (b), add a third bulb to the circuit.

The circuit may include up to three batteries (in series).
If bulbs go out when you disconnect another bulb, change the circuit.
Keep trying new arrangements until two bulbs are always lit, even when a third bulb is removed.
When everything works, draw a diagram of the circuit and label the parts.

2. **Taking Notes** As you try different ideas, make accurate drawings of each attempt, even if it doesn't work. That way, you won't repeat the same design.

3. **New Directions** Did the instructions from TMT easily lead you to success? If not, you need to rewrite them. Keep what worked, and write new instructions that describe what you actually did. Choose your words carefully. Make the new directions as clear and simple as you can. Add more steps where needed and change the wording to make it simpler. (Perhaps a numbered list of steps would help.) Also include a brief description of the difference between series and parallel circuits and a diagram of the correct circuit.

Copyright © Pearson Education, Inc., or its affiliates. All Rights Reserved.

Name ______________________ Date ____________ Class ____________

Conclusion

Let's see what you learned about electric circuits in your home.

1. There are two kinds of circuits. In one kind, all the bulbs go out when one bulb is removed. In the other kind, a bulb can be removed while all other bulbs remain lit. What are the names for these different circuits?

____

____

2. What will happen to the brightness of the first two bulbs if you add a third bulb in series? (If you aren't sure, try it.)

____

____

3. What will happen to the brightness of the first two bulbs if you add a third bulb in parallel?

____

____

4. Which type of circuit do you have in your home? How do you know?

____

Write a letter to the director of research and development at TMT. Tell the director what you liked about the kits and what you didn't like. (Try to be polite and constructive.) Include your new set of instructions with the letter.

Copyright © Pearson Education, Inc., or its affiliates. All Rights Reserved.

Stuck at the Top

Investigation Overview

- The Scenario in this investigation is based on a real incident that took place at Keansburg Amusement Park, in New Jersey. It was determined that the incident was caused by rust on the rails, which increased the coefficient of friction.
- Prior to the investigation, you will need to purchase enough foam pipe insulation for your class. Each student pair will need one six-foot length of insulation, cut in half lengthwise, to produce two model roller-coaster tracks. Each pair will also need one heavy ball and one light ball of similar diameters, such as a golf ball and table tennis ball.
- Before beginning the investigation, review with students the formulas for gravitational potential and kinetic energy (Gravitational potential energy = Weight × Height; Kinetic energy = $\frac{1}{2}$ × Mass × Speed^2).
- Begin by having your students read the Scenario and Steps 1–3. Answer any questions.
- Proceed with the investigation but have students stop when they reach the Conclusion. Students should discover that the two balls behave in a very similar manner. (If there is a slight difference, it is most likely caused by a difference in the coefficients of friction.)
- Discuss with your students what has happened and why. Remind students that potential energy is equal to kinetic energy and write the equations on the board, set equal to each other. Make sure your students notice that, if you replace PE_g with mgh and KE with ½ mv^2, mass appears on both sides of the equation and can be canceled. That means mass is not a factor.

SCORING RUBRIC	
SCORE 4	Student's report includes a conclusion about the cause of the incident, accurately describes the experimental results, and explains how the results support the stated conclusion.
SCORE 3	The report contains all information required for a score of 4 but contains minor errors, or does not clearly connect the results to the conclusion.
SCORE 2	The report contains the required information, but there is a significant error, or the student did not fully participate in the team's effort.
SCORE 1	The report is partially incomplete and/or indicates only a minimal understanding of the investigation, or the student did not adequately contribute to the group.

Extension Activities

Cooperative Learning Have students brainstorm as many different kinds of amusement park rides as they can. Then have students work in pairs to describe the energy transformations that occur on each ride. Conclude with a class discussion that summarizes what students learned about energy transformations. Have each group choose one unique ride to discuss with the class.

Field Trip Many amusement parks sponsor a special day called "Physics Day," when they invite teachers to bring their students armed with accelerometers and devices for measuring height by triangulation. Arrange a field trip to your local amusement park and have students conduct age-appropriate physics activities as they experience the various rides there.

Copyright © Pearson Education, Inc., or its affiliates. All Rights Reserved.

Name ______________________________ Date ____________ Class ____________

Stuck at the Top

Purpose To investigate the amount of potential energy a roller coaster needs to make it over a hill

Materials
- 6 feet of pipe insulation, cut lengthwise
- masking tape
- 2 balls with similar diameters and different masses

Scenario

FIREFIGHTERS RESCUE CHILDREN STUCK ON ROLLER COASTER

Investigators to Determine Cause of Malfunction

SOMERDALE, NJ – With its low prices and family-friendly atmosphere, Kenny's Amusement Park has been a favorite summer tradition in New Jersey for nearly 30 years. With attractions including four roller coasters, bumper cars, and a water park, Kenny's stands for good, old-fashioned thrills, excitement, and fun. But is it safe?

Around 5 P.M. on Monday evening, a 12-year-old boy and 8-year-old girl got more excitement than they expected. Their four-person car on the popular Whirlwind roller coaster stalled on the tracks at the top of the highest hill, leaving the frightened children trapped for nearly an hour as firefighters worked to rescue them.

No one involved in the incident was hurt, but the ride will remain closed until state inspectors can determine what caused the car to stop on the tracks. When asked to comment on the incident, Ken Smarmy, owner of Kenny's Amusements, Inc., stated that the two small

(Story continued on page B6)

Ken Smarmy, owner of Kenny's Amusement Park, told officials that the ride malfunctioned because the two children did not weigh enough to keep their car moving. He said that it is against park policy to allow partially empty cars to run on the track, and he fired the ride's attendant immediately after the incident. However, some of Mr. Smarmy's employees have accused him of ignoring complaints that many of the rides need repairs and better maintenance. Is it true that there was not enough weight in the roller coaster car to keep it moving, or is that just Smarmy's excuse?

You and your partner are roller-coaster engineers. It's your job to find out whether the children's weight was the cause of the problem. Then, report your findings to the New Jersey inspectors.

Procedure

1. **Making It to the Top** A roller coaster car must have plenty of kinetic energy at the bottom of the first hill. Not only does the car need to climb to the top of the second hill, but it also must have enough energy left over to keep moving along the track. Use the materials supplied by your teacher to design a model roller coaster that has one drop and a hill that is lower than the drop. Using the heavier ball, find a starting point on the drop hill that always allows the ball to make it over the second hill. Mark the starting point with masking tape.

Copyright © Pearson Education, Inc., or its affiliates. All Rights Reserved.

Procedure *(continued)*

2. **A Lightweight Hypothesis** When the boy and girl got stuck on the Whirlwind, they were the only two people riding in a four-person car. Perhaps with only two small passengers, the car wasn't heavy enough. If you test a lightweight ball at the starting point you marked on your roller coaster, will it make it over the hill? (This is your hypothesis.)

   ____

3. **Why Do You Think So?** A hypothesis is not a guess. A scientist bases a hypothesis on observations or theory. State the reason(s) you think your hypothesis is correct.

   ____

   ____

4. **Try It Out** Place the lighter ball at the start point and let it go. Test it two or three times. Use a complete sentence to describe what happened.

   ____

5. **Evaluate Your Hypothesis** Was your hypothesis supported by the results? Explain. (A hypothesis is never proven! It is either supported or not supported by the results of an experiment.)

   ____

Conclusion

Let's see what you learned about kinetic and potential energy.

1. What type of energy is the motion of an object? ______________________
2. What type of energy does an object store internally? ______________________
3. Which idea describes a change from potential energy to kinetic energy?

   ____

4. Not all of a roller coaster's energy transfers back and forth between potential energy and kinetic energy. According to the law of conservation of energy, however, the leftover potential energy must exist somewhere. Identify another form of energy that both potential and kinetic energy can become.

   ____

The New Jersey Department of Community Affairs is responsible for the safety of carnival and amusement park rides. Its roller-coaster inspectors are eager to see the results of your investigation. The director wants to either make the Whirlwind roller coaster an adult-only ride, or further investigate the claims of Ken Smarmy's employees. Write a report describing your results and explain what recommendation you will make based on your results.

Copyright © Pearson Education, Inc., or its affiliates. All Rights Reserved.

Please Drop In

Investigation Overview

- Free-fall times presented in the table on the student page were calculated based on the 9.8 m/s^2 acceleration caused by the force of gravity.
- Prior to the investigation, obtain enough materials for students to work in pairs.
- Demonstrating Newton's second law requires that a constant force be exerted over a long enough time period to observe a change in velocity. The force of gravity is the best candidate, but the acceleration due to gravity requires relatively large drop heights to measure drop times with sufficient accuracy. Test the designs in a location where students can drop masses from a height of at least two meters.
- Discuss as a class the number of washers to use for the mass. Help students conclude that each group should use the same mass. As students collect data, check on the accuracy of their measurements.
- Provide students with large plastic bags that they can use to create a parachute. Students may need several attempts to perfect their designs. Emphasize that there can be more than one good parachute design. To test for landing accuracy, choose a height and drop location. Draw a bull's-eye as the target. You may wish to assign points to the various rings of the target and turn the investigation into a competition.

SCORING RUBRIC	
SCORE 4	Student report includes all relevant data, a description of the design and results, and a recommendation for the design that best meets the goals of speed and accuracy. The student took a leadership role in the investigation.
SCORE 3	Student report contains all information required for a score of 4 but with minor errors. The student fully participated in the investigation.
SCORE 2	Student report is missing a required piece of information, or the student did not fully participate in the investigation.
SCORE 1	Student report conveys minimal understanding of Newton's second law of motion, or student did not make a significant contribution to the group.

Extension Activities

Cooperative Learning Have students work in groups to create presentations for the amusement park company. Presentations should include visual aids, address both the design and testing process, and provide a recommendation for a parachute design.

Guest Speaker Arrange to have a mechanical engineer speak to your class about how he or she uses Newton's laws of motion during the design process and what kind of tests are used to evaluate a design.

Copyright © Pearson Education, Inc., or its affiliates. All Rights Reserved.

Name ______________________ Date ____________ Class ____________

Please Drop In

Purpose To investigate falling objects and design a safe parachute ride for an amusement park

Materials

- paper clip
- large metal washers
- string
- stopwatch
- plastic bag
- scissors

Scenario

A famous amusement park company has hired your engineering company to design a parachute ride for their newest park. They want the ride to be fun, but they also want it to be safe and reliable. The parachute should drop quickly, but not so quickly that it injures the riders. Also, the parachute must land in a small area directly below the release point. If the parachute drifts too far from the target, it could crash into other rides or people.

Before you can send the amusement park your design, you have to do some experimenting. How will you find the perfect balance of accuracy and speed?

Procedure

1. **Fall for Accuracy** Slide some washers onto a paper clip. Your teacher will demonstrate how you can safely drop this mass from a high place. Measure the drop height in meters from the bottom of the washers. The height should be at least two meters.

____

2. **Timing the Fall** Use a stopwatch to measure the free-fall time for the mass. Repeat for a total of five trials. Calculate and record the average free-fall time.

____

3. **Gravity and Acceleration** Find your drop height on the table to the right. Your drop time should be close to the time on the table. If it is not, check your height measurement and try again. Notice that the free-fall time for a drop height of four meters is less than twice the free-fall time for a drop height of two meters. This means that objects do not fall at a constant velocity. The velocity of an object increases as the object falls. This acceleration is caused by the force of gravity.

Drop Height (m)	Free-Fall Time (s)
2.00	0.639
2.10	0.655
2.20	0.670
2.30	0.685
2.40	0.700
2.50	0.714
2.60	0.728
2.70	0.742
2.80	0.756
2.90	0.769
3.00	0.782
3.10	0.795
3.20	0.808
3.30	0.821
3.40	0.833
3.50	0.845
3.60	0.857
3.70	0.869
3.80	0.881
3.90	0.892
4.00	0.904

Copyright © Pearson Education, Inc., or its affiliates. All Rights Reserved.

Procedure *(continued)*

4. **Adding a Parachute** Make a parachute out of a plastic bag. Fasten it to the washers using string. Start the parachute at the same drop height as you did for the free-fall trials (measured from the bottom of the washers). Measure and record the parachute drop times. Repeat for five trials. Calculate and record the average drop time.

____

5. **Perfecting Your Parachute** You may redesign your parachute in any way. Your goal is to have the longest drop time possible and still have an accurate landing.

6. **My Parachute Worked Best!** When all groups have demonstrated their parachute drops, notice which designs worked best. Infer why some designs worked better than others.

____

____

Conclusion

Let's see what you learned about falling objects.

1. Compare the free-fall time of the free-falling washers to the free-fall time of washers hanging from the parachute. Use these times to figure out which washers had the greater acceleration. Explain your reasoning.

____

____

2. Recall that Newton's second law states that the net force on an object is equal to the mass of the object multiplied by the acceleration of the object. Which set of washers was acted upon by the greater net force?

____

____

3. The gravitational force that Earth exerts on an object, also called weight, depends on the mass of the object. Did the weight of the washers ever change during your experiment? Explain what caused the change in net force when you added the parachute. (*Hint:* Remember the different types of friction.)

____

____

Now write a report that explains your results and makes a recommendation to the amusement park company. Describe the parachute you designed and the results of your tests. Include your data in a table. Based on your own results and what you observed for other teams' designs, recommend the best parachute design for the ride. Be sure to discuss both the speed and accuracy of the ride design.

Copyright © Pearson Education, Inc., or its affiliates. All Rights Reserved.

Is the North Pole Really the South Pole?

Investigation Overview

- The geographic North Pole really is a magnetic south pole. The North Pole was named that way because the skinnier, north end of the compass needle points in that particular direction. However, the north end of a bar magnet, like the compass needle, would point to a magnetic south pole.
- Students should conduct this investigation in pairs or small groups. Each group will need one paper clip, one compass, two bar magnets, a collection of refrigerator magnets, several nonmagnetic objects, and a copy of a local map showing your school and a compass rose.
- Caution students that using a bar magnet too close to a compass can reverse the polarity of the compass needle.
- Prior to the investigation, check each compass to make sure that its needle points toward Earth's geographic north. Move away from other magnets, electrical cords, and electrical devices, which will attract the compass needle. If the polarity of the compass is reversed, fix it by holding the compass so that its needle is horizontal, and move one pole of a bar magnet along the compass needle.
- Begin the investigation by having students read the Scenario and Steps 1–4. Answer any questions, and then instruct students to begin.
- Once students reach Step 4, they may need guidance in determining which way is north. Help students properly orient their maps so that they can determine which direction your classroom faces.

SCORING RUBRIC	
SCORE 4	Student's notes clearly and logically explain that the North Pole is actually a magnetic south pole, and why a compass shows the North Pole as "north."
SCORE 3	Student's notes explain the confusion regarding the North Pole but with one or two minor errors.
SCORE 2	Student's notes contain a significant error, or the explanation is somewhat confusing.
SCORE 1	Student's notes convey only a minimal understanding of the investigation.

Extension Activities

Cooperative Learning Have students work in groups to design, build, and test electromagnets. Hold a competition to see which team can construct the strongest magnet.

Field Trip Arrange a field trip to a location where students can observe the use of magnets in technology. Examples of such technology include large electromagnets used for lifting cars, electromagnetic locks, and electric motors.

Copyright © Pearson Education, Inc., or its affiliates. All Rights Reserved.

Name ______________________ Date ____________ Class ____________

Is the North Pole Really the South Pole?

Purpose To investigate the magnetic poles of Earth

Materials

- compass
- two bar magnets
- paper clip
- refrigerator magnets
- nonmagnetic objects
- map of the community
- index card

Scenario

Magnets are everywhere. In your home there are magnets you can see and hidden magnets you don't see. If you're like most people, you probably have several magnets on your refrigerator door. They are holding up coupons, pictures, and reminder notes. Those are the visible kind of magnets. Did you know that every electric motor has at least two magnets inside it? Those are hidden magnets. But the biggest magnet of all is right under your feet. Earth itself is a huge magnet, and the detector that proves it's a magnet is a compass.

You have read about magnets in your textbook. Today a student in your class asked an interesting question.

> Since opposite magnetic poles attract, and since the north end of a compass needle points to the North Pole, isn't Earth's North Pole really the South Pole?

Some students laughed, and the student who asked the question was embarrassed. But your teacher said this was a very good question and has challenged your class to come up with a logical answer.

Procedure

1. **If the Paper Clip Sticks ...** Humans cannot taste, smell, see, hear, or feel the presence of a magnet. But we can detect magnets using metals such as iron and steel. Metals only work as detectors if the magnetic field is strong enough. Your teacher will give you an assortment of objects. Use a paper clip to check which of the objects are magnets.
2. **It Takes One to Know One** Magnets themselves make good magnet detectors, too. A magnet will attract or repel another magnet. In that way, a magnet can tell you something about the magnet it detects. Test this out with two bar magnets. Which ends attract and which ends repel?

Attract ______________________

Repel ______________________

Copyright © Pearson Education, Inc., or its affiliates. All Rights Reserved.

Name ______________________ Date ____________ Class ____________

Procedure *(continued)*

3. A Compass Is a Magnet Detector Use a compass to investigate the magnetic field around one of the bar magnets. Which end of the compass points toward the south pole of the bar magnet, and which end points toward the north pole? (Be careful not to let the compass touch the bar magnet. A touch can change the poles of the compass needle.)

End pointing to south pole ______________________

End pointing to north pole ______________________

4. Where on the Map Does the Compass Point? Examine the map your teacher gave you. The north arrow on the map points in the direction of Earth's North Pole. When you stand facing north, which end of your compass points toward the North Pole of Earth?

____

Conclusion

Let's see what you learned about magnets and Earth's poles.

1. Name two magnet poles that attract one another.

____

2. Which end of a compass needle points toward the south pole of a bar magnet?

____

3. Which end of a compass needle points toward Earth's North Pole?

____

4. Is Earth's North Pole a magnetic north pole or a magnetic south pole?

____

Your science teacher thinks your discovery will surprise many people. How can you tell the world about it without confusing people? A reporter from your local paper is coming this afternoon to interview you about your discovery. Think about what you want to say and organize the order in which you would say it. Write your ideas on an index card so that you won't forget them when you are being interviewed.

Copyright © Pearson Education, Inc., or its affiliates. All Rights Reserved.

The Mayor Is Worried

Investigation Overview

- Students may require help converting travel times to speed in miles per hour. You may wish to illustrate the conversion with the following example:

$$\frac{0.5 \text{ mile}}{60 \text{ sec}} \times \frac{60 \text{ sec}}{1 \text{ min}} \times \frac{60 \text{ min}}{1 \text{ hr}} = \frac{1{,}800 \text{ miles}}{60 \text{ hrs}}$$

$$= 30 \text{ miles/hr}$$

- The best route is: left from the firehouse, left on Peach Promenade, left on Cat Court, left on Lemon Lane, and left on Dog Drive. This route adds the least number of seconds to the trip. It takes 110 seconds to travel this route, 50 more than the direct route without speed bumps, and 110 seconds before the flashover point.
- If students have trouble calculating speed in this investigation, you may want to allow students to work in pairs and check their calculations. However, students should still prepare individual reports.

SCORING RUBRIC	
SCORE 4	Student writes a letter beginning with the provided sentence and includes all required information as described in the Conclusion.
SCORE 3	Student letter includes the required information but with minor errors or omissions.
SCORE 2	Student letter is missing a significant piece of required information, or a piece of information is incorrect.
SCORE 1	Student letter conveys minimal understanding of the investigation.

Extension Activities

Assignment Have students measure the average speed between their homes and the school. They can base the calculation on walking, riding a bicycle, riding in a car, or any other mode of transport.

Cooperative Learning Divide the class into four teams and assign one role to each team: city council, firefighters, citizens in favor of speed bumps, and citizens opposed to speed bumps. Have each team research the issue from the perspective of their group and select a spokesperson to participate in a mock hearing. While other teams develop their cases and produce audiovisual aids, the city council team should investigate the role of the city council in your community. This activity should end with a vote by the members of the city council.

Guest Speaker Have a city planner or civil engineer visit your class to discuss instances where scientific knowledge (especially knowledge of force and motion) has influenced development decisions.

Copyright © Pearson Education, Inc., or its affiliates. All Rights Reserved.

Name ________________________ Date ____________ Class ____________

The Mayor Is Worried

Purpose To calculate travel time and speed

Materials
- pen or pencil
- calculator (optional)

Scenario

Speeding on neighborhood streets has been a problem since cars were invented. Communities across the country are now adding "traffic calming" devices to slow speeders. One device that forces drivers to slow down is the speed bump. If a driver speeds over the bump, not only will it give the driver a large jolt, but it can damage the car.

Your city council is considering installing speed bumps in some neighborhoods. Some people are afraid, however, that speed bumps won't just slow speeders. They will slow fire trucks and ambulances, too. The mayor is one of those worried people. It currently takes about 60 seconds for a fire engine to drive to his house at 5900 Dog Drive. How long will it take when the speed bumps are installed?

You are a civil engineer at the company the city hired to solve its speeding problem. The mayor has asked you to explain how the proposed speed bumps will affect the fire department's response times. Specifically, you must select five different routes between the fire station and the mayor's house (including the route currently used by the fire department) and prepare a report with your recommendation to the mayor.

Proposed Speed-Bump Placement

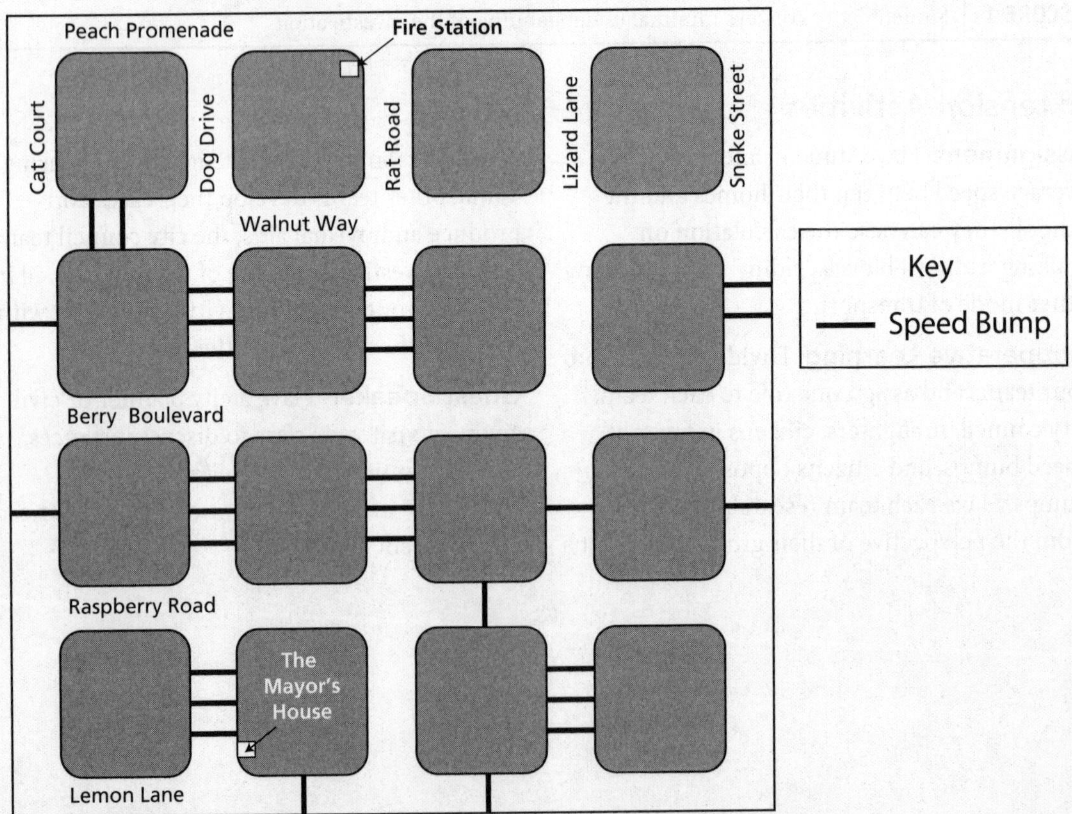

Copyright © Pearson Education, Inc., or its affiliates. All Rights Reserved.

Name ______________________________ Date______________ Class______________

Procedure

1. **Calculating Speed** Speed is the distance and object travels over a unit of time. To calculate the speed between two points, you need to divide the distance by the time. One city block in your town is 1/10 of a mile (0.1 mi). The mayor's house is five blocks away from the fire station. To get to the mayor's house, the fire department currently takes Rat Road for three blocks, turns right on Raspberry Road, and left on Dog Drive. According to the mayor, it takes a fire truck 60 seconds to cover that distance. Calculate the average speed without speed bumps and record it in your notebook.
2. **Adding Speed Bumps** Research shows that each bump adds about 10 seconds to emergency-response times. You have determined that it takes 10 seconds for a fire engine to cover one city block. Each turn adds another 5 seconds. Now calculate the time it will take a fire truck to travel the current route to the mayor's house with speed bumps.
3. **Alternate Routes** Next, select four routes that look like they may be faster than the route in Step 1. Give each route a name, and then calculate its time and distance. Record all results in your notebook.
4. **Slower Speeds?** Calculate and record the average speed for each alternate route.

Conclusion

Let's see what you learned about the relationship of distance, time, and speed.

1. What is the average speed in miles per hour of a fire truck following the direct route to the mayor's house, without speed bumps?______________________________
2. What is the travel time and average speed with speed bumps?______________________________

____

3. Did you find a better route? If so, describe that route and give its distance, time, and average speed.

____

____

The point at which the site of a fire explodes in flames is known as the *flashover point*. It takes an average of 3 minutes and 40 seconds for a small room with a wastebasket fire to reach its flashover point. With this time in mind, write a letter with your recommendation for the mayor. Describe the three main reasons for your recommendation. Support your recommendation with your data, including

- the calculated average speed of fire trucks traveling each route
- the calculated time lost by the trucks on each route
- a comparison of each route to the original route without speed bumps

Copyright © Pearson Education, Inc., or its affiliates. All Rights Reserved.

Where Is the Battery?

Investigation Overview

- Although students will write individual scripts, they should conduct the experiment together in small groups. Prior to the investigation, obtain a tile, carpet scrap, and two thermometers (one labeled *A* and the other *B*) for each group. (You may be able to obtain free scrap tiles and carpet squares from home supply stores.)
- The day before you conduct this investigation, place the tiles and carpet squares in a cool place in your classroom.
- Begin by having students read the Scenario and Steps 1–3. Answer any questions, divide the class into groups, and have them begin the experiment.
- Discuss student answers to the Conclusion before allowing them to begin writing their responses. Be sure to emphasize that it is thermal energy (heat), not temperature, that flows from one place to another.
- Be prepared to point students to the pages in their textbook about conductors and insulators.

SCORING RUBRIC	
SCORE 4	Student script clearly and accurately explains why tile feels colder than carpet. The language used is appropriate for a second-grader.
SCORE 3	Script includes all information required for a score of 4 but is not written for a second-grader or contains minor errors.
SCORE 2	Script contains a significant error or omission.
SCORE 1	Script is largely incomplete or conveys only a minimal understanding of heat transfer.

Extension Activities

Assignment Have students keep a personal thermal diary for one day. Every time they feel that heat is flowing to them (making them feel warmer) or away from them (making them feel colder) they should list the time of day, the activity in which they are engaged, the heat source, and the heat receptor (i.e., the part of the body that senses the heat).

Cooperative Learning An important step to reducing home energy consumption is installing or upgrading insulation. Have students work in groups to create pamphlets describing for homeowners the three main types of insulation (polystyrene, cellulose, and fiberglass), and how each one reduces the transfer of thermal energy between spaces.

Guest Speaker Have an architect or contractor speak to your class about the different design features or products frequently used to reduce the flow of thermal energy through a home.

Copyright © Pearson Education, Inc., or its affiliates. All Rights Reserved.

Name ______________________ Date ____________ Class ____________

Where Is the Battery?

Purpose To investigate thermal energy transfer in the bathroom

Materials
- ceramic tile
- carpet square
- 2 thermometers
- duct tape

Scenario

On your local radio station, you are known as "The Science Answer Person." Your show has a simple format. The audience sends questions to you, and you answer them on the air. That sounds easy, doesn't it?

Most of the questions you receive are easy to answer, but some questions are hard to answer in words that young children will understand. This is one of those questions. Today the father of a second-grader sent the following question:

> Hi, Science Answer Person,
>
> My 7-year-old son came out of the bathroom today carrying the bathroom rug. He was looking at the bottom of it very closely, so I asked him what he was looking for. He said, "Where's the battery?"
>
> "Why do you think it has a battery?" I asked.
>
> "Because the floor is so cold, but the rug is warm."
>
> I know the rug doesn't have a battery, but I do not know why it feels so much warmer than the tile floor. Aren't they the same temperature? Please help.
>
> Signed, Mr. Cold Feet

Of course, Mr. Cold Feet is right. The rug and the tile are the same temperature. How can you prove it and explain to a second-grader what is really happening?

Procedure

1. **Colder Than I Thought** Your teacher will give you a tile and a piece of carpet that sat in a cool place for the same length of time. Touch each of them. Which one feels colder? Does it feel a lot colder or just a little bit colder?

   ____

2. **Keep It Standard** In this investigation, you will use two thermometers to measure and compare the temperatures of the tile and the carpet square. If the thermometers do not report the same temperature under the same conditions, you must correct for the error. Read the thermometers as they sit on your desk. Do they both show the same temperature? If they show different temperatures, calculate the difference between the two readings. Record which thermometer has a lower reading and the difference in the two temperatures. This number will be called the Correction Factor. Add this number to all readings of the lower thermometer as you complete the investigation.

   Lower thermometer (*A* or *B*) ______________ Correction Factor ______________

Copyright © Pearson Education, Inc., or its affiliates. All Rights Reserved.

Name ______________________ Date ____________ Class ____________

Procedure *(continued)*

3. **Taking Their Temperatures** Use duct tape to attach the bulb of one thermometer to the tile and the other to the carpet. After three minutes, record the temperature of each. (Be sure to add the Correction Factor if needed.)

   Tile: ______________________ Carpet: ______________________

4. **The Readings** What is the temperature difference between the tile and the carpet? Would you consider the tile and carpet the same temperature? Explain.

   ____

5. **Why Does the Tile Feel Colder?** This did not come as a surprise to you, The Science Answer Person, but the temperatures are the same (or very close). Why does the tile feel colder? (*Hint:* Before you answer, read about conductors and insulators in your textbook.)

   ____

   ____

Conclusion

Let's see what you learned about the transfer of thermal energy.

1. When you touch a cold object, in which direction does thermal energy flow?

   ____

2. Is temperature the same as heat? Explain.

   ____

   ____

3. When a hot object is placed in cold water, the temperature of the hot object will decrease and the temperature of the cold water will increase. When will the flow of heat stop?

   ____

4. If you place an object that is room temperature in room-temperature water, what energy transfer will happen? Explain.

   ____

   ____

It's time to prepare the script for tomorrow's show. In the script, you must explain why the tile feels colder than the carpet even though they are the same temperature. Remember that your answer is for a child, so keep your explanation simple. If you use scientific terms, explain what they mean.

Copyright © Pearson Education, Inc., or its affiliates. All Rights Reserved.

Help! I'm Trapped Under Here!

Investigation Overview

- Have the students read the Scenario and review Steps 1–4. Answer any questions, and then have them begin. After a few minutes, have students share their lists with a partner. After pairs share their ideas, create a master list. The list may include many items but must include the weight of the car, weight of the rescuer, mechanical advantage needed, distance from the fulcrum to the input force, and distance from the fulcrum to the output force.
- Have all students use the same car weight (3,000 pounds) and the same distance from fulcrum to output force (one meter).
- Before students can use the formula to figure out the total length of the lever they will need, they must calculate the Mechanical Advantage required using the equation below:

$$\text{mechanical advantage} = \frac{\text{weight of car}}{\text{weight of student}}$$

However, rather than telling your students the formula, ask them for suggestions and do not be too eager to give them the answer. Also, remind students that they will be calculating the distance from the fulcrum to the input force based on their own weight, and then they will add the two distances to find the total length of the lever they will need.

SCORING RUBRIC	
SCORE 4	Student states on an index card three correct facts about levers and mechanical advantage that would be helpful in an emergency. One of the points identifies which class of lever is most helpful in an emergency and explains why.
SCORE 3	Student states three correct facts about levers and mechanical advantage that would be helpful in an emergency. The student states which class of lever is most helpful but does not provide justification.
SCORE 2	Student states two correct facts about levers and mechanical advantage that would be helpful in an emergency.
SCORE 1	Student states only one correct fact about levers and mechanical advantage that would be helpful in an emergency.

Extension Activities

Assignment Crevasse rescue with a pulley: Mountain climbers often have to walk across glaciers that have deep crevasses. Pulling a fallen climber out of a crevasse requires a lot of strength—or a simple machine. The machine most commonly used is a pulley. Have your students work in three-person teams to design a pulley system they could use to rescue a climber in an emergency.

Field Trip Arrange a field trip to a construction site near your school. Make sure that your students will be able to observe from a safe distance. Have students work individually to list all the simple machines they see, and then work together in pairs to estimate the mechanical advantage of each machine.

Copyright © Pearson Education, Inc., or its affiliates. All Rights Reserved.

Name ______________________________ Date______________ Class______________

Help! I'm Trapped Under Here!

Purpose To investigate the use of a lever in an emergency

Materials
- small notebook
- index card

Scenario

You are a rescue worker. Although you work in a fire station, you are not a firefighter. You are a first responder. Your training has included a number of different rescue situations. However, your most common job involves carefully removing a victim trapped in or under a car during a vehicle accident. In your work, you have the help of many different machines. Even when a motor powers them, they are all based on levers, pulleys, wedges, or other simple machines.

Last week, you and your partner rescued a man trapped under a compact car. You used a pulley system to lift the car while your partner and a firefighter pulled the man to safety. When you returned to the station, the captain asked you an interesting question: What would you have done if you had not had a pulley or other rescue equipment?

Procedure

Hydraulic Rescue Tools

Emergency rescue workers often use hydraulic rescue tools to cut, pry open, and even lift vehicles to free a victim trapped inside. The tools are powered by a hydraulic pump, but they use levers to create mechanical advantage.

1. **How Long?** You agree with your partner that a first-class lever could do the job, but you're not sure how long it should be to lift a compact car.
2. **Things To Consider** Think about all of the factors that you must consider before you can solve this problem. Make a list in your notebook of everything you can think of.
3. **Share and Add** Show your list to your partner. Add to your list anything your partner thought of that you missed. Be sure to remove anything that you both agree does not belong.
4. **Making a Class List** Create a master list together with your class. Make sure that the list only includes those things that must be considered.
5. **Calculating the Mechanical Advantage** First, you need to determine the necessary mechanical advantage of the lever. Work with your partner to predict how to calculate the mechanical advantage. Compare your prediction to the equation below and then calculate.

   Weight of car: 3,000 pounds

   Your weight: ______________________________

   $$\text{Mechanical advantage} = \frac{\text{Weight of car}}{\text{Your weight}}$$

   Mechanical advantage needed: ______________________________

Copyright © Pearson Education, Inc., or its affiliates. All Rights Reserved.

Name ______________________________ Date__________ Class__________

Procedure *(continued)*

6. **Using Your List and the Formula** Next, use your calculated mechanical advantage to calculate the required distance from the fulcrum to the input force. Use a different formula for mechanical advantage shown below to solve the problem.

$$\text{Mechanical Advantage} = \frac{\text{Distance from fulcrum to input force}}{\text{Distance from fulcrum to output force}}$$

Distance from fulcrum to output force: 1 meter

Distance from fulcrum to input force: ______________________________

Full length of the lever: ______________________________

Conclusion

Let's see what you have learned about using a lever to rescue a person trapped under a compact car. Answer the following questions.

1. Is a first-class lever a realistic way to lift a car off a trapped person? Explain.

____

____

2. What everyday object could you successfully use for a lever that is the length you have calculated? ______________________________

3. If you had several people to help you, how could your lever change? Explain.

____

____

4. Another option is to use a second-class lever, with the ground under the car as the fulcrum. Would a first-class or second-class lever be able to generate a greater input force? Explain.

____

____

____

You have been invited to appear on the evening news at your local TV station. You wil have one minute to discuss your most recent rescue, and another minute to tell ordinary people how to help a person trapped under a heavy object. The second minute is critical! On an index card, list three points you want to make during the second minute. Be sure to recommend the class of lever that would be most helpful to lift a car off a trapped person and justify your decision.

Copyright © Pearson Education, Inc., or its affiliates. All Rights Reserved.

Catching the Waves

Investigation Overview

- Students will work in small groups to complete this investigation. Each group will require measuring tape and at least one small battery-operated AM radio. (FM radios will also work.)
- Begin the investigation by assigning students to groups and having them read the Scenario and Procedure. Answer any questions.
- Before students begin the Procedure, turn off all fluorescent lights and other electrical devices in the room. You will turn the lights back on when students are ready to perform Step 4.
- After everyone has completed Step 4, turn on all electrical devices in your classroom. For Step 5 students will name, measure, and record the electromagnetic radiation (EMR) strength of five electrical devices. (NOTE: Outlets and dimmer switches can emit EMR.) Tell your students that the easiest way to measure the strength of a signal is to measure the distance to the point where a sound begins. The farther away the radio is when it detects a signal, the stronger the source.

SCORING RUBRIC	
SCORE 4	Student writes a script that clearly and correctly states the radio is not broken, explains why the radio made the noise, and suggests moving the radio away from the dishwasher.
SCORE 3	Student script contains all information required for a score of 4 but contains minor errors.
SCORE 2	One piece of required information is missing or incorrect.
SCORE 1	The script indicates only a minimal understanding of the investigation.

Extension Activities

Assignment An AM radio can serve as a lightning detector. As a thunderstorm approaches, tune the radio to a place between stations. Listen carefully for crackling sounds, which are caused by radio waves emitted by a bolt of lightning. Students may notice that some of the lightning bolts the radio detects will not be visible to them. These may be lightning bolts that are high in the thunderstorm cloud or far away in another thunderstorm cell.

Cooperative Learning Have students work in teams to investigate the role that radio frequency plays in detecting different EMR emitters. Measure the EMR strength of each emitter already identified to see if their relative strengths remain the same at the different frequencies.

Guest Speaker Arrange for an electrician to speak to your class about the importance of EMR detection in his or her work. If possible, have the speaker bring and demonstrate the use of some of the equipment used in the field to detect EMR.

Copyright © Pearson Education, Inc., or its affiliates. All Rights Reserved.

Name ______________________ Date ____________ Class ____________

Catching the Waves

Purpose To investigate how different electrical devices emit radio waves

Materials
- portable AM radio
- measuring tape

Scenario

On your local radio station, you are known as "The Science Answer Person." Your show has a simple format. The audience e-mails you questions, and you answer them on the air. It sounds easy, doesn't it?

You know your science, so most of the questions are easy to answer. However, explaining them in words a child will understand is difficult. Today the father of a third-grader e-mailed the following question from his daughter:

> Hi, Science Answer Person,
>
> Two weeks ago, I gave my 8-year-old daughter an old portable radio. I put new batteries in it, and it was working well until yesterday. That's when it broke. She had it in her pocket as she was helping me load our dishwasher. As she stood in front of the dishwasher, a squealing noise in her earphones became so loud she couldn't hear the station anymore.
>
> My daughter said, "Daddy, my radio broke." I listened, and she was right. She asked me to explain why it broke, but I couldn't. Is it possible the dishwasher broke her radio?
>
> Signed, Confused Father

You've seen this happen before. The dishwasher did cause the squealing noise, but it did not break the radio. The radio should be fine as soon as it's moved away from the dishwasher and any other electrical device that emits electromagnetic radiation (EMR). EMR waves are created anywhere electrical power is turned on and off rapidly. You will have to figure out a way to explain this to "Confused Father". Before you begin writing him back, you decide to test your hypothesis.

Procedure

1. **You Need a Portable AM Radio** A battery-operated AM radio makes a good detector of low-frequency EMR. Your teacher will divide the class into teams and give each team an AM radio.

2. **Finding No Station** The EMR that interfered with the daughter's radio was strong enough to block the station she was listening to. But some EMR interference is weak. In order to detect weak EMR, tune the radio to a spot between stations.

3. **Turn Down the Volume** Even between stations, there may still be noise. Turn the volume down until you can barely hear the noise.

Copyright © Pearson Education, Inc., or its affiliates. All Rights Reserved.

Name ______________________ Date__________ Class__________

Procedure *(continued)*

4. **Use the Radio as an EMR Detector** Listen carefully as your teacher turns the fluorescent lights back on. Do you hear anything? Move the radio closer to a fluorescent light. What happens?

____

____

5. **Finding the Strongest EMR Source** Measure and record the EMR strength of the fluorescent lights. To determine the strength, figure out how far you can move the radio away from the lights before the sound stops. Measure the farthest distance you can hold the radio from the lights without losing the sound. Once you have recorded the EMR strength of the lights, repeat this procedure for four other electrical devices.

Electrical Device	EMR Strength (distance from radio)
fluorescent lights	

Conclusion

Let's see what you learned about electromagnetic radiation and radio waves.

1. All electromagnetic waves travel at the same speed in a vacuum. What characteristics of electromagnetic waves can be different?

____

2. When you detect EMR with a radio, are you detecting relatively short or long wavelengths? Explain.

____

3. What characteristic do AM radio stations vary when transmitting radio waves? What characteristics do they keep constant?

____

4. Which radio waves have more energy: AM or FM? Explain.

____

It's time to prepare the script for tomorrow's show. In the script, you must answer Confused Father's question. Explain why the radio made the squealing noise when it was close to the dishwasher. Suggest how he can show his daughter that the radio still works.

Copyright © Pearson Education, Inc., or its affiliates. All Rights Reserved.

Seeing in the Dark

Investigation Overview

- This activity directly attacks the common misconception that if we wait long enough, we can see in a totally dark room.
- This activity requires that you prepare your classroom in advance. You must be able to dim the lights until all color vision fades. Make the light level as low as possible in your classroom without making it totally dark. If you can still see more than one color, use a different room.
- Step 2 should be assigned as homework. The day before you plan to begin the investigation, ask your students to find a place in their homes that can be made totally dark.
- The day of the investigation, review the Scenario and Procedure, and answer any questions. Then dim the lights in the classroom in three or four stages. After each stage, show three brightly colored sheets of paper (red, green, and blue) in random order and have students record the colors they see. Turn the lights back on, tell your class the correct sequences, and ask which color they got wrong first.
- Make sure all students were able to make a place in their homes totally dark. Have students discuss the places they found and steps they took to make the places totally dark. Stress that students will need total darkness for the assignment. The goal is to see if their eyes will eventually adapt to total darkness. (Note: They should test their vision by having an object to look at. Many people will be able to "see" their own hands in total darkness because the brain knows the hand is there and will actually create a perceivable image on the visual cortex.)
- The next day, hold a class discussion about the results. Explain that, although the human retina changes to adjust its sensitivity in very low light, there is a limit. A single rod cell responds to a single photon of light, but the optic nerve only sends a signal to the brain if between five and nine photons strike a rod cell in less than 0.1 second.

SCORING RUBRIC	
SCORE 4	The script includes an opening statement explaining that rod cells allow us to see in dim light but do not respond to color. There is a logical discussion that concludes Sammy could not have seen the color of the cap.
SCORE 3	The script meets all content requirements for a score of 4 but is sloppy or contains errors.
SCORE 2	The script describes how rod cells work but does not explain how that information discredits the witness.
SCORE 1	The script does not correctly explain the function of rod cells or adequately relate the information to the credibility of the witness.

Extension Activities

Assignment Have your students draw and label a diagram of the human eye in cross section.

Guest Speaker Have a police spokesperson tell one or two true stories about the role of science in investigation. If they have a story that involves light, color, or the working of the human eye, make sure they tell that story, too.

Copyright © Pearson Education, Inc., or its affiliates. All Rights Reserved.

Name ______________________ Date ______________ Class ______________

Seeing in the Dark

Purpose To use a lightproof room to investigate how human eyes work in the dark

Materials
- totally dark room
- flashlight or lamp with a switch
- brightly colored cards (red, green, and blue)

Scenario

Have you ever arrived at a movie theater after the movie started? If you entered in the daytime, you could barely see the rows, the seats, or the people who were already there. Then an amazing thing happened: Your eyes adjusted. Your pupils grew larger to let in more light, and your retinas became more sensitive. Things that were invisible became visible. You could see in the dark. Or could you?

Your eyes take time to adjust to dim light, but how long does it take? Can you see colors in the dark? Can you see when there's no light at all?

You have been thinking about these things because of the murder case you're working on. You are a defense lawyer. Your client, Willy the Weasel, has been arrested based solely on the testimony of an eyewitness. The witness, an old man named Sammy the Snitch, told police that it was totally dark when the murder went down. It was so dark that the murderer couldn't even see that Sammy was there. But Sammy had been in the room long enough for his eyes to adjust. He claimed to see everything, including the green baseball cap the murderer was wearing.

It was the green cap that led police to your client—no fingerprints, no DNA, no strands of hair … just the green cap. When Willy was arrested, he was standing on a street corner near the crime scene. He was wearing a green cap!

Willy says he's innocent. He says he never hurt anyone. He says he didn't even know the victim, Big Joey the Fish. It's up to you. You have to convince a jury that Sammy the Snitch is lying.

Procedure

1. **Where'd the Color Go?** Your teacher will make your classroom darker in stages. After each dimming of the light your teacher will show you three brightly colored cards, and you will record the colors you see in the order they are presented. (Do not guess. If two or three colors look the same to you, it's okay to write the same color more than once or to place a "?" on your answer sheet.)

   ____

   ____

   ____

2. **Check Your Answers** Your teacher will give you the correct color sequences. At what stage were you no longer able to see the colors?

   ____

Copyright © Pearson Education, Inc., or its affiliates. All Rights Reserved.

Name ______________________ Date ____________ Class ____________

Procedure *(continued)*

3. How Dark Is Dark? Yesterday, your teacher asked you to find a place in your house that can be made totally dark. Find a partner and describe the place you found. Tell how you know it is totally dark. Did you have to do anything to block the last bits of light?

____

4. A Dark Assignment Tonight for homework, sit in the dark place you found and time how long it takes for your eyes to adjust to the darkness. You may wish to take a radio or music player. Record the time here:

____

Conclusion

Let's see what you learned about how your eyes work in the dark.

1. Which light-sensitive cells work best in bright light?

____

2. These cells are sensitive to three primary light colors. Name them.

____

3. Which light-sensitive cells work in very dim light?

____

4. Is it possible to see in total darkness?

____

____

____

Now use what you have learned about low light and color vision to plan the defense of your client—Willy the Weasel. Write the script you will follow in your opening statement to the jury. In the script, explain to the jury why Sammy could not possibly have seen the color of the murderer's hat.

Begin your script with these words: "Your honor and members of the jury, my client—Willy the Weasel—has been charged with the murder of Big Joey the Fish. Although this was a violent crime, my client is innocent. I am prepared to prove that the eyewitness account you just heard cannot be true. Sammy the Snitch could not have seen the color of the murderer's cap because ________."

Copyright © Pearson Education, Inc., or its affiliates. All Rights Reserved.

Seeing with Your Ears

Investigation Overview

- Prior to the investigation, obtain a stopwatch, blindfold, and two different noisemakers (e.g., clicker, bell, whistle).
- Begin the investigation by having students read the Scenario. You may wish to show students video footage of Ben Underwood using echolocation, which is available on the Internet.
- Discuss the Scenario and make sure everyone understands the principle behind echolocation. Students have probably learned about animals (e.g., bats, dolphins, whales, and shrews) that use echolocation to sense their surroundings.
- Discuss echoes, what they are, and how they happen. Ask your students for examples of when and where they have heard echoes. Emphasize that sound is reflected from some surfaces but absorbed by others.
- Have students read the Procedure and list three obstacles, and then compile a class list of obstacles.
- Work with your students to design and build an obstacle course. Barriers should be high enough to reflect sounds at ear level. Make the course simple enough so that everyone can complete it. A simple "T" maze made of stacked desks works well.
- Students will need to make a data table in their notebooks to record the trials through the obstacle course. The data table should include a column for each trial (or each student), noise type, and time. You may want to create this data table ahead of time and make copies for the class.

SCORING RUBRIC	
SCORE 4	Student writes an e-mail that names the student with the best time, and gives his or her time and the sound source used. The e-mail is well written and includes a discussion of the average class time and the average times for each sound source.
SCORE 3	Student's e-mail includes all information required for a score of 4 but contains minor errors.
SCORE 2	Student's e-mail identifies the fastest student, but other pieces of information are missing or incorrect.
SCORE 1	Student's e-mail indicates only a minimal understanding of the investigation.

Extension Activities

Assignment Have each student research an animal that uses echolocation for navigation and write a brief summary describing the importance of echolocation to the animal.

Field Trip Arrange a trip to a large movie theater, auditorium, or concert hall where a spokesperson can explain to your students about the various design features that contribute to the acoustic properties of the room.

Copyright © Pearson Education, Inc., or its affiliates. All Rights Reserved.

Name ______________________________ Date____________ Class____________

Seeing with Your Ears

Purpose To investigate how using echolocation can determine surroundings

Materials
- 2 different noisemakers (clicker, bell, whistle)
- blindfold
- stopwatch

Scenario

An Amazing Ability

Ben Underwood lived with his family in Sacramento, California. Like any other teenage boy, he played basketball, rode his bike to school, played video games, and chased his brothers up and down the stairs in their home. But unlike most boys, Ben was blind.

Ben was born with two normal, healthy eyes. When he was only two years old, a rare cancer began to grow in one of them. His doctors tried to treat the cancer, but they could not stop the tumor's growth. The only way to save Ben's life was to operate, which would leave Ben blind.

About a year after the operation, Ben began to "see" again. One day while riding in the car with his mother, Ben pointed out a large building. How did Ben know the building was there? He couldn't see the building, but he could hear it. As Ben listened to the noise of the traffic, he could hear the changes in the sounds as they bounced off the buildings. Ben was seeing the buildings with his ears!

As Ben grew older, he learned to "see" the world around him by using *echolocation*, which is the process of using echoes to locate objects. By making clicking sounds with his mouth and listening to the clicks as they echoed off objects, Ben could locate walls, furniture, and even small objects. He was so good at sensing the world around him that he did not need a guide dog or a cane to walk around.

Unfortunately, Ben's cancer returned, and he died at the age of 16. Before he died, scientists were able to study his amazing ability. They discovered that Ben's brain had learned to convert sound into visual information. Can you teach your brain to use echoes to see? Are some sounds better for seeing than other sounds? These are the questions you must answer.

Procedure

1. **Obstacles Are Easy to Find** To test your ability to use echolocation, you will construct a simple and safe obstacle course in your classroom. An obstacle is something that gets in your way. List three obstacles that you might use:

   ____

2. **Creating Obstacles** Your teacher will ask for obstacle ideas and list them for everyone to see. Then, as a class, you will use the list to create a simple obstacle course.

Copyright © Pearson Education, Inc., or its affiliates. All Rights Reserved.

Procedure *(continued)*

3. **Navigating the Course** One at a time, each student will wear a blindfold and try to navigate the obstacle course by making noises and listening for echoes. Your teacher will time how long each student takes to complete the course. The students can make noises with a noisemaker or by clicking with their mouths. Record the results in a data table.

4. **Summarizing the Class** Calculate the average time it takes to go through the course. To do this, add all of the times and then divide by the number of trials.

   ____

5. **Which Sound Source Worked Best?** Now calculate the average times for each type of sound. Did one sound work better than the others did?

   ____

Conclusion

Let's see what you learned about echolocation.

1. How does echolocation work?

   ____

   ____

2. How was Ben able to "see" with his ears?

   ____

   ____

3. Why do you think Ben's brain learned to use echolocation?

   ____

4. Describe a situation in which echolocation could help you to "see."

   ____

   ____

The scientists at the University of California, Santa Barbara who were working with Ben Underwood are looking for another subject. Write an e-mail to the scientists in which you identify the student with the fastest time in your experiment. Be sure to include data. What was the average time for all students going through the obstacle course? What was the average time for each sound source? What was the best student's time, and what sound source was he or she using?

Copyright © Pearson Education, Inc., or its affiliates. All Rights Reserved.

Rogue Wave

Investigation Overview

- Before beginning this investigation, obtain graph paper and a copy of the Student Edition for each student. You may want to collect images and video footage of the wreckage of the *Edmund Fitzgerald*, clips of news reports of the disaster, and images of rogue waves to show the class.
- Begin the investigation by having students read the Scenario. When everyone has finished reading, show the class the images you collected.
- Next, have students read Steps 1–3. Answer any questions, distribute graph paper, and have students begin.
- If students need to review constructive interference, be prepared to tell them where they can find the relevant information in the Student Edition.

SCORING RUBRIC	
SCORE 4	Student creates a graph that shows four waves ranging in height from 13 to 26 feet, which together add up to a height of 85 feet. The graph is neat and labeled correctly.
SCORE 3	Student's graph includes all information required for a score of 4 but may contain a few minor errors.
SCORE 2	Student's graph contains a significant error or shows more than four waves.
SCORE 1	Student's graph conveys only a minimal understanding of the investigation.

Extension Activities

Assignment Have students write a brief paragraph that explains how constructive and destructive interference are mathematically identical.

Cooperative Learning Form teams of students and assign them to research and create a video to accompany the song, *The Wreck of the Edmund Fitzgerald* by Gordon Lightfoot.

Field Trip Arrange a trip to a local body of water where ships are docked. Have a harbormaster or port authority spokesperson discuss the role that high waves play in sail/no sail decisions.

Copyright © Pearson Education, Inc., or its affiliates. All Rights Reserved.

Name ______________________ Date__________ Class__________

Rogue Wave

Purpose To investigate how constructive interference can produce rogue waves

Materials
- Student Edition
- graph paper

Scenario

TRAGEDY ON LAKE SUPERIOR

It was late on the afternoon of November 9, 1975, when the ship, *Edmund Fitzgerald,* left Superior, Wisconsin. The *Fitzgerald* was fully loaded with iron ore as it began its crossing of Lake Superior. The voyage was supposed to end at the steel mill on Detroit's Zug Island.

On November 10, the *Fitzgerald* hit an awful storm. Winds were over 58 mph. Thirty-five foot waves crashed over its deck. When conditions became too much for Captain McSorley, he headed for shelter in Whitefish Bay on the lake's Canadian side, but they never made it.

The captain's last words were, "We are holding our own." Only a few minutes later the *Edmund Fitzgerald* broke in half and sank—no distress call was sent. The captain, the 28-man crew, and one of the largest ships to ever sail on the Great Lakes now rest under 530 feet of water only 17 miles from the entrance to Whitefish Bay.

The sinking of the *Edmund Fitzgerald* is the most famous disaster in the history of Great Lakes shipping. Why it sank is still a mystery. Some think it was a rogue wave.

You are an oceanographer specializing in rogue waves, or large, spontaneous waves. A science reporter for the *London Times* newspaper is writing an article about a rogue wave that hit the North Sea oil platform on New Year's Day, 1995. She has asked you to explain how rogue waves form.

Rogue Waves

Rogue waves are very tall, steep waves that appear and disappear suddenly and without warning. On New Year's Day, 1995, waves were averaging 13 to 26 feet when an oil platform in the North Sea was suddenly damaged by a single monster wave over 80 feet tall. In 2000, a 95-foot-tall rogue wave was reported. More recently, one was estimated to be 110 feet tall. No one knows the maximum height a rogue wave can reach.

The steepness of a rogue wave can be an even greater problem than its height. Hitting a nearly vertical wall of water is dangerous, but sliding down the other side is like racing down the steepest hill of a very tall roller coaster.

Procedure

1. What Causes Rogue Waves?
Scientists are still studying how and when rogue waves form, but one known cause is constructive interference. Use your textbook to find information about constructive interference.

Copyright © Pearson Education, Inc., or its affiliates. All Rights Reserved.

Name ______________________ Date__________ Class__________

Procedure *(continued)*

2. **Constructing a Monster** When the crests of two waves come together, their heights add together. What happens if the crests of three or more waves combine?

____

____

3. **Creating a New Year's Day Monster** The rogue wave that hit the oil platform was an 85-foot wave. The reporter wants to know how such a big wave formed if the average wave height was between 13 and 26 feet that day. She must think that only two waves can come together at the same time. You know that actually two or more waves can overlap. What is the least number of 13- to 26-foot waves that could have combined to create an 85-foot rogue wave?

____

Conclusion

Let's see what you learned about waves and wave interference.

1. How is wave height measured?

____

____

2. What is constructive interference?

____

____

3. What is destructive interference?

____

____

4. Constructive interference can involve two or more waves. Can destructive interference also involve more than two waves? Explain.

____

____

The *London Times* reporter wants a diagram to include with her article. She wants the diagram to show how a set of waves with different heights could produce the 85-foot rogue wave that hit the North Sea oil platform. Your diagram should be in the form of a graph. Use the smallest number of 13- to 26-foot waves needed to produce an 85-foot wave. Give your graph a title and be sure to label the *x*- and *y*-axes. Make sure that your graph, title, and labels are neat and correct.

Copyright © Pearson Education, Inc., or its affiliates. All Rights Reserved.

Science Inquiry and Processes

Science, Society, and You: Casting a Vote That Makes Sense (pp. 1–3)

Procedure

1. No; all landfills will eventually leak.
2. An aquifer is an underground layer of cracked rock or other porous material that is saturated with water.
3. The water in an aquifer is extracted for drinking water.
4. Sample table:

Costs	Benefits
May pollute four towns' drinking water	Landfill will last 20 more years
Effects may not be known for many years	No evidence of increased cancer
Every landfill eventually leaks	Reduces cost of removing towns' waste

Conclusion

1. Answers may vary. Sample: It is important for a voter to be informed about an issue before voting. If the issue includes scientific terms, it is the voter's responsibility to learn about the science involved.
2. Answers may vary. Sample: Knowing how an aquifer provides drinking water to the towns caused me to vote *no* on my ballot because polluting the aquifer could affect thousands of people's health.

Scientific Inquiry: Bias, Anyone? (pp. 4–6)

Conclusion

1. An exaggerated claim is hard to support with scientific data.
2. Answers may vary. Samples: The sample size is too small. The scientist failed to acknowledge a possible variable in the study.
3. Answers may vary. Sample: It is possible for a scientist to be unbiased when working on privately-funded research. However, the special group might be funding the research with a certain experimental result in mind, which could bias the scientist's research.
4. The finding is likely to be unbiased because it was peer-reviewed to check for any existing inaccuracies or bias.

Technology and Engineering: This Isn't Science! (pp. 7–9)

Conclusion

1. Science
2. Technology
3. Technology uses science principles to solve problems.
4. Engineering

Tools of Science: Messy Data (pp. 10–12)

Procedure

Students' graphs will vary. Check that the axes are labeled correctly, scatterplot is accurate, median points are correctly plotted, and the final trend line is adjusted slightly downward.

Conclusion

1. Scatterplot
2. The median is the midpoint in a set of ordered data.
3. The line is not affected by extreme data points because the median does not depend on the values of the most extreme data.
4. Answers may vary. Sample: Not all trend lines are exactly the same because each group adjusted its line differently for the in between median point. The most accurate trend line belongs to the group that created the scatterplot carefully and best adjusted the trend line for the in between median point.

Copyright © Pearson Education, Inc., or its affiliates. All Rights Reserved.

Ecology and the Environment

Ecosystems and Biomes: Fantasy Food Chain (pp. 13–15)

Conclusion

1. Producers are the source of all food.
2. The bottom level
3. The top level
4. Decomposers consume the wastes and remains of other organisms.

Energy Resources: Light Bulbs Can't Use Much Energy (pp. 16–18)

Procedure

1-4. Answers will vary and depend on the bulbs in each student's house and the community's energy costs. Check student calculations for accuracy.

Conclusion

1. Answers will vary. Check students' work for accuracy.
2. An incandescent bulb uses electricity to heat a filament until it glows; a fluorescent bulb uses electricity to excite mercury atoms, which causes the phosphorus coating to give off light.
3. Because they convert a higher percentage of the electricity used into visible light.

Land, Air, and Water Resources: The Problem with Runoff (pp. 19–21)

Conclusion

1-3. Answers will vary and depend on the card assigned and location of your school.

1. Sample: Yard and garden waste; grass Sample: Grass clippings on walkways and sidewalks
2. Sample: Roof surfaces because our school has a large roof whose downspouts empty into the parking lot.
3. Sample: The school could extend the downspouts to a grassy area or build drains that carry the rainwater away.

Populations and Communities: That Can't Possibly Work! (pp. 22–24)

Procedure

8. and 9. Answers will vary. Check that students' data is reasonable and actual size is accurate.

Conclusion

1-4. Answers will vary and depend on experimental results and actual population size. Sample answers are given.

1. Sample: My estimate was very close because it was off by only three animals.
2. Sample: My estimate was too low.
3. Sample: I could recapture more animals in each round or perform more recaptures.
4. Sample: No; most groups in my class had estimates that were close to the actual population size.

Resources and Living Things: Some Resources Are Worth Saving (pp. 25–27)

Conclusion

1. Sustainable means using a resource in ways that will maintain the quality of the resource for a certain period of time.
2. Answers may vary. Sample: Wind; wind power is almost always available.
3. Answers may vary. Sample: Coal; solar energy could replace coal as a source of fuel.
4. A larger population needs more natural resources, which increases our ecological footprint.

Copyright © Pearson Education, Inc., or its affiliates. All Rights Reserved.

Cells and Heredity

Cell Processes and Energy: Just Count the Bubbles (pp. 28–30)

Procedure

5. and 6. Answers will vary. Check that students' answers are reasonable and that the number of bubbles decreases as the bulb moves further from the test tube.

Conclusion

1. To increase the carbon dioxide in the water
2. Oxygen
3. Photosynthesis
4. Light energy + carbon dioxide + water $\longrightarrow$ glucose + oxygen

Cells: The Cell Game (pp. 31–33)

Conclusion

1. Cell wall, chloroplast
2. Lysosome
3. Chloroplast, endoplasmic reticulum, Golgi apparatus, lysosome, mitochondria, nucleus, vacuole
4. Sample: Cilia; paramecium

Change Over Time: Worms Under Attack! (pp. 34–36)

Procedure

2. and 3. Answers will vary and depend on the results of your class.

Conclusion

1. Tan pickworms were easier to spot in the grass.
2. There would be more green pickworms than tan ones because they survived predation from the hawks better.
3. The addition of hawks makes the environment more favorable for green pickworms.
4. The opposite result would occur. Tan pickworms would be more common.
5. Darwin would explain the adaptations as a response to environmental change.

DNA: The WWGP Is Coming (pp. 37–39)

Conclusion

1. Sugar and phosphate molecules
2. Adenine, cytosine, guanine, thymine
3. Thymine
4. Guanine
5. A complete set of genetic information that an organism carries in its DNA

Genetic Technology: We All Have It, So It Must Be Dominant! (pp. 40–42)

Procedure

1. and 3. Answers will vary and depend on the students' traits.

Conclusion

1. and 2. Answers will vary and depend on class totals.
3. No; the frequency of the trait does not tell you whether it is dominant or recessive.

Genetics: Tay-Sachs (pp. 43–45)

Procedure

2. 25%; 50%; 25%

Conclusion

1. Answers may vary. Sample: Has anyone in your family ever been diagnosed with Tay-Sachs Disease?
2. Recessive; the trait is not present in the heterozygous parents.
3. No; the disease is linked to chromosome #15, which is not a sex chromosome
4. It only takes one carrier parent to give birth to a carrier child.

Copyright © Pearson Education, Inc., or its affiliates. All Rights Reserved.

The Diversity of Life

Animal Behavior: Saved by a Life Cycle (pp. 46–48)

Procedure

3. Answers may vary. Sample: Larva stage; introduce a predator of the mosquito to the local water source

Conclusion

1. Complete metamorphosis
2. Egg, larva, pupa
3. Adult
4. Suck blood from a bird or mammal

Animal Movement: Mealworm Migration (pp. 49–51)

Procedure

5-8. Answers will vary. Check students' work.

Conclusion

1. Answers may vary. Samples: To obtain food, to defend themselves, to find protection, to maintain homeostasis, to find a mate
2. Skeletal, nervous, muscular; the nervous system receives and processes a signal, the muscles contract, and the skeleton moves.
3. No; there is no reason to believe that seasonal changes caused the observed movements.
4. Legs

Animals and Energy: The Stomach Stone Controversy (pp. 52–54)

Procedure

3. They don't have grinding teeth.

Conclusion

1. Chewing increases the surface area of food particles.
2. The type of teeth an animal has depends on what it eats. Carnivores have sharp teeth to tear meat, while herbivores have flat teeth to grind plants.
3. Pencil-like; shredding
4. Answers may vary. Sample: Since sauropods did not have wide teeth for grinding like most herbivores, they may have needed a gizzard to help break down their food.

Animals: Fantasy Zoo (pp. 55–57)

Conclusion

1-4. Answers will vary and depend on the group chosen. Samples are given.

1. Fish
2. Bilateral symmetry
3. Vertebrate
4. Ectotherm; it produces little internal body heat, and its body temperature changes with temperature changes in its environment.

Living Things: Mom's Car Must Be Alive (pp. 58–60)

Procedure

2. Answers will vary. Sample: Reproduction; a car is a nonliving thing because it cannot produce offspring.

Conclusion

1. Cellular organization, growth and development, reproduction
2. Chemicals of life, energy use, response to surroundings
3. Growth is the process of becoming larger; development involves the changes that occur as an organism grows.
4. Asexual involves one parent; sexual involves two parents.

Copyright © Pearson Education, Inc., or its affiliates. All Rights Reserved.

The Diversity of Life *(continued)*

Plants: Plants in Space (pp. 61–63)

Procedure

2. Vascular with seeds; they absorb carbon dioxide, release oxygen, and provide food.
3. Sample: Angiosperms, such as apples or corn. They are a good choice because the colonists can eat them right from the plant.

Conclusion

1. Carbon dioxide
2. Oxygen
3. Photosynthesis
4. Vascular plants with seeds

Viruses, Bacteria, Protists, and Fungi: How Could That Be? (pp. 64–66)

Procedure

4. 64,000 μm^3; 64 μm^3
5. 1000
6. $\frac{1}{1000}$

Conclusion

1. Intestines
2. $\frac{10}{1000} = \frac{1}{100}$
3. Answers will vary and depend on students' weight.
4. Answers will vary. Samples: Cheese, yogurt, buttermilk, sour cream

Copyright © Pearson Education, Inc., or its affiliates. All Rights Reserved.

Human Body Systems

Bones, Muscles, and Skin: Muscle Fatigue (pp. 67–69)

Procedure

2-6. Answers will vary. Results should show a decrease in performance from Trial 1 to Trial 4.

7. Answers will vary. Sample: 11%; 19%; 6%; 9%

Conclusion

1. Voluntary
2. Skeletal
3. Tendons
4. Sample Answer: Muscle fatigue is an overuse injury; warming up your muscles and tendons before using them repeatedly will help prevent fatigue.

Circulation: Oh No! My Heart's Beating Too Fast! (pp. 70–72)

Procedure

3-4. Answers will vary and depend on the students' pulses.

Conclusion

1. 69 beats per minute
2. Answers will vary. The average should be noticeably higher, as much as 90 beats per minute.
3. Because the contractions of the heart cause pulses of blood flow, the pulse will be the same as heart rate.
4. Answers may vary. Samples: Age, body size, medication use, fitness level, emotions, body position, air temperature. The primary reason Question 1 doesn't match Question 2 is age.

Digestion: Eating for Success (pp. 73–75)

Procedure

2-3. Answers may vary and depend on the food students eat.

Conclusion

1. Answers may vary. Sample: Vegetables; they are rich in vitamins and minerals.
2. Answers may vary. Sample: Grains; my body will produce too much glucose.
3. Exercise and other activity require more calories.
4. Answers may vary. Sample: These foods are high in sugars and fats.

Endocrine System and Reproduction: Stay Calm if You Can (pp. 76–78)

Procedure

3. Check that students' survey questions are appropriate.

Conclusion

1. Emotional
2. Physical
3. Adrenal
4. Answers may vary. Sample: Extended periods of stress can cause adrenal fatigue. The adrenal glands no longer perform their functions, which can lead to problems with blood sugar, blood pressure, and the immune system among other functions.

Human Body: Working Together Is the Key (pp. 79–81)

Procedure

5. Answers will vary and depend on the system chosen. Check students' charts for completeness and accuracy.

Copyright © Pearson Education, Inc., or its affiliates. All Rights Reserved.

Human Body Systems *(continued)*

Conclusion

1-4. Answers will vary and depend on the system chosen. Sample answers are given.

1. Circulatory; heart, blood vessels, blood
2. Transports oxygen, nutrients, and wastes
3. Excretory
4. Remove waste; the circulatory system carries wastes, such as carbon dioxide, away from cells.

Immune System and Disease: The Pandemic Starts Here (pp. 82–84)

Procedure

1-5. Answers will vary and depend on class behavior.

Conclusion

1. Yes; the flu can spread even if no symptoms exist yet.
2. Answers may vary. Sample: Bacteria; tetanus
3. A flu shot consists of weakened or killed flu viruses that trigger your immune response to produce antibodies.
4. No; antibiotics kill bacteria, but the flu is a virus.

Nervous System: Hit the Ball or You're Out! (pp. 85–87)

Procedure

1-5. Answers will vary. Check students' work for accuracy.

Conclusion

1. Answers may vary. Sample: Relaxing before each trial improved my performance by .03 seconds.
2. The eyes see the ruler drop and send a message to the brain. The brain sends a message to the spinal cord, which relays the message to the muscles that close the fingers (which are in the forearm). The muscles close to catch the falling ruler.
3. Yes; the batter sees the ball, and the brain sends a message through the spinal cord to the muscles (arms, hips, and legs) involved in swinging at the baseball.
4. No; You can improve your reaction time with relaxation, repetition of the action, or activities that require quick reaction time, such as video games.

Respiration and Excretion: Dialysis Works, Too (pp. 88–90)

Procedure

2-5. Sample chart:

	Testing for Salt		Color		Looking fo "Red Cells'	
	Simu-lated Blood	Water	Simu-lated Blood	Water	Simu-lated Blood	Urin
Before	+	–	red	colorless		
After	+	+	red	yellow	yes	no

Conclusion

1. Excretory; to remove waste products from the body
2. Urine; urea
3. Wastes build up in the body

Copyright © Pearson Education, Inc., or its affiliates. All Rights Reserved.

Earth's Structure

Earth: No Shoes in This Box (pp. 91–93)

Procedure

Answers will vary. Sample answers are given.

1. No
2. No; 10%
7. No
6. Yes; yes
9. Yes

Conclusion

Answers may vary. Sample answers are given.

1. Two diagrams were very close, but only after you rotate one of the drawings.
2. No; although you can predict the interior shape of the box, you must open it to know what's inside.
3. Science can predict the interior of Earth using indirect observations and measurements, but we must actually visit the interior to know for sure.

Earthquakes: High-Priority Earthquake Zones (pp. 94–96)

Procedure

1-3. Answers will vary and depend on the date and the criteria chosen. Check students' work.

Conclusion

Answers will vary and depend on the date chosen. Sample answers are given.

1. All but one of the earthquakes in the last seven days occurred in a high risk area.
2. Yes; in Minnesota
3. Yes; near Lake Superior.
4. The states on the west coast, such as California, Washington, and Alaska, are located near a plate boundary.

Minerals and Rocks: My Rock Tells a Story (pp. 97–99)

Conclusion

All answers will vary and depend on the rock chosen. Sample answers are given.

1. Igneous rock
2. From cooled lava or magma
3. On or beneath Earth's surface
4. The rock has large crystals so it probably formed from slow cooling magma.

Plate Tectonics: Flight 7084 to Barcelona (pp. 100–102)

Conclusion

1. An undersea mountain chain where new ocean floor is produced
2. Plate tectonics
3. Rough
4. Steep-sided valleys or molten material

Volcanoes: Jane Versus the Volcano (pp. 103–105)

Conclusion

1. At the edge of tectonic plates
2. An area where material from Earth's mantle rises through the crust and melts to form magma; in the middle of tectonic plates
3. Cinder cone, composite volcano, shield volcano
4. Composite and shield volcanoes; ash, cinders, and bombs

Copyright © Pearson Education, Inc., or its affiliates. All Rights Reserved.

Earth's Surface

Erosion and Deposition: Dunwich Is Done (pp. 106–108)

Procedure

Diagrams and explanations will vary and depend on the beaches made and direction of waves.

Conclusion

1. Longshore drift
2. Sample Answer: A sandbar is caused by incoming waves carrying sand; a barrier beach forms when storm waves pile sand above sea level; a spit is the result of deposition by longshore drift.
3. Headland; beach

Geologic Time: Goodbye, Columbus (pp. 109–111)

Procedure

1. Yes; parchment was once the skin of a live animal.
2. Yes; both the tree bark and the grapes used to make the ink were once alive.
4. and 5. Student estimates should be as close to 570 as possible.

Conclusion

1. About 5,730 years
2. All living objects share the common element carbon, so carbon-14 dating only works for objects that contain carbon. After 50,000 years, so little carbon-14 remains that it would be difficult to detect any carbon from the object.
3. Answers may vary. Sample: Uranium-lead dating can be used because the half life of uranium-235 is about 700 million years.

Mapping Earth's Surface: The Fire Trucks Are Coming! (pp. 112–114)

Conclusion

1. A satellite image is recreated from digital information gathered by satellites and colored digitally, while a photograph is an image recorded on light-sensitive material.
2. The scale tells you the ratio between the distance on the map and the actual distance.
3. The legend describes the pictures and/or symbols used in the map.

Weathering and Soil: In Memory of Winifred (pp. 115–117)

Procedure

2. Sample: Cause Column: plant growth, abrasion, oxidation, acid rain. Not a Cause Column: release of pressure, freezing and thawing, animal actions

Conclusion

1. Mechanical and chemical
2. Answers may vary. Sample: Carbon dioxide is the most likely cause of gravestone damage because most of the gravestones in my area are made from marble and limestone.
3. Answers may vary. Sample: Freezing and thawing is the least likely cause of gravestone damage because I live in a warm climate.
4. The particles of stone that are weathered away are removed by wind, water, ice, or gravity. They become part of the soil around the gravestone.

Copyright © Pearson Education, Inc., or its affiliates. All Rights Reserved.

Water and the Atmosphere

Atmosphere: Mile-High Baseball (pp. 118–120)

Procedure

1. Sample: Air density because gravity is almost the same everywhere on Earth.
4. Answers will vary. Check students' data tables for reasonable answers.

Conclusion

1. Less air density; the change in air density is greater than the difference in gravity in Denver.
2. Because Denver is further up in the atmosphere
3. Sample: Since there is less air density, the ball collides with fewer air molecules so air resistance is less allowing the ball to travel further.
4. Answers may vary. Sample: The higher air pressure in a baseball stadium below sea level would result in higher air density, which would cause the baseball to collide with more air molecules and travel a shorter distance.

Climate and Climate Change: What Causes our Climate? (pp. 121–123)

Conclusion

1. Latitude determines the temperature zone; higher altitude decreases temperature; nearby bodies of water moderate temperature; and ocean currents warm the cool air above them.
2. Prevailing wind direction determines the humidity; mountain ranges interrupt prevailing winds and determine where precipitation falls.
3. Answers will vary and depend on the location of your town.

Fresh Water: My Water Smells Like Gasoline (pp. 124–126)

Conclusion

1. Porosity is the space between particles, expressed as a percentage of the amount of space in a known volume of material.
2. Permeability is the measure of the speed with which a liquid or gas passes through a substance, expressed in liters per minute.
3. Answers will vary and depend on experimental results. Sample: Garden soil
4. Answers will vary and depend on experimental results. Sample: Sand
5. Sample answer: The layer of clay is less permeable than the soil above it, which will help prevent the gasoline from reaching the aquifer deep underground.

Oceans: Cutting Corners Doesn't Always Save (pp. 127–129)

Conclusion

Answers will vary and depend on the shoebox harbors created. Samples are given.

1. A smooth, nearly flat region of the deep-ocean floor; no; the harbor is not deep-ocean floor.
2. A steep-sided mountain rising from the deep-ocean floor; no; the harbor is not deep-ocean floor.
3. A steep incline of the ocean floor leading down from the edge of the continental shelf; no; the chart does not show any sharp changes in ocean depth.
4. A deeper part of a river or harbor; yes; the chart shows one part of the harbor that is deeper than the rest.

Copyright © Pearson Education, Inc., or its affiliates. All Rights Reserved.

Water and the Atmosphere *(continued)*

Weather: Predicting the Weather is No Sport (pp. 130–132)

Procedure

3–5. Answers may vary. Check students' work against the daily weather.

Conclusion

1. Low pressure
2. West to east; the rotation of Earth
3. Answers will vary and depend on the location and chosen week.

Copyright © Pearson Education, Inc., or its affiliates. All Rights Reserved.

Astronomy and Space Science

Earth, Moon, and Sun: Smearing Causes Seasons (pp. 133–135)

Procedure

1–3. Height and width will vary. Check any student calculations for accuracy.
4. The base and/or the height of the trapezoid should be significantly larger than the original measurements.
7. Straight; the area is less, so the energy concentration is greater.
8. Small area

Conclusion

1. The same amount of solar energy is spread over a larger surface area in the winter.
2. Slanted; straight; there is less direct sun on the United States in the winter and more in the summer.

Exploring Space: Asteroid Smasher (pp. 136–138)

Conclusion

1. The thrust of the rubber bands transferred energy to the rocket causing it to move forward with a certain velocity.
2. The closer the launch angle was to 45 degrees, the greater the distance traveled.
3. It can fly off into space.
4. The pencil is not technically a rocket because a rocket expels gas in one direction to move the rocket in the opposite direction.

Solar System: Do Planets Float? (pp. 139–141)

Procedure

3. Check students' data tables for accuracy.

Conclusion

1. Mercury, Venus, Earth, Mars, Jupiter, Uranus, Neptune
2. Saturn
3. Saturn will float because its density is less than that of water.
4. There is only a relationship between volume and density if mass is constant. In that case, if volume increases, then density will decrease.

Stars, Galaxies, and the Universe: The Last Survivors (pp. 142–144)

Conclusion

1. Medium mass, or main sequence
2. Birth, main-sequence star, red giant, planetary nebula, white dwarf
3. About 4.6 billion years
4. About 5 billion years

Copyright © Pearson Education, Inc., or its affiliates. All Rights Reserved.

Introduction to Chemistry

Acids, Bases, and Solutions: Ice Cream, You Scream (pp. 145–147)

Procedure

5. No
6. Answers may vary. Temperature should be above freezing.
8. Answers may vary. Temperature should be below freezing.

Conclusion

1. It lowers the freezing point.
2. Answers may vary. Sample: The energy came from the mixture; the ice-cream mixture got colder.
3. Water is the solvent, and salt is the solute.

Atoms and Bonding: Bonding Super Heroes (pp. 148–150)

Procedure

1. Answers may vary. Sample chart:

Ionic	Covalent
electron transfer	electron sharing
high melting point	lower melting point
conducts electricity	doesn't conduct electricity
hard and brittle	

Conclusion

1. valence electrons
2. share
3. ions
4. Sodium oxide; Magnesium chloride; Aluminum sulfide

Chemical Reactions: The Pipeline Is Burning (pp. 151–153)

Procedure

2. $CH_4 + 2O_2 \rightarrow CO_2 + 2H_2O$
3. Methanol: $2CH_3OH + 3O_2 \rightarrow 2CO_2 + 4H_2O$
   Gasoline: $2C_8H_{18} + 25O_2 \rightarrow 16CO_2 + 18H_2O$
   Hydrogen: $2H_2 + O_2 \rightarrow 2H_2O$

Conclusion

1. 4
2. 6
3. Exothermic; this reaction releases energy in the form of heat and light, which provide power for our homes and buildings.
4. Law of conservation of mass

Elements and the Periodic Table: The Element Museum (pp. 154–156)

Conclusion

1. Sample table:

Chemical Symbol	Atomic number	Atomic mass	Number of protons	Number of neutrons	Nu[illegible] elec[illegible]
Ge	32	72.59	32	41	32

2. Metalloid
3. Boron, silicon, arsenic, antimony, tellurium, astatine; on either side of the zigzag line that separates the metals from the nonmetals

Matter: What a Mass (pp. 157–159)

Procedure

2. and 3. Mass and volume will vary.
4. Approximate densities (g/cm^3): Aluminum: 2.7; Brass: 8.5; Copper: 8.9; Steel: 7.8

Copyright © Pearson Education, Inc., or its affiliates. All Rights Reserved.

Introduction to Chemistry *(continued)*

Conclusion

1. 8 g
2. Less than one; brass has a density of 8.5 g/cm^3, and it does not float.
3. Steel; its constant is closest to 8 g/cm^3.
4. Density

Solids, Liquids, and Gases: My Glass Is Leaking! (pp. 160–162)

Procedure

1-4. Answers may vary. Sample table:

Trial	Number of ice cubes	Temperature (°F)	Condensation?
1	Empty glass	71	No
2	0 (cold water only)	47	No
3	1	45	No
4	2	41	No
5	3	36	No
6	4	33	Yes

4. 34 °F

Conclusion

1. Vaporization
2. Condensation
3. Vaporization
4. Dew point

Copyright © Pearson Education, Inc., or its affiliates. All Rights Reserved.

Forces and Energy

Electricity: My House Is Wired! (pp. 163–165)

Conclusion

1. Series and parallel
2. In a series circuit, the resistance increases, so the current and brightness decrease.
3. In a parallel circuit, the resistance decreases, so the current and brightness increase.
4. Parallel circuit; when you turn off one light switch, the other lights remain lit.

Energy: Stuck at the Top (pp. 166–168)

Procedure

2-3. Answers will vary. Accept all hypotheses that are based on concrete observation and theory. Samples are given.

2. No
3. A lighter ball will not travel as quickly and will therefore not make it over the hill.
4. The lightweight ball made it over the hill.
5. Answers will vary and depend on the hypothesis chosen in Steps 2-3. Sample: No; the lightweight ball made it over the hill, which does not agree with my hypothesis.

Conclusion

1. Kinetic energy
2. Potential energy
3. Energy transformation
4. Answers may vary. Sample: Thermal energy transformed by friction

Forces: Please Drop In (pp. 169–171)

Procedure

1-5. Answers will vary and depend on the drop height chosen. Check students' work.

6. Answers may vary. Sample: The parachute that worked best used a medium-sized parachute. The larger parachutes moved too far from the target, and the smaller parachutes fell too quickly.

Conclusion

1. The washers without the parachute had the greater acceleration because they needed a shorter time to fall.
2. The washers without the parachute.
3. No; the change in net force must have been caused by an upward frictional force from air pushing on the parachute.

Magnetism and Electromagnetism: Is the North Pole Really the South Pole? (pp. 172–174)

Procedure

2. Unlike; alike
3. North; south
4. North

Conclusion

1. North pole and south pole
2. North
3. North
4. South

Motion: The Mayor Is Worried (pp. 175–177)

Procedure

1. 30 mi/h
2. 2 minutes, 30 seconds;
3. Answers may vary. Check students' work.
4. Answers may vary and should depend on the students' answers to Step 2.

Conclusion

1. 30 mi/h
2. 2 minutes, 30 seconds; 12 mi/h

Copyright © Pearson Education, Inc., or its affiliates. All Rights Reserved.

Forces and Energy *(continued)*

3. Answers may vary. Sample: Take Rat Road for one block, turn left on Walnut Way, turn right on Lizard Lane, turn right on Raspberry Road after two blocks, turn left on Rat Road, turn right on Lemon Lane, and turn right on Dog Drive; distance: 0.7 miles; time: 2 minutes; average speed: 21 mi/h

Thermal Energy and Heat: Where Is the Battery? (pp. 178–180)

Procedure

1. Tile; a lot colder
2. Answers may vary. Sample:
   Lower-reading thermometer = A
   Correction factor = 2°F;
3. Answers will vary and depend on the temperature of the room. Check that students added the correction factor.
4. Answers will vary. Sample: 3°F; yes, that is close enough to consider the same temperature.
5. Tile is a better conductor of heat than carpet. The transfer of heat from your feet to the tile is quicker than it is to the carpet, which results in a cold feeling.

Conclusion

1. From you to the cold object
2. No; temperature is a measure of how hot or cold something is compared to a reference point; heat is the transfer of thermal energy from a warmer object to a cooler object.
3. When the temperatures are equal
4. Nothing; heat only flows if there exists a warmer object and a colder object.

Work and Machines: Help! I'm Trapped Under Here! (pp. 181–183)

Procedure

2. Answers may vary. Samples: Weight of car, weight of person, location of fulcrum
5. and 6. Answers will vary. Sample:

$$\text{Mechanical advantage} = \frac{3000 \text{ pounds}}{88 \text{ pounds}} = 34.1$$

Distance from fulcrum to input force = 34.1 ft
Full length of the lever = 35.1 ft

Conclusion

1. No; a lever that long would be too heavy and cumbersome.
2. Answer may vary. Sample: Telephone pole
3. Increasing the number of people increases the force on the lever, which decreases the mechanical advantage required and therefore decreases the length of lever needed.
4. Answers may vary. Both first-class and second-class levers have advantages and disadvantages depending on a variety of circumstances. Samples: The first-class lever is more helpful because I cannot pull up with the same force as my entire body weight; the second-class lever is more helpful because I can use the ground to push off and input more force.

Copyright © Pearson Education, Inc., or its affiliates. All Rights Reserved.

Sound and Light

Electromagnetic Waves: Catching the Waves (pp. 184–186)

Procedure

4. Answers may vary. Sample: Yes; the buzzing sound became louder as I moved closer.
5. Charts will vary and depend on the electrical devices chosen.

Conclusion

1. Wavelength and frequency
2. Long; radio waves have the longest wavelength for electromagnetic waves.
3. Amplitude; frequency, wavelength, and speed
4. FM; FM waves have a higher frequency, which means they carry more energy.

Light: Seeing in the Dark (pp. 187–189)

Procedure

1. and 2. Answers will vary and depend on the students' eyesight.
3. Answers may vary. Sample: Put a towel under the door
4. Answers may vary. Sample: 6 minutes, 10 seconds

Conclusion

1. Cones
2. Red, green, and blue
3. Rods
4. No; rods only allow you to see in very dim light, not total darkness.

Sound: Seeing with Your Ears (pp. 190–192)

Procedure

1. Answers may vary. Samples: desk, student, wall of classroom
4. Data table and average will vary and depend on the results of the class.
5. Answers may vary. Sample: Yes; the whistle produced the best results because it made a louder echo.

Conclusion

1. Echolocation works because sound waves reflect off surfaces.
2. His brain converted sounds into visual information.
3. Answers may vary. Sample: Ben's brain adapted and used his other senses to receive visual information.
4. Answers may vary. Sample: Echolocation could be helpful if the electricity went out in my house at night or if I was camping on a moonless night.

Wave Characteristics: Rogue Wave (pp. 193–195)

Procedure

2. They also add together.
3. 4

Conclusion

1. From trough to crest
2. Waves combine to form a wave with a larger amplitude than any individual wave's amplitude.
3. Waves combine to form a wave with a smaller amplitude than any original wave's amplitude.
4. Yes; any number of waves can interfere with each other and add or subtract heights (and energy).

Copyright © Pearson Education, Inc., or its affiliates. All Rights Reserved.